The Nature of Copyright

L. Ray Patterson & Stanley W. Lindberg

Foreword by Robert W. Kastenmeier

The Nature of
Copyright

A Law of Users' Rights

The University of Georgia Press   Athens & London

© 1991 by L. Ray Patterson and
Stanley W. Lindberg
All rights reserved
Published by the University of Georgia Press
Athens, Georgia 30602
Designed by Richard Hendel
Set in Baskerville and Gill by
Tseng Information Systems, Inc.
Printed and bound by Thomson-Shore, Inc.
The paper in this book meets the guidelines for
permanence and durability of the Committee on
Production Guidelines for Book Longevity of the
Council on Library Resources.

Printed in the United States of America
95 94 93 92 91 C 5 4 3 2 1
95 94 93 92 91 P 5 4 3 2 1

Library of Congress Cataloging in Publication Data
Patterson, L. Ray (Lyman Ray)
    The nature of copyright : a law of users' rights /
L. Ray Patterson, Stanley W. Lindberg.
        p.   cm.
    Includes bibliographical references and index.
ISBN 0-8203-1347-5 (alk. paper). — ISBN 0-8203-1362-9
(pbk. : alk. paper)
    1. Fair use (Copyright)—United States.   2. Fair use
(Copyright)—United States—History.   3. Copyright—
United States.   4. Copyright—United States—History.
I. Lindberg, Stanley W.   II. Title.
KF3020.P37   1991
346.7304'82—dc20
[347.306482]   90-28430
                              CIP
British Library Cataloging in Publication Data available

Contents

Part Four. Conclusions

Foreword

This is a book that needed to be written and now needs to be read. It does something that no other law book I know of has done: it provides a framework to serve as a basis for interpreting the 1976 Copyright Act against the backdrop of copyright history and its constitutional roots. This is the unique perspective set forth by L. Ray Patterson and Stanley W. Lindberg, the former a nationally respected professor of law and the latter an esteemed author and editor. I am personally familiar with the dedication of Professor Patterson to the study and understanding of copyright law and to his measurable contributions to copyright policy-making and literature. And I am pleased to become familiar with the work of Professor Lindberg in this book.

As a former national legislator who devoted more than three decades of professional life to the enactment of copyright legislation, I have been acutely aware that while the legislative branch enacts laws, the judiciary interprets them. My experience has been that—at least in the field of copyright—courts do not always interpret the law that legislators thought they enacted, for legislators and judges necessarily view legal issues from different perspectives. The legislator makes laws for society as a whole; the judge decides disputes between specific individuals. In enacting copyright legislation, Congress starts with the intellectual-property clause of the Constitution. In deciding copyright cases, however, a judge starts with the facts of a single case and goes back to (and usually stops with) the Copyright Act. Most judges give Congress the benefit of a doubt, presuming that Congress acted within its constitutional grant of power in passing the statute. But that presumption goes too far if it serves as a substitute for analyzing provisions of the Act. Congress can properly enact copyright statutes only as the copyright clause permits, and courts can properly interpret those statutes only in light of that clause.

We must remind ourselves that the legislative and judicial branches are separate and autonomous, but each is subject to different pressures and processes in a democratic society. The Congress is majoritarian in its decison-making, whereas the courts are antimajoritarian. In passing legislation, Congress is always subject to political pressures and the lobbying of special interests. The copyright industry is composed of and represented by politically active, sophisticated, and knowledgeable people; in attempting to persuade Congress, they are doing only what every citizen has a right to do. To say that lobbyists and lawyers shape the language of many copyright bills is only to recognize reality, but some of the shaping is very subtle, and judges have not only a right but a duty to consider the impact of particular influences in the legislative process.

Furthermore, the question of statutory interpretation often involves the question of what Congress *did*, not what Congress *intended*. But to determine the former it is often necessary to consider the latter. Most words have multiple meanings, and a single word of several meanings may make a great deal of difference in the interpretation of a statute. Yet courts have been strangely reluctant to engage in a contextual reading of the 1976 Copyright Act. The major reason, I believe, has been the lack of any framework of fundamentals to serve as a basis both for drafting and for interpreting copyright legislation. Therein lies the importance of this book, which provides that framework.

When I speak about copyright fundamentals, I mean those basic propositions, policies, and principles that underlie all copyright issues. Although Anglo-American copyright has a 450-year history, its fundamentals have rarely been recog-

nized or articulated. Even the most basic issue of copyright—
the nature of copyright itself—remains a matter of dispute.
The question is whether copyright is a natural-law property
right of authors or society's grant of a limited statutory monopoly. There are proponents of both theories, and each side
can bring forth many arguments to support its position. The
authors of this book take the position that only copyright as
the grant of a limited statutory monopoly can serve as the basis
for a soundly integrated copyright law. They have made a very
persuasive case, based on the simple but fundamental insight
that copyright is a body of law which must accommodate the
interests of three groups in our society: authors, distributors
(including publishers), and consumers.

Persons in all three of these groups use copyrighted materials, of course, but for different purposes. The author
uses copyrighted material in the creation of new works; the
distributor disseminates copyrighted material in the marketplace; the consumer uses copyrighted material in the home,
in the classroom, and in the office. In general terms, then, we
can say that the author makes a creative use, the distributor
a commercial use, and the consumer a personal use of copyrighted materials (which may or may not have commercial
implications).

Since the creative and personal use of copyrighted materials
may come into conflict with the goal of distributors and entrepreneurs to control commercial use, the balancing of competing interests is no small task. To complicate matters, members
of the various groups may have different positions at different times. An author, for example, may wish to be free to
quote others liberally, but may not want to be so quoted without compensation. A publisher may wish to publish portions
of another's book, but not wish to return the favor. Only the
consumer's position is consistent: he or she wishes to be free
to use material. The problem, of course, is made all the more

complicated by the fact that copyright is a law that deals with the flow of information, the lifeline of a free society. And all the while economic implications are expanding rapidly in a global marketplace.

The complexity of these problems requires that we deal with the issues in terms of the basic policies and principles. The authors argue that copyright cannot be treated as being primarily a property right, because property is essentially a bilateral concept—between the property owner and everyone else. Only if copyright is viewed as a statutory grant can it be seen as more regulatory than proprietary. I suggest that the authors must be right if we are to avoid the consequences of the paradox of copyright: a legal concept that is intended to encourage the dissemination of information being used instead as an instrument of censorship.

These issues find their most controversial manifestation in the doctrine of fair use, which may be the most difficult problem Congress faced in enacting the 1976 Copyright Act. In retrospect, we may have relied too much on a nineteenth-century concept to deal with twentieth-century problems. Even so, if we approach the problems in terms of fundamentals, the fair-use provision that was enacted into law can serve well. This can be done if courts will recognize fair use as a generic term encompassing three species of use: creative use, competitive use, and consumer use.

This foreword is not the place to delineate these concepts, which are developed more fully in this book. I will say only that if the 1976 Copyright Act is read as a whole, and is read in light of the intellectual-property clause of the Constitution, it will support them. One who reads this book with care will understand.

Professors Patterson and Lindberg do not provide here all the answers to copyright problems, but they do something even more important—they enable readers to ask the right

questions. The book serves generally to promote the understanding of copyright law, but more importantly it offers direct
assistance to participants in the lawmaking and judicial processes, whether they represent private or public interests.

Some of the authors' questions are provocative, and so are
some of their tentative answers. I do not agree with everything
that they have written. But I strongly feel that this book contributes to a sound and informed debate on the issues, a debate necessary for wise and balanced congressional decision-
making and fair judgments by the federal courts consistent
with the bedrock copyright law.

I commend the book to copyright lawyers, to legislators and
their staffs, to judges, and to all those whom copyright is ultimately intended to benefit—the American citizens who use
copyrighted materials for the promotion of their own learning, but who have no lobbyist in the halls of Congress to plead
their case for the right of personal use in their homes, schools,
libraries, and offices.

Robert W. Kastenmeier

Acknowledgments

As is usual in any undertaking of this scope, we are indebted to many others who helped at various stages. We are grateful in particular to C. Ronald Ellington, Dean of the Law School, and William F. Prokasy and Delmer D. Dunn, Vice-President and Associate Vice-President for Academic Affairs at the University of Georgia, for their steadfast support and encouragement, and to Margaret K. Park and Stephen Corey for their sound advice and criticism. Special thanks are due to Craig Joyce of the University of Houston Law Center for his challenging and perceptive assessments of our manuscript as it evolved—and to Roberta Carver, whose patience and secretarial skills monitored the manuscript through its many drafts. None of these kind people, nor any of the others who offered support, can be held responsible, of course, for any errors or excesses that survive in the version now presented—and, of course, copyrighted—by the coauthors.

The Nature of Copyright

Knowledge is, in every country, the surest basis of public happiness.
— George Washington

Property has its duties as well as its rights.
— Benjamin Disraeli

The Role of Copyright in American Life

Copyright plays a significant role in the life of nearly everyone in our society. Magazines and books, music, plays, movies, television broadcasts, even computer programs—all are copyrighted, and how we use them is often influenced by our perceptions of copyright. Yet despite copyright's impact on our lives, relatively few people have sufficient knowledge or understanding of what it is—and far too many hold major misconceptions about what copyright means. The term *copyright* itself is often erroneously viewed as being self-defining, meaning "the right to copy," and related misinterpretations have begun to receive wide public circulation. A recent article in *Newsweek*, for instance, asserts confidently, "The primary purpose of copyright law is to protect authors against those who would pilfer their work."[1] But this is *not* copyright's announced purpose—even though protecting authors is indeed one of the incidental functions of copyright. Moreover, such oft-repeated fallacies, many of them now generally accepted, pose serious dangers to the integrity of copyright law.

The primary purpose of copyright—as stated explicitly by the framers of the U.S. Constitution and subsequently interpreted by federal courts and Congress—is to promote the public welfare by the advancement of knowledge. With the specific intent of encouraging the production and distribution of new works for the public, copyright provides incentive for creators by granting them exclusive rights to reproduce and distribute their work. But these rights are subject to important limitations—nearly all of them related to the basic purpose of advancing knowledge for the general welfare of society. From its statutory beginnings in early-eighteenth-century England, copyright has been the product of a precarious attempt to balance the rights of the creators—and those of their publishers—with the rights of users, present and future.

The most frequently mentioned (but least understood) limitation on the rights granted to copyright holders is the doctrine of fair use, a vital component of the rights many users do not realize they have. There would be no problem, of course, if all people could agree on what is fair, and it is tempting to argue that all we need to resolve the problem is the application of more common sense. As the eminent critic Jacques Barzun points out:

Quotations being for a purpose, the purpose declares itself in the context and in no other way. If I write about the drama, I may quote three pages from Shaw and be no plagiarist. If I quote for ornament, I should be brief. And if I begin, "As Churchill aptly says . . ." following it up with his Collected Speeches, I should be jailed. Makers of anthologies, plainly, must ask and pay for the privilege of reprinting copyrighted work. In any given instance, the law's reasonable man can tell what is going on. If the law avers that it cannot, then "the law is a ass." (By permission of Charles Dickens's heirs and assigns.)[2]

Yet all rules of law contain implied extensions and implied limitations and are therefore subject to interpretation. The more general the rule, the more leeway for interpretation (and often the greater need). Fair use, as it appears in the current statute, is a classic illustration of a very general rule—it is, in fact, a legal principle most uncomfortably cast as a rule—and interpretations are almost certain to vary widely.[3] Not surprisingly, copyright owners tend to give the fair-use doctrine a narrow reading, while users naturally take a broader view. In short, one cannot expect universal agreement concerning what is and what is not fair use—even by the courts, where rulings on fair use are often overturned on appeal and decisions frequently have strong dissenting opinions.

The unfortunate truth is that copyright is a confused and confusing body of rules. Traditionally viewed as a law for authors and artists, copyright was actually originated by publishers and has a long history of having benefited entrepreneurs much more than creators. A major purpose of this book is to explain the vagaries of history that caused this anomaly, and thus to justify a new—and long overdue—perspective of copyright law: copyright as a law for consumers as well as for creators and marketers. All three of these groups—authors, publishers (or other entrepreneurs), and customers—are users of copyrighted materials, which is why the copyright law consists of three parts: a law of authors' rights, a law of publishers' rights, and a law of users' rights.

Although not generally realized, and indeed often obscured by legal jargon, this truism merely reflects the fact that copyright rules determine the rights of all individuals in the creation, dissemination, and use of copyrighted works. The point becomes apparent if we were to assume an unlikely scenario: the existence of only a single book in a universe populated by one author, one publisher, and one user. A copyright law that defines the author's rights in relation to that book necessarily defines also the duties of the publisher and the user in relation to that same book. This would be the case even if the law did not articulate the rights of each, since to define one person's rights in relation to a work is to define the rights of all other persons relevant to that same work.

The mythical universe of one author, one publisher, and one user brings to the fore the impact that copyright law may have on what can be called the learning right of all persons— a right predicate to the right of livelihood upon which life, liberty, and the pursuit of happiness depend. Nor should the lesson be lost simply because there are now many books, many authors, many publishers, and many users. The cornucopia of copyrighted works today—including such esoterica (in terms of traditional copyright) as musical recordings, live television broadcasts, and computer programs—does not change the analysis, because in any given situation, copyright continues to define the relationship of one creator, one publisher/entrepreneur, and one user to the single work in question.

The importance of copyright law in the implementation of the learning right is made apparent by the fact that the U.S. Constitution empowers Congress to enact copyright statutes, one of the few instances in which that document prescribes a subject of congressional legislation. Significantly, the grant of power is limited, for Congress can grant copyright only to authors. The entrepreneur's component of copyright law is thus derived from the authors' rights. And the law of users' rights is by and large an unwritten law, being a by-product of the limitations on the rights of the author and the publisher as copyright owners. This fact, however, should not be allowed to obscure its importance within the tripartite thesis of copyright law, a thesis that must be implemented if copyright is to fulfill its policy of promoting learning.

This fundamental policy, mandated by the Constitution, means that ideas must be free for all to use: copyright does not protect ideas themselves—only their expression. In other words, copyright deals with the packaging and dissemination of ideas, whether in the form of a book, a motion picture, a painting, a television program, or a computer database. Ideas are information, information is learning, and learning is part of culture. In a larger sense, then, copyright law is the law governing access to the culture of our society in all its aspects—social, political, economic, educational, and artistic. Logic tells us that if this law were to grant rights only to creators and purveyors of the materials of culture, the law would be treating culture as consisting of products that are ends in themselves rather than as a process relevant to both the amenities and essentials of a civilized society.

In light of the impact that copyright law has on the daily lives of all, our charge that copyright law is a confused and confusing body of law is a serious one, and our claim that it contains a law of users' rights is unique. Consequently, a brief word of explanation is in order. This book is essentially a report on a search for the correct premises of copyright, not a detailed manual of copyright law annotated with case citations. Because modern American copyright is the direct lineal descendant of a concept created by book publishers in England some 450 years ago, we will begin our analysis at that point and trace its development in England until it was transported to the United States immediately following the American Revolution. After that, however, we will focus almost exclusively on U.S. copyright law. Our primary concern throughout will not be with copyright rules arising out of litigation but with the historically tested copyright policies and principles underlying them, from which those rules should be—but are not always—derived. There are three reasons for this approach:

First, much of the current confusion in copyright law—confusion we treat as a given—comes from conflicting judicial decisions. But in our legal system, case law is binding only in the jurisdiction of the court rendering it. Copyright law is a matter of federal law, and there are thirteen federal circuit courts of appeal in the United States, twelve of which are entitled to render copyright decisions (even if contrary to decisions in other circuits). Only the copyright decisions of the U.S. Supreme Court are binding nationally, and indeed, that Court is one of only two authoritative sources of copyright law in the United States. The other is Congress.

Second, confusion in the law also results from the fact that copyright law—for all its importance—is only a small portion of the law with which judges must deal daily. Given the breadth of their efforts, they lack the luxury of time to delve deeply into what for many judges is an arcane subject. Copyright may very well be the only law they deal with that can be traced directly back to its origins in sixteenth-century England. Yet because copyright in origin was the product of a new communications technology (the printing press), and because copyright today has been extended to products of other new communications technology (television and the computer), the early history of copyright has a particular contemporary relevance. Copyright for television and the computer today serves precisely the same function that copyright for the printing press served originally—to give entrepreneurs a monopoly of their products—with little regard to, or concern for, the "authors" who produce the product. The lessons to be learned from the history of copyright—which records periodic struggles by society to limit the power of publishers—are relevant to the same problems engendered by today's publishers and other copyright entrepreneurs. Time has changed neither the function of copyright nor the evils of an unchecked monopoly.

Third, and most important, the ultimate source of confusion in copyright law is a distressing ignorance of copyright fundamentals, evidenced by virtually all parties concerned. As time has passed, awareness of the nature and purpose of copyright has dimmed, in part through general apathy, and the fundamentals are now largely obscured. That process did not occur unaided, however, for it has been vigorously cultivated by copyright owners in promoting an industry-oriented view as to the rights copyright entails.

Courts can give binding interpretations to statutory laws only if proper cases are presented to them, and it is the copyright owners who largely determine which cases will be presented. But interpretation of the copyright statute is not limited to the courts and, indeed, is a task that copyright owners have regularly undertaken with some measure of zeal—stating their views publicly in the form of propositions that appear to be statements of law. Consider, for example, the following statement published by the Copyright Clearance Center (an organization to license the copying of copyrighted materials) in its promotional literature: "Copyright law in the United States *requires that users of copyrighted materials obtain authorizations from copyright owners*" (emphasis added).

That statement is only partially true, which (given its knowledgeable source) makes it essentially false. Although *some* users must obtain prior authorizations, many are not so required; yet the term *users* as employed here, having no modifier, is clearly intended to be read as *all* users—and must therefore be adjudged as being intentionally misleading or, in legal terms, fraudulent. In truth, section 107 of the 1976 Copyright Act expressly permits the fair use of copyrighted materials (including use by copying) *without* authorization of the copyright owner, although many users of copyrighted materials are misled by canards like the one just cited.

During the legislative considerations leading to the Copyright Act of 1976, Congressman Robert W. Kastenmeier and the House subcommittee responsible for copyright legislation attempted to gather a consensus opinion regarding what constitutes permissible fair use for educational purposes. Three ad hoc committees of citizens were assembled to deal with the classroom use of printed material, of music, and of audiovisual material. The results of the first two of these committees' deliberations were received in time to be incorporated within the legislative history attached to the Copyright Act of 1976. The third committee, dealing with audiovisual material, reported later; its suggested guidelines were entered into the *Congressional Record* of 14 October 1981. A fourth set of guidelines, dealing with educational use of computer software, was subsequently generated by the software industry and has been widely circulated in the academic community.[4]

None of these published guidelines addresses questions dealing with competitive or other noneducational fair use, however, and there is legitimate reason to question their value even for their announced educational applications. In our opinion, all of them are far more restrictive than justified by either fair-use precedents or the statute itself, and some are dangerously misleading in their official-sounding assertions. One of the deceptive attractions of such documents is that they offer "safe" specifics (for example, how many lines of a poem or how many words of prose one may copy without obtaining permission from the copyright owner). But such quantifying of the qualitative factors of fair use unduly limits what the law actually states, even as it conflicts with the basic policies and principles that inform copyright—thus serving mainly to intimidate users and inhibit the advancement of knowledge. Users need to realize that, even though these classroom guidelines are frequently cited as if they were law (and as if their restrictions extended well beyond the educational setting), they are in no way part of the legal statute itself and should not be viewed as such.

The two sets of guidelines in the House report (those for classroom copying of books and periodicals and for the educational use of music) carry notice that they express only "minimum standards of educational fair use" and state clearly that they are "not intended to limit the types of copying permitted under the standards of fair use." Regrettably, however, statements of *minimum* standards invite (and all too often receive) interpretation—both by copyright owners and by risk-averse users—as *maximum allowable limits*. Even more disturbing, the later sets of guidelines (those for the use of audiovisual materials and for computer software) in no way acknowledge their status as minimum standards; in fact, they reflect distortions of copyright policies and principles by almost totally disregarding fair-use provisions of the law and by treating copyright as if it were a plenary property right (that is, an unregulated, natural right).

Such restrictive and misleading guidelines offer a serious threat to user rights, but they illustrate all too well a valuable lesson in American jurisprudence. Most Americans think of law as consisting of written rules in the form of legislative statutes or court decisions. But law also grows out of what people actually do, that is, out of custom. Even the most comprehensive legal statute is skeletal in content, while court decisions tend to be fact-intensive (resolving disputes between litigants over specific, concrete issues). Between these two poles, therefore, there is an enormous amount of room for private action, and consistent private action can essentially "make" law by reshaping existing customs (or even creating new ones) that may subsequently be honored by the courts.

When the conduct in question involves economic interests, those most directly affected often take the lead in making private pronouncements concerning the kind of actions that are legal and permissible. This is precisely what has happened in the matter of the use and fair use of copyrighted materials. Corporate copyright owners and others with vested interests—including licensing agents, broadcasting and publishing associations, and so on—have used the skeletal statute, section 107 of the 1976 Copyright Act, to influence and promulgate guidelines that purport to implement that law but instead often constitute self-aggrandizement at the expense of the public interest.

Another aspect of the custom-making process may be observed in the increase of extended, intimidating copyright notices accompanying works, whether published, broadcast, or software "licensed." More and more common are statements like "No part of this publication may be reproduced, stored in a retrieval system, or transmitted in any form or by any means, electronic, mechanical, photocopying or otherwise, without the prior written permission of the copyright owners." Unfortunately, because of their *in terrorem* effect, such baselessly exaggerated copyright notices, along with constant references to the restrictive guidelines, tend to work. The threat of a lawsuit is a powerful inhibitor, even though infringement actions are rarely brought against individuals. And the minimum guidelines in the House report, although of no binding legal effect, can be very persuasive (and may all too easily be misconstrued as maximum allowable standards) when cited to a busy court.

It seems clear that many copyright holders are actively promoting the notion that users may quote or reproduce copyrighted material only at the sufferance of the copyright owner. If such fallacies go unchallenged long enough, they are likely to become a substitute for the truth. It is important, therefore, that all overly restrictive and spurious guidelines—along with false-claim copyright notices—be directly refuted. One of the main objectives of this book is to refute them with a simple truth: users have rights that are just as important as those of authors and publishers—and these rights are grounded in the law of copyright. To employ the fair-use provisions of the copyright act is not to abuse the rights of the author or copyright owner; indeed, the very purpose of copyright is to advance knowledge and thus benefit the public welfare, which is exactly what fair use—properly employed—does.

Underlying all of the misconceptions and confusions concerning copyright are several key theoretical issues that will be explored in greater detail later in the book. Central among them is the long-standing debate over the nature of copyright itself, which in legal terms boils down to this: Is copyright a natural-law property right of the author by reason of creation of a work? Or does copyright exist only as a concession by society, that is, as a statutory grant of a limited monopoly? As we will demonstrate, the weight of evidence overwhelmingly supports the limited-monopoly interpretation, which indeed serves as the basis for the 1976 Copyright Act. Nevertheless, arguments based on the alternate theory continue to arise in court cases, regularly contributing to the confusion surrounding the law.

If we phrase this central issue in a slightly different way—Is copyright a proprietary concept or is it a regulatory con-

cept?—the confusion is compounded, for although copyright
is far more regulatory than is commonly perceived, it is also
proprietary. That is, copyright is a highly regulated property
right that can most accurately be described as a regulatory-
proprietary concept.

The problem is that both the regulatory and the proprietary
premises are available to use in dealing with copyright issues,
and the choice of which to use has not been uniform. As might
be expected, copyright owners and others with vested interests in the resulting industry choose the proprietary premise
and in general downplay or ignore the regulatory premise.
Congress, on the other hand, has enacted copyright legislation
on the basis of the regulatory premise, as a review of the copyright acts from 1790 to 1976 demonstrates. And courts have
varied in their approach. In the nineteenth century, courts
treated copyright as the grant of a limited monopoly that required strict construction of the copyright statute; contemporary courts tend toward the proprietary premise and rule
accordingly.

This modern trend can be accounted for in part historically, since the application of copyright to any new technology
has generally led to an expansion of the proprietary premise. Understandably, perhaps, courts during this century have
tended to be sympathetic to the electronic copyright, still in its
early stages, just as courts were sympathetic to the print copyright in eighteenth-century England after it was first codified.
But contemporary courts still following the proprietary trend
are acting contrary to the design of the 1976 Copyright Act.
Indeed, the regulatory pattern of the current act is so clear
that the judicial treatment of copyright as more proprietary
than regulatory is a mystery that can be explained only by
judicial confusion as to the nature and purpose of copyright.

A related and contributing factor to the overall legal confusion is what could be called the jurisprudential flaw of copy-

right: the failure of courts to distinguish—and to treat as separate entities—the original work, the copyright of that work, and a subsequent copy of the work. The distinction between, for example, the manuscript of a novel and the copyright of that novel—or between either of them and a book that is the physical embodiment of the novel—is clear enough as a matter of fact and reason, but the distinction has not been clear as a matter of law.

The problem comes into sharper focus if one thinks in terms of ownership. An author initially owns the work he or she has created, the manuscript containing that work (the only copy), and the copyright to that work (upon its creation "fixed in any tangible medium of expression"). When the author assigns the copyright to a publisher, the publisher owns the copyright but not the work. When the publisher publishes the work, the purchaser of a copy of the book owns that copy but nothing more. This seemingly elementary analysis, however, has been confused because of a common tendency to equate the ownership of rights with ownership of the physical object. Historically the transfer of the physical object was deemed to transfer the rights it embodied. Therefore, when the author transferred the manuscript, the author was deemed to have transferred the ownership of the work; and since upon publication the publisher acquired the copyright of the work (which he or she owned by reason of assignment), the ownership of copyright was equated with ownership of the work. (The ownership of a copy of the published work only has never been considered to be a matter of consequence.)

Prior to the 1976 Copyright Act this equation of ownership of copyright with ownership of the work was manifested in the rule that copyright was indivisible, that is, that copyright could be transferred only as a whole, not in part. (This was a judicial construction of the copyright statute that its language did not require, but twentieth-century courts have steadily refused to

distinguish between the ownership of a work and the ownership of the copyright of the work.) The 1976 Copyright Act,
however, explicitly makes copyright divisible and thus makes
the distinction clearer. That act also clarifies the distinction
between ownership of the copyright and the ownership of a
physical object, such as a work in which the copyrighted work
is embodied.

Our position here is that the frequent failure of courts to
distinguish clearly the work, its copyright, and a copy of the
work—while interpreting copyright statutes that utilized those
very distinctions—is the root problem behind much of the
confusion in copyright law. Under all U.S. copyright acts, copyright is a series of rights granted in relation to a given work
for a limited period of time. And under all those acts, when
the copyright term ends, the copyright ceases—even as the
work itself continues to exist: the clearest proof of a difference
between a work and its copyright. Unfortunately, when attor-
neys and courts get caught up in hair-splitting interpretations
of rules, these basic distinctions almost never get considered.

Our intent in this book is to inform as many people as possible—writers, publishers, judges, and users—of the fundamentals of copyright, how it developed, and why. All Americans need to realize that the copyright law is the infrastructure
supporting the progress of learning in our free society—and
that if it is to serve this crucial function, the law must take into
account not only rewards for creators and disseminators but
also reasonable rights for the users who provide those rewards.
In the pages that follow we attempt to provide a balanced
view of copyright by examining it in historical context and by
analyzing the rules of copyright in light of its basic policies
and principles. Special emphasis throughout will be on users'
rights—far less publicized or known than those of authors
and copyright owners—although we offer here no formal set
of specific guidelines for personal or fair use of copyrighted

materials. Since a single user may, at different times, make significantly different uses of exactly the same copyrighted material, all personal- and fair-use determinations must be made on an individual-case basis. And according to the copyright act, the determination of what constitutes legitimate personal or fair use calls not for the counting of words or lines but for informed users willing to employ common sense in the exercise of rights they clearly have under law—and for informed courts willing to recognize that copyright is not simply a plenary property right.

Our claim is not that the positions taken in this book reflect all case precedents but rather that they are both internally consistent *and* consistent with the historic policies, principles, and rules of copyright, and in that sense reflect the law. We believe it is reasonable to hope that, with a better understanding of copyright and the legal limits on the use of copyrighted works, users will be more likely to respect those limits. It is equally reasonable to hope that, given the analysis of copyright provided and supported here, all parties—authors, publishers, users, and judges—will recognize users' rights as far more important than most of us have been led to believe.

PART ONE

Copyright in Context

A well regulated propriety of Copies among Stationers, makes Printing flourish, and Books plentifull and cheap.
—Stationers' Petition to Parliament (April 1643)

Books seem to me to be pestilent things, and infect all that trade in them . . . with something very perverse and brutal. Printers, binders, sellers, and others that make a trade and gain out of them have universally so odd a turn and corruption of mind that they have a way of dealing peculiar to themselves, and not conformed to the good of society and that general fairness which cements mankind.
—John Locke

Copyright in the Beginning

A Publisher's Right

In 1557, eighty years after William Caxton had introduced the printing press into England, Philip and Mary (Tudor) granted the guild of stationers a royal charter, thereby creating the Stationers' Company. As one of the livery companies of the City of London—all of which were essentially incorporated craft guilds—the stationers immediately proved to be a valuable ally of the government in its campaign to suppress dissent by controlling the output of the press (which, indeed, had been Mary's motive in granting the royal charter).

The stationers were businessmen who manufactured and sold books, and to them press control was a means to their own ends—government protection of their market monopoly. As Edward Arber, commenting on "the virulence of their trade competition," has said: "We must think of these printers and publishers as caring chiefly for their crowns, half-shillings and silver pennies. They bore the yoke of [governmental] licensing as best they could, but only as a means to hold themselves harmless from the political and ecclesiastical powers. Their business was to live and make money; and keen enough they were about it."[1] These were the men who created the stationers' copyright—the first English copyright, and thus (by way of an indisputable series of causally related events) the direct antecedent of the modern American copyright.

That copyright in the beginning was a publisher's right is hardly surprising; indeed, it is remarkable that later it somehow came to be generally known as an author's right. This shift in how copyright was perceived will be examined primarily in the next chapter, but it is essential first to concentrate on the origins of copyright and the nature of the stationers' copyright as a publisher's right. For regardless of conventional wisdom, which has long viewed copyright as belonging to authors, copyright began and continues to function much the same as it did for its originators, that is, primarily to protect the publisher's marketing of works.

The Stationers' Copyright

The complex details of the history of the Stationers' Company (the membership of which included bookbinders, printers, and booksellers) and the stationers' copyright will not be examined in depth here, for—apart from the fact that they have been related by others and can be found in the transcripts of records—only certain aspects of any historical development survive to influence the future.[2] Thus it is irrelevant for present purposes that not all books printed in England during the time of the stationers' copyright were registered with the company, that the incidents of copyright may have varied during its long history, or even that no one can precisely determine the date of its beginning (which almost surely preceded the grant of the charter to the Stationers' Company). The vital fact is that the stationers' copyright lasted for almost two centuries and clearly provided the basic legal structure that its successor, the statutory copyright, inherited and carried forward—first in England, then in the United States.

Although the specific source of the idea for the stationers' copyright is not revealed by the records of history, it may well have been the printing patent, which was granted by the sovereign in the exercise of the royal prerogative and preceded the trade practice that resulted in the stationers' copyright. The monarch's grant of letters patent was not limited to printing; it could be for any trade, since such a grant was a source of income for the sovereign. But the earliest printing patents, for which the grantee was willing to pay a desirable sum, granted the exclusive right to publish books that had an assured market—such as the *ABC Book* (the first schoolbook for English children), the Bible, and law books.

If the sovereign could grant the exclusive right of publication, it was logical for stationers to agree to a similar right among themselves. And since the right to print and publish books was essentially limited to the members of the guild (later company) of stationers, the exclusive right of individual members to publish a particular book was relatively easy to enforce. The basic requirement was to establish a record of who was entitled to print a work by registering the title of the manuscript (the "copy"), thus identifying the owner.[3]

In assessing the stationers' copyright some three hundred years after its demise, it is important to view it in proper perspective, and there are several points to aid one in doing so. First, one should understand the nature of that copyright, which was granted by a group of businessmen who agreed to allow one of them the exclusive right to publish a specific work *in perpetuity.* The right could be secured only by an entry of the title of the work in the company register for a fee that came to be sixpence.[4] A typical entry was as follows:

Quarto die Julii

Edward White/ Entred for his Copie vnder the wardens handes, a ballad intituled/
> A *Dittie worthie to be viewed of all people declaringe the dreadfull comynge of CHRIST to Judgement and howe all shall appeare before his presence* . . . . vjd[5]

The "copy," or manuscript, belonged to the individual stationer, clearly indicating that in the beginning the word *copy* in *copyright* was used as a noun, not a verb. (The term *copy right* itself does not appear in the register books until the 1670s.) How the stationer acquired ownership of the copy from the author was, by and large, of no concern to the wardens, whose responsibility it was only to register the copies. In fact, who created a given work was irrelevant, since authors, not being members of the company, had no role in the stationers' copyright. Copyright, in short, originally had to do with the manufacture and sale of books, not the creations of authors.

Second, the Stationers' Company, as a London company, had the power of self-regulation. The major officers were the master and wardens, with the central component of its internal machinery being a court of assistants, which promulgated company ordinances (subject to approval by government officials) and resolved copyright disputes between its members.[6] This meant, of course, that issues concerning stationers' copyright were not litigated in the common-law courts. Copyright was thus initially shaped not by the common law but by members of the industry.

Third, the stationers—good businessmen intent on protecting their monopoly of the book trade—were acutely sensitive to the fact that their ordinances were binding only on members of their company, and that in fact their copyright was essentially a matter of private law. As a result, one theme dominates the history of the stationers' copyright: the continual efforts of the stationers to obtain *public* law support for their *private* copyright by petitioning for laws regulating the press that made it a crime for anyone to print books in violation of the stationers' copyright.[7]

Copyright and Censorship

The stationers' desire for legal copyright protection coincided fortuitously with the government's perceived need to gain control over "the dangerous possibilities of the printed word."[8] It had been Henry VIII's break with the Roman Catholic church in the 1530s that had contributed most to creating conditions of instability, unrest, and religious strife in England. Henry was succeeded in 1547 by his Protestant son Edward VI, who was succeeded by his Catholic half-sister Mary Tudor (wife of Philip of Spain), who was succeeded by her Protestant half-sister Elizabeth I—all within the space of eleven years. It was Philip and Mary's desire to prevent the publication of "seditious, heretical, and schismatical" materials that finally led to their granting to the Stationers' Company in 1557 a royal charter that limited most printing to members of that company and empowered the stationers to search out and destroy unlawful books.[9] But Mary's Protestant successor, Elizabeth I, renewed that charter in the first year of her reign for the same reasons that Mary had granted it initially.

Despite Elizabeth's long reign (1558–1603), the religious unrest continued with her successors: James I; his son Charles I (who lost his head to the Puritans); Oliver Cromwell, who ruled during the Interregnum; the pro-Catholic Charles II; and finally his brother, the avowed Catholic James II, whose actions precipitated an end to the religious controversy in 1688. The continuous political unrest proved beneficial to the stationers, for without it (and the various monarchs' perceived needs for censorship) the stationers' copyright probably would not have survived as long as it did. Less than twenty-five years after the Glorious Revolution of 1688 assured the Protestant succession, Parliament displaced the private stationers' copyright with a public statutory copyright.

Throughout this period, decrees of press control were continually in force—even during the Interregnum, when Parliament enacted ordinances to replace the censorship decrees of the Court of the Star Chamber. Promulgated during Elizabeth's reign were the Star Chamber decrees of 1566 and 1586, and during the reign of Charles I, the Star Chamber Decree of 1637.[10] Despite the relatively short life of the 1637 decree (because of the demise of the Star Chamber in the 1640 Revolution), it turned out to be the most important. Parliament had filled the void during the Interregnum with the ordinances of 1643, 1647, and 1649, but the importance of the 1637 decree is that it was essentially reenacted by Parliament as the Licensing Act of 1662, two years after Charles II ceased his travels and ascended to the throne.[11] Although the Licensing Act contained a sunset provision—it was to expire by its own terms after two years—it was actually renewed continually until 1694, when Parliament finally refused to renew it again.[12]

The stationers' role in promoting these various regulations was continuous and ongoing, because regulation of the press meant protection for their copyrights. "Whatever other problems may have exercised the minds of whatever combination of Master, Wardens and Assistants," according to the historian Cyprian Blagden, "the fundamental and perennial worry was the protection of copyright."[13] One of their earliest achievements in this regard was acquiring "[t]he right to search—nominally for seditious or heretical books—but really for infringements of copyright."[14] And one of their most notable achievements was the Star Chamber Decree of 1637.

The earlier Star Chamber Decree of 1586 had given the stationers a large part of the power they wanted, particularly for the protection of copyright, but there were still many cases of pirated editions—especially of popular and less expensive books. And the government had been unable to halt the printing or importing of works critical of King Charles I's administration. Consequently, on 11 July 1637, the Privy Council approved in Star Chamber a decree "Concerning Printing," which the attorney-general had drawn up. ("For his Loue & kindnes to the Company," the stationers soon after voted to give the attorney-general twenty pounds—a payment to a public official that reflects fairly transparent motives.) As Blagden notes in his history of the Stationers' Company: "There is no doubt that the 1637 Decree, like that of 1586 and like the grant of the Charter in 1557, was promoted by the Company for the benefit of stationers and obtained the sanction of the Government because it promised more effective safeguards than those already in existence, against the printing and distribution of schismatical publications which were, as on previous occasions, becoming sources of extreme embarrassment."[15]

The Star Chamber Decree of 1637 was revived in the form of the Licensing Act of 1662, and the stationers continued their support of press control as a means of protecting their copyrights, working in "uneasy partnership" with Sir Roger L'Estrange, the Surveyor of the Press.[16] According to Blagden, "Urged on by L'Estrange, the Wardens seized Quaker pam-

phlets and Catholic books and had them burned in the gar-
den at Stationers' Hall or damasked [defaced or destroyed];
and in the Michaelmas Term 1681 no fewer than twelve cases
were pending, seven instituted by the Crown and only five by
the Wardens who were known to send warning of impend-
ing searches to such members of the Company as were fool-
ish enough to be caught dealing in unlicensed books yet not
knavish enough to handle counterfeit primers." [17]

By promoting censorship and press control the stationers
were utilizing the best means available to protect their "property." The government was not really interested in copyright
as property, only as an instrument of censorship. And that is
our point. As a device to control the distribution of printed
material, copyright was ideal, since it combined so well the
interest of the government with the self-interest of the copyright owners. And though it may come as a surprise to many,
American copyright still retains the features that once made it
such an effective device of censorship. Indeed, the 1976 Copyright Act betrays the origins of copyright as such in that it gives
courts a similar power to burn and damask offending copies—
in a clause that would have pleased Sir Roger L'Estrange, even
though its language is less direct than the Surveyor of the Press
might have desired.[18]

Human nature has not changed much in three hundred
years. Copyright owners today are no more willing than the
stationers were in seventeenth-century England to put the
public interest ahead of their private-property concerns.
The Stationers' Company has its American successors in the
media conglomerates, who control the use of the nation's air
waves courtesy of governmental licenses—and then control
the use of the material they present over those airwaves courtesy of a copyright law they have had an active role in shaping.
In many respects the stationers' copyright can be regarded as
the grandsire of today's corporate copyright.

To understand why this is so, one need only trace the story of copyright after the 1694 demise of the Licensing Act of 1662, which meant that the only copyright in force was left without support in the public law. No longer was it a criminal offense to print books in violation of the stationers' copyright. The "death" of copyright, however, was not universally mourned, for by this time the publishers had become dominant in the Stationers' Company and had established what was known as the "booksellers' monopoly," based on the perpetual nature of the stationers' copyright. The ownership of the major copyrights was limited to small groups of booksellers known as the Congers.[19] (Although the copyrights were sold at auction, apparently only booksellers with the appropriate credentials were allowed to participate.) Contemporary reports suggest that the monopolists were notorious, powerful, and ruthless in protecting their self-created prerogatives. And it seems clear that growing resentment against the monopoly—much more than against censorship—led to Parliament's refusal to renew the Licensing Act.[20]

The Statute of Anne

The end of legally sanctioned censorship after 1694 meant that the booksellers had no public protection for their private stationers' copyrights, and in the following years they frequently petitioned Parliament for relief.[21] Their first efforts were to secure full reinstatement of censorship laws, but when these attempts failed, the booksellers tried a new tactic: they sought legal protection not for themselves but for authors, who would be expected to convey their copyright to the bookseller as in the past. This tactic succeeded in 1710, and the result was the Statute of Anne, which carried the full title of "An act for the encouragement of learning, by vesting the copies of printed books in the authors or purchasers of such copies, during the times therein mentioned."[22] A relatively short statute of eleven sections, it actually dealt with three copyrights: the stationers' copyright (which was extended for twenty-one years); the printing patent (which was not to be affected by the statute, but which was no longer significant); and the new statutory copyright.

Although the Statute of Anne ostensibly provides for an author's copyright, the main beneficiaries were the booksellers, because the law made copyright assignable to others. It may be anachronistic to call this a catch-22 situation, but the label is otherwise appropriate in every way. Since an author had to assign the copyright in order to be paid—otherwise, no bookseller would publish the work, and without a printed book there could be no copyright—the benefit of the statute to authors was minimal.

There were, however, two notable aspects of the Statute of Anne. The first was that it transformed the stationers' copyright—which had been used as a device of monopoly and an instrument of censorship—into a trade-regulation concept to promote learning and to curtail the monopoly of publishers. Arguing that the new statutory copyright benefited authors appears to have been a canard of the booksellers to enable them to hide behind authors while retaining their old power. If so, Parliament perceived the ruse and turned the tables on the monopolists, using the author primarily as a decoy to create a copyright that was really a trade-regulation concept.[23]

Indeed, when the first English copyright act is interpreted in light of the history that led to its enactment, the almost inescapable conclusion is that it was designed as a trade-regulation statute intended to destroy (and prevent the recurrence of) the booksellers' monopoly. A comparison of the new statute with the Licensing Act of 1662 strongly suggests that the draftsmen used the latter as the starting point for their efforts in order to erase the undesirable features of the stationers' copyright that had made it an instrument of censorship and monopoly.[24]

The features of the Statute of Anne that justify the epithet of trade regulation included the limited term of copyright, the availability of copyright to anyone, and price-control provisions. Copyright, rather than being perpetual, was now limited to a term of fourteen years, with a like renewal term being available only to the author (and only if the author were living at the end of the first term). Since authors normally assigned copyrights to booksellers, the provisions meant that the work of any author who died during the initial term would go into the public domain without a renewal term—consistent with the antimonopoly purpose of the statute.

Copyright, which had theretofore been limited to members of the Stationers' Company, was made available to anyone. Indeed, the statute even contained an alternative provision for securing copyright if the stationers refused registration. The ordinary means for securing the statutory copyright continued to be the same as it had been for the stationers' copyright; the alternative method was by advertisement in the *Gazette*, the legal newspaper.

The statute also contained price-control provisions, although they seem never to have been invoked. Obviously created in response to the high prices the booksellers had charged, the price controls may have served their intended purpose merely by existing.

Creation of the Public Domain

An even more notable aspect of the Statute of Anne was its creation of the public domain for literature. From our vantage point in history, so far removed from the stationers' copyright, it is difficult to realize that the perpetual nature of early copyright had essentially precluded the existence of such a public domain. Under the old system, all literature belonged to some bookseller forever, and only literature that met the censorship standards as administrated by the booksellers could ever appear in print. Moreover, the whole system—so amenable to both the governing authorities and the stationers who enforced it by their own regulations—lay completely beyond the jurisdiction of the common-law courts.

The public domain resulted from three rules in the Statute of Anne: the requirement of the creation of a new work in order to obtain copyright (which protected extant works against recapture); the limited term of copyright (which ensured that all copyrighted works would eventually be free for any to publish); and the limited rights granted to the copyright owner: to print, publish and vend (which limited the copyright owner's control of the use of the work after it was purchased by the consumer).

These two aspects of the Statute of Anne—copyright as trade regulation and the creation of the public domain—constituted a watershed recognition of the public interest that copyright serves. First, the publishers were limited in their use of copyright as a support for their monopoly. Second, the public was assured not only of access to copyrighted works at a fair price but eventually of ownership of the work in the public domain.

The design of the Statute of Anne was thus a remarkable feat of legal architecture—with one fatal flaw that prevented its immediate success in destroying the booksellers' monopoly. Because the old stationers' copyrights were "grandfathered" for twenty-one years, the booksellers could (and did) continue business as usual. The monopolists were thus made a present of time, the most precious of commodities, which (as we will show in the next chapter) they used to great advantage. When the Statute of Anne was finally given its definitive judicial interpretation in the House of Lords' decision of *Donaldson v.*

Beckett—some sixty-five years after its enactment—time had obscured its design, and the lords may have partially misperceived the carefully wrought plan of Parliament that was the Statute of Anne. Consequently, copyright, though it continued to function as a publisher's right, came to be conceived of as an author's right.

The laws of conscience, which pretend to be derived of nature, proceed from custom.
— Montaigne

Ignorance never settles a question.
— Benjamin Disraeli

Copyright Changes

An Author's Right?

The stationers' perpetual copyright finally expired in 1731, after its twenty-one-year reprieve by the Statute of Anne. The statutory copyright then became the sole legal protection for the right of exclusive publication, which was now limited to two terms of fourteen years each. By 1731, those books first published when the copyright act went into effect had already exhausted their initial term; and by 1738, even if they had been renewed, they were in the public domain after only twenty-eight years. In theory, the booksellers' monopoly was approaching its end.

But as is often the case, theory foundered on the reefs of reality. The booksellers viewed perpetual copyright as the basis of their livelihood, and they were not willing to sacrifice it on the altar of public interest merely because a statute purported to deprive them of their property. Still, it would be better to have their position supported by statute than not, and once again they sought relief from Parliament.[1] When this effort at rescue by legislation failed, they turned to the courts and attempted to obtain the judicial creation of a substitute for the stationers' copyright: a perpetual common-law copyright for the author. Their assumption was that authors would assign this new copyright to the booksellers in accordance with custom, an assumption justified by their control of the market. If authors wanted their books to be sold, they would do as the bookseller wished. The author's common-law copyright would thus displace the statutory copyright and provide a support for the booksellers' monopoly as secure as the earlier stationers' copyright.

The judicial efforts of the monopolists resulted in a forty-year campaign that came to be known as the Battle of the Booksellers—quite possibly the most long-lasting and notable instance of intellectual combat in Anglo-American jurisprudence. Although the forty-year controversy was filled with continual litigation, there were only two decisions that had any lasting importance. These were the cases of *Millar v. Taylor*, a King's Bench decision, and *Donaldson v. Beckett*, a House of Lords decision.[2]

Millar v. Taylor

In 1767, Andrew Millar, a bookseller, brought an action in the Court of King's Bench against Robert Taylor for printing

James Thomson's long poem *The Seasons*, which Millar had purchased from the author in 1729. The plaintiff had duly entered his copy in the Stationers' Register, but the period of protection granted by the Statute of Anne had expired. There were two questions in the case: Did the author of a book have a copyright at common law after publication? Was this right taken away by the Statute of Anne? The court ruled three to one in favor of the plaintiff, answering the first question yes, the second no.

Justice Willes relied on the charter and bylaws of the Stationers' Company, the various Star Chamber decrees that had earlier regulated the press, the ordinances passed by Parliament during the Interregnum, and the Licensing Act of 1662 to support the author's common-law copyright. The fault in his use of this evidence, as Justice Yates pointed out in dissent, was that it was irrelevant. None of these matters provided any protection for the author, and since the outdated stationers' copyright had been limited to members of the company, no author would even have been qualified to have that copyright.

The majority's other reasons for supporting the common-law copyright, however, are more complex and more persuasive. These reasons had to do primarily with the natural right of a person in the property he or she creates. On this point, the opinions of Justice Aston and Lord Mansfield are particularly interesting. Justice Aston, after discussing the concept of property, concluded that "a man may have property in his body, life, fame, labours, and the like; and, in short, in anything that can be called his."[3] Later, he commented, "I do not know, nor can I comprehend any property more emphatically a man's own, nay, more incapable of being mistaken, than his literary works."[4] Lord Mansfield, in speaking of the author's common-law copyright before publication, said that the right is not found in custom or precedent, but is drawn

[f]rom this argument—because it is just, that an author should reap the pecuniary profits of his own ingenuity and labour. It is just, that another should not use his name, without his consent. It is fit that he should judge when to publish, or whether he ever will publish. It is fit he should not only choose the time, but the manner of publication; how many; what volume; what print. It is fit, he should choose to whose care he will trust the accuracy and correctness of the impression; in whose honesty he will confide, not to foist in additions: with other reasonings of the same effect.[5]

These were sufficient reasons to protect the copy before publication, he argued, and the same reasons should apply after the author has published. Lord Mansfield's argument was best summed up in the following statement: "His [an author's] name ought not to be used, against his will. It is an injury, by a faulty, ignorant and incorrect edition, to disgrace his work and mislead the reader."[6] At this point, however, Mansfield treated ownership of the copyright as ownership of the work. The major fallacy in his argument, then, was that it ignored the crucial fact that when an author assigned the copyright to a publisher, as was usually the case, he signed away those very rights that Mansfield said compelled a recognition of his perpetual copyright.

In a dissenting opinion, Justice Yates contended that there was no common-law copyright of the author, because one cannot have a property "in the style and ideas of his work" at common law. The only copyright, he said, was the statutory copyright under the Statute of Anne. "The Legislature indeed may make a new right. The Statute of Queen Ann. has vested a new right in authors, for a limited time: and whilst that right exists, they will be established in the possession of their property."[7] Yates thus implied but did not clearly state a distinction between the ownership of the work and the ownership of the copyright of that work.

The opinions in the *Millar* case treated copyright as an author's right. On this point, Yates in dissent differed only in noting that the author's copyright was a statutory, not a common-law, copyright. Yet, in light of the earlier history of copyright, all the opinions missed the basic point: copyright remained essentially a publisher's right; authors had nothing to do with its development.

Donaldson v. Beckett

Millar v. Taylor was not appealed, but it lasted as a precedent for only five years. Millar himself died in June 1768, while his case was pending, and the executors of his estate sold his copies at auction on 13 June 1769. Thomas Beckett and fourteen partners purchased in shares for £505 the copyrights of works by James Thomson, including the poems upon which the *Millar* case had conferred the author's perpetual common-law copyright.

Under the Statute of Anne, however, the copyrights of the poems had expired in 1757 at the latest. Alexander Donaldson (who had been excluded from the sale of Millar's copyrights) then claimed the right to publish the works free of charge and allegedly sold several thousand copies of *The Seasons* printed in Edinburgh. In November 1772, on the authority of the *Millar* case, Beckett and his partners received a perpetual injunction to restrain Donaldson. Their ultimate goal, however, was to have the great question of literary property resolved by the House of Lords, to which Donaldson appealed.[8] The result was the landmark case of Anglo-American copyright law, *Donaldson v. Beckett.*

The lords in the *Donaldson* case directed that five questions be put to the judges of the common-law courts, King's Bench, Common Pleas, and Exchequer, for their advice and opinion. The questions and their answers were as follows:

1. Whether an author of a book or literary composition had at common law "the sole right of first printing and publishing the same for sale," and a right of action against a person printing, publishing, and selling without his consent. Advised, yes by a vote of eight to three.

2. If the author had such a right, did the law take it away upon his publishing the book or literary composition; and might any person thereafter be free to reprint and sell the work? Advised, no by a vote of seven to four.

3. Assuming the right of common law, was it taken away by the Statute of Anne, and is an author limited to the terms and conditions of that statute for his remedy? Advised, yes by a vote of six to five.

4. Whether an author of any literary composition and his assigns have the sole right of printing and publishing the same in perpetuity by the common law. Advised, yes by a vote of seven to four.

5. Whether this right was restrained or taken away by the Statute of Anne. Advised, yes by a vote of six to five.[9]

The questions fall in two groups: the first three apply only to the author, the last two to the author and his assigns. The fourth question dealing with the author and his assigns was apparently intended to make sure that the *Millar* case—which had held that the author could assign his common-law copyright—was specifically reconsidered.

On the basis of these published responses, American courts and commentators assumed that (and have since acted as if) the House of Lords had held that the author had a common-law copyright.[10] Recent scholarship, however, demonstrates that such a reading of *Donaldson* is wrong, and that in fact the lords did not so hold.[11] The opinions of the common-law judges were advisory only, and after hearing them, the lords debated the case and by a vote of 22 to 11 reversed the grant of the injunction.[12]

The reason for the misreading is simple enough: an over-reliance on the account of the case in volume 4 of Sir James Burrow's *Reports of Cases Argued and Adjudged in the Court of King's Bench*, which was the most widely circulated report and thus the one most readily available in the United States.[13] The report in Burrow, however, is incomplete, presumably because "at the time of the *Donaldson* decision it was a contempt punishable by imprisonment to publish any statements made by a member of Parliament in the course of parliamentary business."[14] Moreover, the report of *Donaldson* in Burrow consists of only ten pages and appears as an appendix to the report of *Millar v. Taylor*, which is slightly over one hundred pages in length. Anyone reading *Millar* first, followed immediately by the answers to the questions in *Donaldson*, would reasonably have concluded that the lords had recognized the common-law copyright—which is what most commentators and judges thought in the early years of American copyright. But a more complete report of the case in *Cobbett's Parliamentary History*, published in 1817, demonstrates why such a conclusion is in error.

Cobbett's report of the proceedings in the House of Lords consists of the arguments of counsel, the opinions of the judges, and the speeches of the lords, of whom only five spoke. A brief excerpt from each will provide the tenor of the proceedings.

Sir John Dalrymple, counsel arguing for Donaldson, contended (among other things) that there was no property in ideas:

If I copy a manuscript, says he, and publish it, I am liable
to a civil action; if I steal a book, to a criminal one; the one
is simply taking ideas, the other a chattel. But, argues he,
what property can a man have in ideas? Whilst he keeps
them to himself they are his own, when he publishes them
they are his no longer. If I take water from the ocean, it
is mine, if I pour it back it is mine no longer.[15]

Solicitor General Wedderburn, counsel for the booksellers,
argued as follows:

Authors, he contended, both from principles of natural
justice, and the interest of society, had the best right to
the profits accruing from a publication of their own ideas;
and as it had been admitted on all hands that an author
had an interest or property in his own manuscript, previous to publication; he desired to know who could have a
greater claim to it afterwards. It was an author's dominion
over his ideas that gave him his property in his manuscript
originally, and nothing but a transfer of that dominion
or right of disposal could take it away. It was absurd to
imagine, that either a sale, a loan, or a gift of a book,
carried with it an implied right of multiplying copies; so
much paper and print were sold, lent, or given, and an
unlimited perusal was warranted from such sale, loan or
gift, but it could not be conceived that when 5s. were paid
for a book, the seller meant to transfer a right of gaining
100l.; every man must feel to the contrary, and confess
the absurdity of such an argument.[16]

Justice Ashurst's opinion is an example of the opinions of
the judges favoring the author's common-law copyright.

[He] accorded in opinion with the Justice Nares, after trac-
ing the nature of literary property, and producing many

cogent reasons to prove that such a claim was warranted
by the principles of national justice and solid reason.
Making an author's intellectual ideas common, was, he
observed, giving the purchaser an opportunity of using
those ideas, and profiting by them, while they instructed
and entertained him; but he could not conceive that the
vender, for the price of 5s., sold the purchaser a right to
multiply copies, and so get 500l. Literary property was
to be defined and described as well as other matters, and
matters which were tangible. Every thing was property
that was capable of being known or defined, capable of a
separate enjoyment, and of value to the owner. Literary
property fell within the terms of this definition. According to the appellants, if a man lends his manuscript to
his friend, and his friend prints it, or if he loses it, and
the finder prints it, yet an action would lie (as Mr. Justice Yeates had admitted), which shewed that there was a
property beyond the materials, the paper and print. That
a man, by publishing his book, gave the public nothing
more than the use of it.[17]

The most cogent statement against the author's common-
law copyright by the judges was that of Lord Chief Justice
De Grey:

The truth is, the idea of a common-law right in perpetuity was not taken up till after that failure (of the booksellers) in procuring a new statute for an enlargement of
the term. If (say the parties concerned) the legislature will
not do it for us, we will do it without their assistance: and
then we begin to hear of this new doctrine, the common-
law right, which, upon the whole, I am of opinion, cannot
be supported upon any rules or principles of the common
law of this kingdom.[18]

Lord Camden was one of the strongest opponents of the author's common-law copyright; indeed, it was at his suggestion that questions 4 and 5 (dealing with the author and his assigns) had been added to the list of questions the lords posed to the judges.[19] Lord Camden lauded De Grey's argument and continued:

> The arguments attempted to be maintained on the side of the Respondents, were founded on patents, privileges, Star-chamber decrees, and the bye laws of the Stationers' Company; all of them the effects of the grossest tyranny and usurpation; the very last places in which I should have dreamt of finding the least trace of the common law of this kingdom; and yet, by a variety of subtle reasoning and metaphysical refinements, have they endeavoured to squeeze out the spirit of the common law from premises, in which it could not possibly have existence.[20]

Lord Camden's speech was lengthy, but perhaps that portion which most clearly rejects the author's common-law copyright is the following:

> Knowledge has no value or use for the solitary owner: to be enjoyed it must be communicated. "Scire tuum nihil est, nisi te scire hoc sciat alter." Glory is the reward of science, and those who deserve it, scorn all meaner views: I speak not of the scribblers for bread, who teaze the press with their wretched productions; fourteen years is too long a privilege for their perishable trash. It was not for gain that Bacon, Newton, Milton, Locke, instructed and delighted the world; it would be unworthy [of] such men to traffic with a dirty bookseller for so much [as] a sheet of a letter press. When the bookseller offered Milton five pound for his Paradise Lost, he did not reject it, and commit his poem to the flames, nor did he accept the mis-

erable pittance as the reward of his labour; he knew that
the real price of his work was immortality, and that posterity would pay it. Some authors are as careless about
profit as others are rapacious of it; and what situation
would the public be in with regard to literature, if there
were no means of compelling a second impression of a
useful work to be put forth, or wait till a wife or children
are to be provided for by the sale of an edition. All our
learning will be locked upon in the hands of the Tonsons
and the Lintons of the age, who will set what price upon it
their avarice chuses to demand, till the public become as
much their slaves, as their own hackney compilers are.[21]

Lord Chancellor Apsley was also against the author's
common-law copyright—a significant opponent, because he
had issued the decree that was in issue. He explained "that he
had made the decree entirely as of course, in pursuance of the
decision upon the right in the court of King's-bench, and that
as what he had decreed, as a chancellor, was merely a step in
the gradation to a final and determinate issue in the House of
Peers, he was totally unbiassed upon the question, and therefore could speak to it as fairly from his own sense of it, as any
one of the judges, or any of the lords present." He was "clearly
of opinion with the appellants [Donaldson]."[22]

According to the report in *Cobbett's Parliamentary History*,
only three other lords spoke on the "Question of Literary
Property": Lord Lyttelton, the bishop of Carlisle, and Lord
Effingham. Of these three, only Lord Lyttelton spoke in favor
of the author's common-law copyright. The bishop of Carlisle "made use of similar arguments with those of lord Camden against the property." Then the report continues, "Lord
Effingham rose last, and begged to urge the liberty of the
press, as the strongest argument against this property; adding, that a despotic minister, hearing of a pamphlet which

might strike at his measures, may buy the copy, and by printing 20 copies, secure it his own, and by that means the public
would be deprived of the most interesting information. Lord
Mansfield did not speak."[23]

In view of the opinions of Lord Camden and Lord Chancellor Apsley, Burrows's terse note at the end of his report
of the case takes on considerable significance: "And the Lord
Chancellor seconding Lord Camden's motion 'to reverse'; the
decree was reversed."[24]

The *Donaldson* decision was widely approved at the time of
its rendering—except by the few monopolists whom it affected
directly, who once again turned to Parliament for relief, con-
tending that in reliance on the *Millar* case they had invested
thousands of pounds in the purchase of old copyrights not
protected by statute. The claims of economic ruin were sufficient to get a bill before the House of Commons, but there
was widespread opposition both inside and outside of Parliament.[25] The authors did not support the booksellers, and
many counterpetitions opposed their claims. The most effective opposition was probably that of various competitors who
"stated that only a few of the London booksellers were affected
by the decision" of the *Donaldson* case.[26]

There is no surviving copy of the bill presented in April
1774, but some responses to it remain on record. For instance,
Mr. Dempster in the House of Commons charged that "this
Bill was not meant to restore the law concerning copyright as
it formerly stood, but as the individual booksellers of London
thought it stood."[27] In spite of such strong opposition, the bill
passed the House of Commons and was sent to the House
of Lords.

Opposition to the bill by the lords was indeed bitter. Lord
Denbigh stated "that the very principle of the Bill was totally
inadmissible, and that it was not necessary to call witnesses,
or to make any inquiry into a Bill that violated the rights of

individuals, and affronted that House." The lord chancellor argued "that the booksellers never could imagine that they had a common-law right, . . . that the monopoly was supported among them by oppression and combination, and that . . . none of their allegations nor any part of the Bill required any further inquiry." And Lord Camden pointed out "that the monopolizing booksellers had robbed others of their property; . . . that they had maintained this monopoly by most iniquitous oppression, and exercised it to the disgrace of printing; that they were monopolists, and if the line of justice and equity were drawn, it would be, that those who had deprived others of their right for a series of years, should make compensation to all those they had injured by such conduct."[28]

The bill was rejected, and so, late in the eighteenth century, the Battle of the Booksellers ended. Copyright had ceased to be recognized as a publisher's right and had come to be known as an author's right. And it was as an author's right that copyright was received into the United States a few years later.

Our conclusion that American courts misread *Donaldson* is, we think, supported by the facts now known; but we also think that the harm resulting from the misreading derived not from the common-law copyright per se but from the misleading effect that right has subsequently had on the courts' perception of the nature of copyright. There was no disagreement among the disputants in the *Donaldson* case regarding whether or not an author's work was his or her property upon creation.[29] The disagreement was over whether the author at common law had the exclusive right to reproduce the work in copies. Whatever one concludes as to the lords' actual holding on this point, there was uniform agreement that the lords had held that the copyright statute superseded this right, even if it had earlier existed. Since the issue of the common-law copyright was never to be litigated in either England or the United States without a copyright statute, the author's common-law copyright was a stillborn concept. Copyright is the right of exclusive publication, whether in perpetuity or for a limited time. Because of the copyright statute, the common-law copyright never meant more than the right of first publication—a right agreeable to the opponents of the author's common-law copyright in perpetuity.

The author's common-law copyright thus came to mean the author's property interest in his or her work prior to publication—an interest that courts would probably have recognized even if the *Donaldson* case had never been decided. The harm from the common-law copyright, then, came not from its content but from its name, because the name gave the law of copyright a dual theoretical basis. The legislative statute notwithstanding, copyright came to be viewed as a natural-law right of the author as well as the statutory grant of a limited monopoly. The result ever since has been confusion as to the nature of copyright: one theory holding that copyright's origin occurs at the creation of a work, the other that its origin exists only through the copyright statute. But there is a significant difference between source and origin. The author's creation is obviously the *source* of copyright; but since copyright comes into existence only under the terms of the statute, the statute itself is its *origin*. The fact that creation of a work is legally a *necessary* condition for copyright did not—until the 1976 U.S. Copyright Act—mean that it was a *sufficient* condition.

Moreover, statutory copyright has long been only nominally a right of the author. The epithet "author's right" itself was a fiction from the start, because authors, by assigning copyright to publishers, assigned their entire interests in the works. Yet, once the phrase achieved currency, publishers were able to argue that copyright was the author's property by reason of creation under natural law, rather than by statutory grant, and that justice therefore required that the rights of copyright be enlarged to protect the author (even though these rights were primarily to benefit the publisher). Copyright as an author's right was and continues to be a fiction.

The booksellers knew this and acted accordingly. Even after the *Donaldson* decision the booksellers acted as if it had been decided in their favor. They simply created their private perpetual copyright by unwritten agreement within the trade. As late as 1791, James Boswell—writing about Dr. Samuel Johnson's *Lives of the Poets*—acknowledged that "The Poets were selected by the several booksellers who had the honorary copy right, *which is still preserved among them by mutual compact,* not withstanding the decision of the House of Lords against the perpetuity of Literary Property" (emphasis added).[30]

The good of the people is the chief law.

— Cicero

The American Constitution is the most wonderful work
ever struck off at a given time by the brain and purpose
of man.

— William Gladstone

Copyright in the

U.S. Constitution

Policies

The 1710 Statute of Anne is the direct ancestor of American
copyright law: its full title identified the fundamental ideas
(the encouragement of learning, copyright for authors, and
limited times) of the copyright clause of the Constitution, and
the statute itself clearly served as the model for the Copyright
Act of 1790, the first U.S. copyright statute.[1] The English copyright was thus received into the United States as an author's

right, both because the language of the statute suggested it, and because of the misreading of the *Donaldson* case.

We do not know to what extent the framers of the Constitution had knowledge of the earlier stationers' copyright and the genesis of copyright as a publisher's right, although it is highly unlikely that historical materials relevant to the stationers' copyright were available in the United States in 1789. Besides, the *Donaldson* case was deemed to have given the Statute of Anne, which had been on the books for almost seventy years, its definitive interpretation by the House of Lords only fifteen years earlier, and that made the early history of copyright seem irrelevant. In any event, the Statute of Anne provided sound policies for copyright that the framers incorporated into the copyright clause.

As used in this context, the term *policy* indicates the goal or purpose to which a proposition of law is directed. In this regard, American copyright law is unique, for the purpose of copyright is specifically stated in the U.S. Constitution, the intellectual-property clause of which grants to Congress the power to enact copyright legislation. Because the clause is a limitation on, as well as a grant of, congressional power, it states both the purpose of and the basic conditions for copyright:

> The Congress shall have power . . . to Promote the Progress of Science and useful Arts, by securing for limited Times to Authors and Inventors the exclusive Right to their respective Writings and Discoveries.[2]

Since the intellectual-property clause also empowers Congress to grant patents, one must read the passage distributively, recognizing that, as there used, the word *science* retains its eighteenth-century meaning of "knowledge or learning." So read, the copyright portion of the clause grants Congress the power to promote learning by securing for limited times to authors the exclusive right to their writings.

This language manifests three policies for copyright: the promotion of learning (because the language so states), the preservation of the public domain (because after a limited time all writings go into the public domain), and the protection of the author (because to achieve the larger goals the author is given an exclusive right).

The Promotion-of-Learning Policy

The ordering of the policies in the clause indicates their priority: the first is that copyright promote learning; the second is that it preserve the public domain; and the third is that it encourage creation and distribution of works by benefiting the author. Logically, the third policy is an instrument for achieving the first two, a logic that Congress has continually reiterated, most recently in the House report on the Berne Convention Implementation Act of 1988, which reads in part:

> Sound copyright legislation is necessarily subject to other considerations in addition to the fact that a writing be created and that the exclusive right be protected only for a limited term. Congress must weigh the public costs and benefits derived from protecting a particular interest. "The constitutional purpose of copyright is to facilitate the flow of ideas in the interest of learning." . . . [T]he primary objective of our copyright laws is not to reward the author, but rather to secure for the public the benefits from the creations of authors.[3]

The constitutional mandate that copyright promote learning is the justification for the grant of the statutory monopoly, which (until the 1976 act) required the publication of a work.

A new work contributed to, and publication made it available for, learning. The purpose of promoting learning was thus accomplished effortlessly in the process of publication.

The keystone of copyright, then, is the promotion-of-learning policy. Without it, there would be no need to distinguish an author's copyright from any other kind of property. Once this central purpose of copyright is recognized, it is much easier to see the functional aspects of the other two policies—the preservation of the public domain and the incentive nature of the rights given to authors.

The Preservation-of-the-Public-Domain Policy

The public domain is not a territory, but a concept: there are certain materials—the air we breathe, sunlight, rain, ideas, words, numbers—not subject to private ownership. The materials that compose our cultural heritage must be free for all to use no less than matter necessary for biological survival.

Copyright, of course, is itself an encroachment on the public domain, in that it gives the author a limited proprietary control over his or her writings composed of ideas and words—materials taken from the public domain. The encroachment permitted, however, requires a quid pro quo and is limited in both scope and time: to be protected, the author must *create* a new work, and that work is protected for a limited time only. The first requirement means that copyright cannot be used to claim ideas or writings already in the public domain; the second means that the work which the author produces eventually goes into the public domain. The copyright policy thus serves not only to preserve but also to enrich the public domain.

Copyright's relevance to the public domain in the long run is similar to copyright's relevance to learning in the short run.

To the extent that copyright encourages new works that are permanent in form, it contributes to the culture of our society for generations unborn, even as it contributes to the reservoir of knowledge for contemporary learning.

The Protection-of-the-Author Policy

The constitutional protection given to authors is "the exclusive Right to their . . . Writings" for a limited period of time. The operative phrase, "exclusive Right," is the means to fulfill the purpose of promoting the "Progress of Science" and was clearly used as a functional term; in the context of the eighteenth century, it meant *the exclusive right to publish.*

Given the English background that is the source of the right, there is no other meaning available. Consider, for example, the following definition from an English treatise on literary property, published in 1828: "Copyright . . . comprises the exclusive right of printing and publishing copies of any literary performance, including engravings, musical compositions, maps, &c."[4] Moreover, the right to be granted was obviously to be a statutory right, and the statutory right in the Statute of Anne was the right to publish; as the title of that act makes clear, copyright then applied only to "printed" books. In the definitive interpretation of the English statute in the landmark case of *Donaldson v. Beckett,* the House of Lords had held in 1774— only thirteen years before the Constitution was drafted—that the publication of a work deprived the author of all common-law rights in his writings except for those granted by statute. On this point, the misreading of the *Donaldson* case was irrelevant. The framers of the Constitution, we can assume, were quite aware of the English ruling and of the difference between common-law and statutory rights; they also knew, of course, that Congress could grant only statutory rights. It follows, then, that the "exclusive Right" which the Constitution empowers Congress to protect is only the author's exclusive right to publish his or her writings.

The Implied Right of Access

Implicit in these three policies is a fourth—that individuals have a right to use copyrighted materials. Such use is necessary to learning, and the author's "exclusive right"—to publish the work—made it accessible for the very purpose for which copyright was granted. Copyright, in short, was a functional concept: its function was to encourage the author to distribute the works he or she created; its purpose was to promote learning. The function served the purpose by inducements, not threats: the Constitution did not give Congress the power to compel authors to publish their works or to accept the benefits of copyright.

Thus, copyright did not require that an author make available for learning every work newly created out of materials from the public domain. He or she could retain a new work in dusty files or consign it to the flames of a fireplace. But copyright was necessary for one to have the exclusive right to market the work, and the corollary to this right was the duty to make that work accessible for the learning of the present and the heritage of future generations. If an author wished to avoid fulfilling this public responsibility, he or she needed only to forgo the benefit of statutory copyright.

The author's freedom of choice—whether or not to seek fame and fortune by a public sharing of the work—gives rise to a clear inference: The framers of the copyright clause intended that copyright be in the nature of a bargain and sale between the American author and Congress to the benefit of the American public. Under the copyright clause, Congress is empowered to determine the terms of the copyright bargain, but it is clear that the statutory grant to the author, like the constitutional grant of power to enact the statute, is to be conditional. That condition is a right of use by the work's audience—first, because the policies of promoting learning and protecting the public domain have an importance superior to the policy of protecting the author; and second, because, whatever his or her genius, any author invades the public domain for the materials to create a new work. Authors are not free to take and recast public-domain materials and use copyright to obtain a private benefit without making the work available, through public access, for the advancement of learning.

In retrospect, the presence of copyright in the Constitution is somewhat anomalous. Men in the process of establishing a central government for a new nation surely had more important concerns than drafting a provision to empower the new legislature to protect the rights of authors when there were so few authors to protect. Indeed, there was even an argument at that time that copyright legislation would be disadvantageous to a new country whose literature came mainly from foreign shores. Since copyright laws were limited by national boundaries, the absence of a U.S. copyright would mean the absence of a tariff for printing the works of foreign authors. (The point was not lost on Congress, which, in the 1790 Copyright Act, limited the protection of American copyright to American citizens and residents, a limitation that survived intact until the 1890s.)

Apart from the fact that the copyright clause is combined with the patent clause, the efforts of two people may explain its existence. One is James Madison, whose learning and intelligence undoubtedly endowed him with a foresight denied lesser minds; and James Madison clearly bears significant responsibility for the copyright clause.[5] Another is Noah Webster, who got the Connecticut legislature to pass a copyright statute in 1783 in order to have copyright protection for his spelling book. Webster is said to have traveled from state to state and induced twelve of the original states—all except Delaware—to enact similar statutes.[6] There was also a resolution in the Continental Congress (probably as a result of Webster's efforts) encouraging the states "to secure to the authors or publishers of any new books not hitherto printed" copyright protection.[7] The resolution is of dual interest, because it would have included the publishers (who were ultimately excluded from the copyright clause), and because James Madison was a member of the committee that presented it.

The exclusion of publishers from the copyright clause is probably explained by concern for the perceived potential of a booksellers' monopoly in this country, the danger of which the copyright litigation in eighteenth-century England had made manifest. The publishers, however, could not be excluded from the copyright equation: the Copyright Act of 1790 included publishers as proprietors of copyright by reason of assignment. This, of course, was necessary because copyright meant the right to print and publish, and without publication (therefore, without publishers) there would be no copyright. The irony is that while the title of the Statute of Anne (the source of the ideas in the copyright clause) made clear the publishers' right to copyright—by reason of purchase—the U.S. Constitution's copyright clause excludes them. The exclusion of publishers can be said to have constitutionalized the fiction of copyright as an author's right, with substantial, albeit subtle, consequences for copyright. As we shall demonstrate later, the fiction proved to be a detriment, not a boon, for authors.

Nevertheless, subsequent history makes clear the wisdom of the framers in empowering Congress to enact copyright legislation. The greater part of that wisdom, however, was in the limitations on the congressional power that the copyright clause imposes. Given the vagaries of the political process—and the historically proven skill of publishers as legislative lobbyists—the limitations were essential if the goals of copyright were to be achieved and retained without being consumed by the monopolistic practices in the book trade.

All sensible people are selfish, and nature is tugging at
every contract to make the terms of it fair.
—Ralph Waldo Emerson

Important principles may and must be flexible.
—Abraham Lincoln

Copyright in the
Nineteenth Century
Principles and Rules

The nineteenth century was the formative era of American
copyright law. The framers' prescience in putting the copyright clause into the Constitution had been a manifestation
of wisdom, not knowledge. Indeed, so meager was the intellectual underpinning for copyright in the new nation that the
First Congress merely copied the English Statute of Anne—
the contents of which it may not have fully comprehended—
to enact the first federal copyright act.

The copyright clause contained the basic policies of copyright, and the Copyright Act of 1790 contained the rules. But policies are not self-executing, and rules are not self-defining. To formulate the principles that would give the rules meaning in light of the policies—and thus to shape the concept of American copyright—became the responsibility of the courts during the nineteenth century.

The importance of the courts' task becomes clearer if we view law as consisting of three levels—policies, principles, and rules—with policies representing the goals, principles serving to implement the policies, and rules serving to implement the principles. Policies, having the broadest reach, are fewest in number; rules, having the narrowest scope, are more specific in intent and largest in number. A major policy of American law, for example, is that governmental censorship is neither desirable nor permissible; a principle to implement that policy is that Congress shall make no law regulating the press; and a rule implementing that principle is that press commentary critical of the government is not actionable. Indeed, the Bill of Rights of the Constitution consists essentially of principles implementing the policy that governmental power shall not be used in an abusive manner against individuals. Consider, for example, the Fourth Amendment prohibiting illegal searches and seizures, the due process clause of the Fifth Amendment, and the protections given the accused in the Sixth Amendment—the right to counsel, to confront witnesses, and so forth.

The term *law* in this context, of course, entails law in all its forms—constitutional, statutory, and judicial. A court, for example, may hold a statutory rule to be unconstitutional because it contravenes a policy manifested by a principle stated in the Constitution. Or Congress may pass legislation to correct what it sees as an improper or excessive judicial application of a principle. Most often, however, the rules are consis-

tent with the relevant principles, and there is no need to resort
to the governing policy (which may be a matter of dispute any-
way). But if a comprehensive statute exists, as in the case of
copyright, courts frequently limit themselves to a reading of
the rule on the presumption that the rule must be a proper
manifestation of the principle reflecting an appropriate policy,
to which it is not necessary to resort. In applying this tradition to copyright cases, however, courts have too often overlooked the basic fact that the copyright clause is a limitation
on, as well as a grant of, congressional power. Copyright law
is unique in that it entails policies stated in the Constitution,
principles formulated by the Supreme Court, and rules enacted by Congress. The schematic ordering, thus, is built upon
constitutional policies, judicial principles, and legislative rules.

    From a utilitarian standpoint, copyright principles serve as
an aid in the interpretation of copyright rules in order to
implement the relevant copyright policies. Copyright principles are thus created by courts in rendering judicial decisions
that interpret ambiguous statutory language. Consider, for example, the rule that the copyright owner shall have the exclusive right to vend a copyrighted work such as a book. Does this
language give the copyright owner the right to resell a book
that has been sold to another? To make the point another way,
does the copyright owner's exclusive right to vend prevent the
purchaser of the book from reselling it?

    There are two possible principles to use in the interpreta-
tion of this statutory language. If copyright were to be interpreted as a natural-law property right of the author, the obvious conclusion would be that the exclusive right to vend means
only and exactly what it says and that the purchaser of the
book cannot sell it without the copyright owner's permission.
But if copyright is recognized as a grant of a limited statutory monopoly, the reasonable conclusion would be that the
copyright owner's right to vend is exhausted with the first sale

of the book, and the owner of the book may sell it whenever he or she wishes. That is what the courts have, in fact, held—a ruling that Congress subsequently codified.[1] The principle that copyright is the grant of a limited statutory monopoly thus provided the basis for interpreting the statutory rule in a manner that implements the policy of promoting learning: without the first-sale doctrine there would be no used-book market for copyrighted works.

The nineteenth century was the era of copyright principles in the United States because statutory interpretation was necessary to the development of copyright law. Identifying these principles is somewhat risky, of course, since by nature principles are malleable. Being primarily a product of inference (because they are seldom articulated as such), principles must be determined by one's perception of the policies, thereby making any individual's identification of a principle subject to dispute by another. Moreover, some principles overlap, and their separate identification is a matter of judgment. Nevertheless, we believe that there are seven interrelated principles of copyright which can be identified with reasonable certainty:

1. *The limited-protection principle:* copyright is a series of rights to which a given work is subject, and therefore protection is limited to these rights;
2. *The statutory-monopoly principle:* copyright is the grant of a statutory monopoly;
3. *The market principle:* copyright protects the work for the market;
4. *The fair-use principle:* copyright does not preclude others from making reasonable use of the work, thus allowing a competing author's use of copyrighted work in creating another work;
5. *The right-of-access principle:* copyright entails the right of public access to the copyrighted work as a quid pro quo

for the statutory grant of monopoly rights when they
are exercised;

6. *The personal-use principle:* copyright does not prohibit an
   individual's personal use of the work; and

7. *The public-interest principle:* copyright is primarily to
   benefit the public interest and only secondarily to
   benefit the author.

The Limited-Protection Principle

The limited-protection principle is to be inferred directly from
the provisions of the 1790 Copyright Act, where copyright
was limited to newly created books, maps, and charts, and the
rights were specified as being to print, reprint, publish, and
vend for a limited time. The limited rights, however, turned
out to be more significant than the limitations on subject matter. The expansion of the subject matter of copyright began
with the 1802 amendment to the copyright statute, but the
rights, especially as to books, remained essentially the same
until the 1909 Copyright Act.

The limited-protection principle meant that *the copyright
owner's rights were limited to those specified in the statute.* Therefore,
a digest, abridgment, or translation of a copyrighted work—
being itself a new work—was not considered an infringement
of the initial work's copyright at that time because it did not
require the printing, reprinting, or publication of that work.[2]

The limited protection granted to copyrighted works was
in part a result of the contemporary economic use of books
(printing and publishing) by reason of then current technology (the printing press), and in part a result of the monopolistic history of copyright. The monopoly concern, however,
was manifested more by the limited term than by the limited rights, for the limited-protection principle deals with the

scope of copyright protection, not its nature. Thus, although the abridgment doctrine and its corollaries have subsequently been eliminated by both court rulings and statute, the limited-protection principle continues to be good law by reason of the Supreme Court in the case of *Baker v. Selden*, decided in 1879.[3]

The issue in that case was the scope of copyright on a book entitled *Selden's Condensed Ledger, or Book-Keeping Simplified*, which consisted of an introductory essay and blank forms. The defendant, in his alleged infringing book, had used the plan but made a different arrangement of the columns and headings. Selden sought to prove that Baker had used the same system, arguing that no one could make such a ledger without using the ruled lines and headings of the system he owned. The Court, however, held that the copyright on the book did not protect the system: "The very object of publishing a book . . . is to communicate to the world the useful knowledge which it contains. But this object would be frustrated if the knowledge could not be used without incurring the guilt of piracy of the book."[4]

The statutory ambiguity was that the statute did not distinguish between copyright protection for the book and copyright protection for the contents of the book. The Court (without so stating) employed the limited-protection principle to resolve the ambiguity by holding that copyright protects the expression, but not the idea—a rule that is now codified in section 102(b) of the 1976 Copyright Act.

The Statutory-Monopoly Principle

By far the most important American copyright principle established in the nineteenth century was the statutory-monopoly principle: that *copyright is the grant of a limited statutory monopoly* rather than (as proposed by the competing theory) a natural-

law right of the author. The Supreme Court made the choice
in *Wheaton v. Peters,* the American counterpart of *Donaldson v.
Beckett,* whose lead the Court followed.[5]

The *Wheaton* case involved a controversy between a former
reporter of Supreme Court decisions, Henry Wheaton, and
his successor, Richard Peters, concerning Peters's desire to
publish the Court's decisions from its inception, which included those already reported, published, and copyrighted by
Wheaton. Also at issue in the case was whether or not Wheaton
had properly complied with the terms of the copyright statute
in securing his copyright, regarding which Wheaton's counsel
argued that, in addition to the statutory copyright, an author
has a common-law copyright in his works after publication by
virtue of natural law. The following excerpts from his arguments (given by the Court reporter) provide an example of
the reasoning:

> In England, beyond all question, an author had, at com-
> mon law the sole and exclusive property in his copy. This
> was decided in Millar v. Taylor, 4 Burr. 2303. This prop-
> erty was placed by its defenders, and they finally pre-
> vailed, upon the foundation of natural right.[6]

> But the question here is as to private right. And the
> question is whether the Constitution takes away a private
> right, or property at common law.[7]

> But what reason can be discovered why the framers
> of the Constitution should wish, or intend to take away,
> or authorize Congress to take away the common-law
> right. . . .

> Will it be said that the public have rights as well as
> the author; and that it is impolitic to allow a perpetual
> right? . . .

. . . No person can have any rights opposed to the author's.[8]

The Court rejected these reasonings, saying:

That an author, at common law, has a property in his manuscript, and may obtain redress against any one who deprives him of it, or by improperly obtaining a copy endeavours to realise a profit by its publication, cannot be doubted; but this is a very different right from that which asserts a perpetual and exclusive property in the future publication of the work, after the author shall have published it to the world.

The argument that a literary man is as much entitled to the product of his labour as any other member of society, cannot be controverted. And the answer is, that he realises this product by the transfer of his manuscripts, or in the sale of his works, when first published.

A book is valuable on account of the matter it contains, the ideas it communicates, the instruction or entertainment it affords. Does the author hold a perpetual property in these? *Is there an implied contract by every purchaser of his book, that he may realise whatever instruction or entertainment which the reading of it shall give, but shall not write out or print its contents?*[9]

The importance of the *Wheaton* case lies in the fact that the principle chosen—the statutory-monopoly principle—determined the nature of American copyright and therefore served as the premise for copyright rules in the future. (Note also that the italicized dictum above, which presaged the *Selden* ruling, is based on a distinction between copyright protection for the work and copyright protection for the contents of the work.) In retrospect it seems clear that if the Court had ruled copyright to be a natural-law property right of the author, the policies in the copyright clause would have been negated, and the copyright statute would have become an exercise in futility.

Even so, the *Wheaton* case suffered from the defect of its virtue, for its holding was a simplistic solution to a complex problem: How to protect the author's interest in his or her work without at the same time providing the bookseller an unregulated monopoly. This monopoly, of course, is based on the fallacy that ownership of the work is ownership of the copyright and vice versa, which can be traced to the *Millar* and *Donaldson* cases. The problem will be examined in greater depth in Chapter 8.

The Market Principle

The market principle—that *copyright protects the marketing of the work*—is consistent with (and could be viewed as an aspect of) the limited-protection and the statutory-monopoly principles. Indeed, the affinity of the market principle with the other two principles may explain why it has seldom been articulated. But it has an independent significance in that it aids in the interpretation of the rights in the 1790 act—"the sole right and liberty of printing, reprinting, publishing and vending" the copyrighted work. Did this language mean that the rights to print, and so on, were independent of the right to vend? Or did it mean the rights were to print *and vend*, to reprint *and vend*, and to publish *and vend*? The limited-protection principle and the monopoly principle support an inference that the latter interpretation was the proper one, and the market principle serves to confirm this interpretation, an interpretation supported by history.

The explanation for the apparent redundancy in the granting of rights is found in the Statute of Anne (its source) and the stationers' copyright (the source of the Statute of Anne).

The English statute in creating the statutory copyright to replace the stationers' copyright provided a transition period
and thus dealt with three classes of works: (1) those works
already printed, as to which the author, or the bookseller *or
printer* who had acquired the copy in order to print or reprint
the same, was to have the sole right of printing for twenty-one
years; (2) those works composed, but not printed and published, as to which the right was to print and reprint for a
term of fourteen years; (3) those works to be composed in the
future, as to which the right would be the same as for those
already composed but not printed. As to all these classes of
works, a person who printed, reprinted, or imported, sold,
published, or exposed for sale any such work without the written consent of the proprietor was subject to penalties.

The language of the statute implies that there is a significant
distinction between the printing of a book and the publishing of a book, the former being performed by a printer and
the latter by a bookseller. And, indeed, there was. In addition
to the "copyright," the Stationers' Company had also created
a "printer's right," which was the right to print copy, a right
separate and distinct from the copyright.[10] As a matter of practice, the vendor of the copyright of works often reserved the
right to print the works that were sold, that is, retained the
printer's right.[11]

The Statute of Anne thus reflects the practice of the trade.
If the author were to be an effective instrument to regulate the
booksellers' monopoly of the book trade, it was necessary to
vest in the author all the rights the stationers had theretofore
controlled. These rights were the right to print (the printer's
right); the right to reprint (because books were printed in "im-
pressions" of limited numbers—often 1,200 copies or less—
and might require reprinting); and the right to publish (that
is, to issue and distribute the printed books). The right to print
was as much a separate economic right as was the right to pub-

lish. Therefore, as the market principle makes clear, the rights to print and reprint were not intended to be independent of the right to vend.

The Fair-Use Principle

In his nineteenth-century classic on copyright, Eaton S. Drone provides a clear and concise statement of the fair-use principle: "It is a recognized principle that every author, compiler, or publisher may make certain uses of a copyrighted work, in the preparation of a rival publication." [12] Despite its longevity, however, the fair-use principle is perhaps the most debated and least understood principle of copyright law. The contemporary confusion results, at least in part, from the failure to recognize the relevance to fair use of a fundamental distinction in copyright law: the copyright and the copyrighted work are two different things. A work can exist without a copyright, but a copyright cannot exist without a work. Obviously, then, there must be a distinction between the use of the copyright and the use of the copyrighted work. The distinction was understood and accepted in nineteenth-century American copyright law, though it seems to have clouded in recent years.

This distinction becomes particularly important when the copyright owner is given an "exclusive" right that the user may also wish to exercise, that is, when there is a concurrent right. In the nineteenth century, there was only one such right, the right to vend the copyrighted work. As discussed above, when the copyright owner claimed that a person's resale of a copy that he had purchased was an infringement of the copyright owner's right to vend, the court held that it was not. The copyright owner's right to vend was limited to the first sale and did not extend to subsequent sales of the same copy. Thus, the first sale constituted a use of the copyright; subsequent sales did not.

Under modern copyright law, the right to vend is encompassed in the right to distribute the copies *publicly*, a right that most users would neither need nor legitimately want to exercise. The concurrent right today is the right "to copy," a right that the user may legitimately wish to exercise, for example, to make a copy of an article for his or her file. In that respect, it is important to appreciate the fact that the fair-use doctrine, as originally created, did not apply to the exercise of concurrent rights of the user but to the exercise of concurrent rights by a competitor. The point requires further explanation.

During the entire nineteenth century, the rights of the owner of the copyright of a book were limited to the right to print, reprint, publish, and vend the book. These rights comprised the copyright, and anyone who, without permission, exercised one of those rights used (that is, infringed) the copyright. But while the use of the copyright required the use of the work, the use of the work did not necessarily involve the use of the copyright. As was noted earlier, for example, under the 1790 Copyright Act a second author could abridge the first author's work and print it without infringing the copyright. The second author was considered as having thus created a different work under the "fair abridgment doctrine," a product of English precedents.[13]

American judges, understandably, did not favor the fair-abridgment doctrine, and in *Folsom v. Marsh*, Justice Story used the occasion to create the fair-use principle as a substitute for it.[14] In *Folsom*, the Rev. Charles W. Upham derived 353 of the 866 pages in his *Life of Washington in the Form of an Autobiography* from letters and documents in Jared Sparks's *Writings of President Washington*, a twelve-volume work of some 7,000 pages. The court rejected the defense that the defendant's work was a lawful abridgment, and then stated the fair-use principle:

> The question, then, is, whether this is a justifiable use of the original materials, such as the law recognizes as no infringement of the copyright of the plaintiffs. . . . It is certainly not necessary, to constitute an invasion of copyright, that the whole of a work should be copied, or even a large portion of it, in form or in substance. If so much is taken, that the value of the original is sensibly diminished, or the labors of the original author are substantially to an injurious extent appropriated by another, that is sufficient, in point of law, to constitute a piracy pro tanto. . . . In short, we must often, in deciding questions of this sort, look to the nature and objects of the selections made, the quantity and value of the materials used, and the degree in which the use may prejudice the sale, or diminish the profits, or supersede the objects, of the original work.[15]

This was the first time that a clear judicial distinction had been made between a use of the work and a use of the copyright, and the *Folsom* ruling established a key copyright principle in America. What's more, the fair-use doctrine—supplanting the fair-abridgment doctrine—was actually an enhancement of the copyright monopoly (not a diminution, as has often been assumed). It is important to realize, however, that the fair-use doctrine then did not apply to an individual's personal use of a copyrighted work; it was promulgated to permit a second author to make a *fair use* of the *copyright* of a work, that is, to exercise a right otherwise reserved to the copyright owner. Since normally only a competitor would wish to use the copyright of a work, the fair-use doctrine originally was, in practical terms, a fair-*competitive*-use doctrine.

The Right-of-Access Principle

The constitutional purpose of copyright—the promotion of learning—requires the right-of-access principle. Recall the dicta from *Wheaton* (that there is no implied contract that prohibits the purchaser of a book from writing out or printing its contents) and from *Selden* (the very object of a book is to communicate to the world useful knowledge). For almost two hundred years, copyright acts gave effect to this principle by the simple mechanism of requiring that a work be published before it was eligible for copyright protection. Once a book is published and placed on the library shelf, access is assured. The de facto implementation of the right-of-access principle made judicial pronouncement of it unnecessary except in dicta, as in *Wheaton* and *Selden*.

With the 1976 Copyright Act, however, publication ceased to be a requirement for U.S. copyright, and the new communications technology enabled owners to profit from copyrighted works (such as materials broadcast by television) that were merely performed, not published. The danger seems clear: television provides only limited public access within a rigid time frame, yet its impact on public opinion—particularly through news reports—is great. Therefore, the right-of-access principle needs to be articulated more clearly. Copyright entails the right of public access as a quid pro quo for the benefits received by the copyright owner in the statutory grant of monopoly rights.

The Personal-Use Principle

The right-of-access principle, in turn, required a personal-use principle; with the former, the purchaser of a book could read it, but without the latter, he could not write out its contents. The predicate of the personal-use principle is that there is a difference between the use of the work and the use of the copyright, and the principle applies only to the use of the work. (The use of the copyright is a matter of fair use.) Thus, the personal-use principle prohibits copyright from being used to inhibit a user's efforts to learn.

The personal-use principle is so much a part of copyright tradition that it has customarily been assumed, seldom articulated. The place to express it, of course, would be in infringement cases, but a copyright infringement action is necessarily one that involves not only the use of the work but also the use of the copyright (that is, a defendant is charged with having exercised one of the rights reserved to the copyright owner). An individual who merely makes a personal use of the work does not interfere with the copyright, and copyright owners do not sue individuals who merely use the work. Therefore, thus far there has been no occasion to enunciate the personal-use principle in copyright cases.

The Public-Interest Principle

The six principles discussed above can be viewed as components of the public-interest principle—that *copyright exists primarily to benefit the public, only secondarily to reward the author*—which is the fundamental principle of American copyright.[16] The English experience with copyright had demonstrated that publishers as businessmen would serve the public interest only to the extent that the public's interest was congruent with their own. It is, of course, in the public interest that copyrighted materials be publicly disseminated, and to the extent that publisher profit is necessary to this end, the profitability of publishers is also in the public interest. But when publishers erroneously state that copyright is the author's natural-law property right in order to justify extracting unreasonable profit, their interest clearly diverges from the public interest.

The proposition argued by Wheaton's counsel—"No person can have any rights opposed to the authors"—is nonsense, but nonsense of a very dangerous kind. And it may well have been this kind of argument that influenced the Supreme Court to render its decision rejecting the natural-law property theory of copyright and accepting the statutory-monopoly theory.

The Court's wisdom in this regard has never been successfully challenged, and because copyright retains characteristics that once made it an effective instrument of monopoly and censorship, the principle that copyright exists primarily to serve the public interest remains a crucial protection against any use of copyright to monopolize the marketplace of ideas. There is good reason, then, for the Supreme Court's continual reiteration of the nineteenth-century principle that copyright rewards the author only to serve the larger public interest.[17]

All the copyright principles discussed above were based for the most part on copyright as manifested in the Copyright Act of 1790. The subject matter of copyright then was limited to maps, charts, and books, the production of which was in the public interest; the term of copyright was limited to two terms of fourteen years each, a limitation that protected the public domain in implementation of the limited-monopoly principle; and the copyright owner was entitled to print, reprint, publish, and vend the copyrighted work, an implementation of the market principle. Congress continued to adhere to the constitutional policies of copyright (as confirmed by the *Wheaton* case) throughout the nineteenth century, which witnessed major revisions of the copyright act in 1831 and 1870. The legislature gradually enlarged the subject matter of copyright (to include musical compositions, engravings, etchings, photographs, works of art, statuary, and so on), but it increased the term of copyright only minimally (the initial term was enlarged to twenty-eight years; the renewal term remained fourteen years), and it held the line on the scope of the copyright owner's rights. Even though it granted the copy-right owner of works of art the right to *copy* them, it limited the copyright owners of books to the right to print, reprint, publish, and vend.

The nineteenth-century view of copyright may have been expressed most clearly in the following judicial dictum distin-guishing the use of the work and the use of the copyright:

> [T]he effect of a copyright is not to prevent any reason-able use of the book which is sold. I go to a book-store, and I buy a book which has been copyrighted. I may use that book for reference, study, reading, lending, copying passages from it at my will. I may not duplicate that book, and thus put it upon the market, for in so doing I would infringe the copyright. But merely taking extracts from it, merely using it, in no manner infringes the copyright.[18]

This dictum amounted to no more than a truism of the day because "the author's exclusive property in a literary composi-tion or his copyright, consists only in a right to multiply copies of his book, and enjoy the profits therefrom, and not in an exclusive right to his conceptions."[19]

As this language implies, courts in the nineteenth century employed but did not articulate the distinction between the copyright and the work. Indeed, the distinction is the basis of the nineteenth-century principles that form the fundamentals of American copyright law. It implied, of course, that there is also a distinction between the ownership of the work and the ownership of the copyright, but the courts did not find it necessary to extend their reasoning that far. One appar-ent reason for their lack of action in this regard was that the subject of copyright litigation was copyright itself—the rights granted by a federal statute to which the work was subject—but ownership of the work was seen as being determined by the common-law copyright, a matter of state law.

The failure to articulate the distinction between the work and the copyright has proved to be the major flaw in nineteenth-century copyright jurisprudence.[20] The courts' narrow reading of copyright led to results that were perceived to be unfair to the author, and Congress was called upon to correct the inequities. After the grant of statutory rights was enlarged in the 1909 act, the distinction between the work and the copyright receded into the background. This unfortunate development and its consequences will be examined further in Chapter 8.

A book's a book, although there's nothing in 't.
— George Gordon, Lord Byron

Every man holds his property subject to the general right of the community to regulate its use to whatever degree the public welfare may require it.
— Theodore Roosevelt

Copyright in the Early Twentieth Century

The 1909 Copyright Act

In 1905, four years before the 1909 Copyright Act was enacted, Thorvald Solberg, the register of copyrights, called for congressional action on copyright, noting that "[d]uring more than a century of legislation upon this subject, a highly technical copyright system has been developed, under which valuable literary and artistic property rights . . . may be rendered nugatory by reason of failure to fully comply with purely arbitrary requirements."[1] Solberg was correct. Throughout the nineteenth century, courts—with some exceptions—had increasingly treated copyright too much as a statutory monopoly, too little as the author's property.

The high-water mark of the nineteenth-century view of copyright actually came in an early-twentieth-century case, *White-Smith Music Pub. Co. v. Apollo Co.*[2] In that 1908 case, the defendant had made perforated music rolls (for pianolas) of plaintiff's copyrighted musical compositions (songs), leading the plaintiff to sue, claiming copyright infringement. Yet the Supreme Court held there was no infringement because the pianola rolls were not legal *copies* of the copyrighted works. At the time—and even from a disinterested distance—the case can be viewed as an implementation of the limited-protection, the statutory-monopoly, and the market principles, as the Court demonstrated in quoting "pertinent language" from an English decision involving similar facts and the same issues:

"The plaintiffs are entitled to copyright in three sheets of music. What does this mean? It means that they have the exclusive right of printing or otherwise multiplying copies of those sheets of music, i.e., of the bars, notes, and other printed words and signs on these sheets. But the plaintiffs have no exclusive right to the production of the sounds indicated by or on those sheets of music; nor to the performance in private of the music indicated by such sheets; nor to any mechanism for the production of such sounds or music.

"The defendants have taken those sheets of music and have prepared from them sheets of paper with perforations in them, and these perforated sheets, when put into and used with properly constructed machines or instruments, will produce or enable the machines or instruments to produce the music indicated on the plaintiff's sheets. In this sense the defendant's perforated rolls have been copies from the plaintiff's sheets.

"But is this the kind of copying which is prohibited by the copyright act; or rather is the perforated sheet made as above mentioned a copy of the sheet of music from which it is made? Is it a copy at all? Is it a copy within the meaning of the copyright act? A sheet of music is treated in the copyright act as if it were a book or sheet of letter press. Any mode of copying such a thing, whether by printing, writing, photography, or by some other method not yet invented, would no doubt be copying. So, perhaps, might a perforated sheet of paper to be sung or played from in the same way as sheets of music are sung or played from. But to play an instrument from a sheet of music which appears to the eye is one thing; to play an instrument with a perforated sheet which itself forms part of the mechanism which produces the music is quite another thing."[3]

The *White-Smith* case was very much in the tradition of *Stowe v. Thomas*, which had been decided in the middle of the nineteenth century, holding that the German translation of *Uncle Tom's Cabin* was not an infringement of the copyright.[4] Sheet music transformed into a player-piano roll was, the court ruled, no more a copy of the music than the translation of a novel was a copy of the novel.

The intuitive reaction to this holding now is likely to be that something was wrong, since the finding seemed to make a mockery of the notion that copyright is an author's right. As noted in the opinion, "from one million to one million and a half" pianola works were manufactured in 1902 alone— presumably with no payment to the composers of the musical compositions. Yet this case serves to demonstrate both the strength and the weakness of nineteenth-century copyright law. The strength involved the judicial development of what have become the basic principles of copyright; the weakness was that no principle emerged to provide protection for the author independent of the publisher.

This weakness derived from the conflation of the author's rights and the publisher's rights that had begun with the *Millar* case in England. And the lack of an author's principle, so to speak, inevitably led eventually to statutory enhancement of the copyright monopoly in an effort to correct the perceived inequities. (For example, Congress subsequently gave the author the right to translate his or her novel, apparently in response to the *Stowe* case.) Yet such enlargements, though nominally to benefit authors, accrued primarily to the advantage of the publishers. In the United States, the process of enlargement began with the amendment of 1802 and proceeded with the 1831 and 1870 copyright revision acts.[5] But the 1909 act, the third major revision of the copyright statutes, was the most significant enhancement of the copyright monopoly and thus marked the turning point in American copyright law.[6]

In the 1909 statute, Congress continued to adhere to the theory that copyright is the grant of a limited statutory monopoly; but while it kept that monopoly narrow in some respects, the legislature enlarged it in other ways. Although Congress chose not to dispense with the "purely arbitrary requirements" about which Register Solberg had complained, it did introduce enough other new developments that the resulting legislation can now be seen as a watershed statute of American copyright.

The 1909 act marks the beginning of a change from the nineteenth-century view that copyright was more regulatory than proprietary to the contemporary consensus—whether or not sound—that copyright is more proprietary than regulatory. The three most important changes the act made were the creation of the compulsory license for musical recordings, the enlargement of the copyright owner's rights to include the right to copy the work, and the enactment of the work-for-hire doctrine, which led to the development of the corporate copyright.

The Compulsory License for Musical Recordings

It is somewhat surprising to realize that copyright, which had been created in response to the invention of the printing press, had existed for some three hundred years before its protection was extended to a product of another new technology. In 1865, Congress amended the 1831 Copyright Act to make photographs copyrightable, presumably because of the efforts of Mathew Brady, the Civil War photographer.[7] This breakthrough required the use of a minor fiction—treating a photographer as an author—and when the issue of the authority of Congress to provide copyright for photographers was litigated, the Supreme Court sustained the fiction, reasoning that the term *author* essentially means a person to whom something owes its origin.[8]

As pictorial representations, photographs are analogous to engravings and etchings, which the 1831 act had already protected—a circumstance that justifies our characterization of this extension as a *minor* fiction. By 1909, however, Edison had invented the phonograph, and clearly there was no analogy for sound recordings in the existing copyright law.[9] In view of the ruling in *White-Smith Music Pub. Co. v. Apollo Co.*, Congress was confronted with the problem of providing composers of musical compositions with the right to benefit from a "mechanical recording" of their songs.[10] The case for composers in 1909 in the United States was just as appealing as the case for authors had been in 1710 in England, but it also presented the perennial problem of copyright: how to benefit the author without creating an unacceptable monopoly of publishers. The

House report openly expressed the concern that, if the grant of right were too broad, there would be serious danger that "the progress of science and useful arts would not be promoted, but rather hindered" by the creation of powerful and dangerous monopolies "prejudicial to the public interests":

> The main object to be desired in expanding copyright protection accorded to music has been to give to the composer an adequate return for the value of his composition, and it has been a serious and difficult task to combine the protection of the composer with the protection of the public, and to so frame an act that it would accomplish the double purpose of securing to the composer an adequate return for all use made of his composition and at the same time prevent the formation of oppressive monopolies, which might be founded upon the very rights granted to the composer for the purpose of protecting his interests.[11]

The fundamental problem of copyright has never been better stated: How can society provide the author with an adequate return and at the same time prevent the formation of oppressive monopolies founded upon the very rights granted to the author for the purpose of protecting his or her interests? Recall that the booksellers in England had created the rights for themselves; the Statute of Anne purported to give these rights to the author, but they were still available to the booksellers by assignment; and *Millar v. Taylor* had made it clear that the rights were assignable in full, thereby conflating the author's and the publisher's interests.[12] *Donaldson v. Beckett* had ostensibly solved the problem by creating the author's common-law copyright prior to publication, leaving the author with only statutory rights after publication.[13] But because the author could assign those statutory rights to a publisher, the problem remained that oppressive monopolies might be founded upon the very rights granted to the author to protect his or her interests—and this had been apparent to the U.S. Supreme Court in *Wheaton v. Peters*.[14] The Court's solution at that point was to limit the author's rights by requiring strict compliance with the terms of the statute.

A more commonsense solution, as we noted in the previous chapter, would have been to differentiate the rights of the author from those of the publisher, and that is precisely what Congress chose to do in the 1909 act in regard to sound recordings. It gave the copyright owner of a musical composition the right to make the first recording of that composition, but it provided that thereafter anyone could, upon the payment of the statutory fee, make a recording of the same composition. Thus was created the compulsory license for musical recordings, which provided protection for the composer of a piece of music but not for the producer of the initial record, who had the role of publisher. (Copyright then did not protect the recording itself; indeed, recordings did not receive copyright protection until 1972.)

Faced with new technology, Congress had found an original solution both to protect the author and to avoid the monopoly of the publisher. Since the danger of oppressive monopoly was from publishers, not authors, it would have been consistent with public policy similarly to treat any author as having a right to receive compensation regardless of who published his or her work. True, most publishers would have insisted on the right of exclusive publication, but a "common-law compulsory license"—even if limited to those cases where the initial publisher's negligence had resulted in the loss of copyright—would have protected the author for the term of the statutory copyright despite any publisher negligence. Such a solution, however, probably never occurred to the justices and, if it had, would doubtless have been dismissed as being fanciful. Judges (like all human beings) are prisoners of their learning.

As to books, there was much prior copyright learning; as to mechanical recordings of music, there was none. Unlike the courts, the 1909 Congress was not hindered by judicial precedents in creating its innovative solution to the problem of the copyright monopoly.

The Right to Copy

The major irony of the 1909 act is that, while Congress was openly concerned about the copyright monopoly in regard to music, it enhanced the copyright monopoly in regard to other works: first, by unwittingly extending to all copyright owners the right to copy copyrighted works; and second, by introducing the work-for-hire doctrine, the first *major* fiction in the copyright statute.

We use the term *unwittingly* here advisedly, for while there is no direct evidence to prove that Congress was unaware of the consequences of extending the copyright owner's existing rights by adding the right to copy his or her work, the circumstantial evidence is compelling. The relevant provision was section 1(a) of the act, which read as follows: "Any person entitled thereto, upon complying with the provisions of this title, shall have the exclusive right: (a) To print, reprint, publish, *copy*, and vend the copyrighted work" (emphasis added). The House report on the bill that became the 1909 act stated: "Subsection (*a*) of section 1 adopts without change the phraseology of section 4952 of the Revised Statutes, and this, with the insertion of the word 'copy,' practically adopts the phraseology of the first copyright act Congress ever passed—that of 1790. Many amendments of this were suggested, but the committee felt that it was safer *to retain without change the old phraseology* which has been so often construed by the courts."[15]

The House report language made it appear that "the insertion of the word 'copy'" was merely a drafting change without substantive consequences. The appearance is deceiving. There is, for example, a substantial difference between the right to publish a book and the right to copy a book or a portion of it. While the exclusive right to publish furnishes the copyright owner of a book adequate protection, it provides little protection for the copyright owner of a work of art, such as etchings, engravings, paintings, and statuary. Thus, although it is appropriate to give the copyright owner of a book the exclusive right to print and publish it, it is more appropriate to give the copyright owner of a work of art the exclusive right to copy it. Indeed, until the 1909 act this distinction had been specified in all copyright acts since 1802, when an amendment to the 1790 act had extended "the benefits [of copyright] to the arts of designing, engraving, and etching historical and other prints."[16]

On this point, the House report's citation of section 4952 of the revised statutes is also misleading. That section (the grant-of-rights section) gave "the sole liberty of printing, reprinting, publishing, completing, *copying*, executing, finishing, and vending," for "any book, map, chart, dramatic or musical composition, *engraving, cut, print*, or photograph or negative thereof, or of a *painting*, drawing, chromo, *statue, statuary*, and of models or designs intended to be perfected as works of the fine arts" (emphasis added). For the correct reading of this section, however, it was necessary to look also to the subsequent sections of the statute that defined the acts of infringement.

Sections 4964 and 4965 of the revised statutes drew a clear line between conduct that infringed a book and conduct that infringed other kinds of works. Section 4964 defined the infringement of a *book*, which included to "print, publish, or import" the book without permission; and section 4965 defined infringement of the *other works*, which included to "engrave, etch, work, copy, print, publish, or import" the work without permission. The right "to copy" in the copyright acts prior to

1909 thus applied only to works of art, as opposed to literary works. Clearly, then, the House report was wrong in claiming that it retained "without change the old phraseology."

The comment does, however, indicate that no change from past precedent in the copyright acts was intended. And, indeed, the language in the 1909 act could still have been construed to avoid the change if the word *copy* had been restricted to and treated as a "word of art," not as a generic term. Thus, an interpretation consistent with the past copyright acts would have been to treat infringement copying as copying for the purpose of marketing the work. In the 1790 act, for example, the rights given were "the sole right and liberty of printing, reprinting, publishing and vending" the copyrighted work.[17] As there was no reason to print, reprint, or publish a book other than to sell it, the rights in the 1790 act thus were surely intended to be the right to print and vend, the right to reprint and vend, and the right to publish and vend the book.[18] With this precedent, it is easy to see that in the 1909 act, the right to copy was the right to "copy and vend." Any other interpretation would have been contrary to the nineteenth-century view of copyright because it would seriously threaten, as it did, the rights of the users of copyrighted works.

Indeed, there is evidence within the 1909 act that such was the interpretation that Congress itself placed on section 1(a). In section 41 it distinguished the copyright from the material object copyrighted in order to ensure that the rights of users would not be defeated.[19] Section 41 of the 1909 act provides:

> The copyright is distinct from the property in the material object copyrighted, and the sale or conveyance, by gift or otherwise, of the material object shall not of itself constitute a transfer of the copyright, nor shall the assignment of the copyright constitute a transfer of the title to the material object; but nothing in this Act shall be

deemed to forbid, prevent, or restrict the transfer of any copy of a copyrighted work the possession of which has been lawfully obtained.

The House report comment on this section explains:

> Section 41 is not intended to change in any way existing law, but simply to recognize the distinction, long established, between the material object and the right to produce copies thereof. The concluding clause in the section, that "nothing in this act shall be deemed to forbid, prevent, or restrict the transfer of any copy of a work copyrighted under this act the possession of which has been lawfully obtained," is inserted in order to make it clear that there is no intention to enlarge in any way the construction to be given to the word "vend" in the first section of the bill. Your committee feel that it would be most unwise to permit the copyright proprietor to exercise any control whatever over the article which is the subject of copyright after said proprietor has made the first sale.[20]

There are two points worth noting about this comment. First, the reference to section 1(a) and the right to vend reinforces the assumption that the members of the committee did not think that the addition of the right to copy had changed "in any way existing law." In their opinion, therefore, the user would continue to have the right to make individual copies as under the 1870 act. Second, this is confirmed by the position of the committee that it would be unwise "to permit the copyright proprietor to exercise any control whatever over the article" after the first sale. Clearly, the right to prevent the user from making a copy would be the exercise of control over the object after the sale, certainly counter to the intent of Congress.

This interpretation, however, has not prevailed in the courts, primarily because the cases that come to trial do not involve individual users, but competitors. Even so, and paradoxically, the very word *copyright* militated against the proper interpretation of the 1909 language. Since—if not before—that statute was enacted, most persons have come to assume that "copy" in the word *copyright* is the verb, not the noun. In fact, it derives from the noun, meaning "manuscript"—a definition established by the stationers in England. Consider, for example, the title of the 1790 act: "An Act for the encouragement of learning, by securing the copies of maps, charts, and books, to the authors and proprietors of such copies, during the times therein mentioned." But the word *copy* is also a generic term, and because it benefited copyright owners to treat it as such (especially after the development of photocopying), the language in section 1(a) of the 1909 Copyright Act was to become the basis for copyright owners to promote a very questionable legal doctrine—that their right to copy a work is exclusive and absolute.

The Work-for-Hire Doctrine

The third major feature of the 1909 Copyright Act that was destined to change copyright law significantly—far more so than was realized at the time—was the work-for-hire doctrine, the basis of the corporate copyright, which was added in a most casual manner. In section 62, defining certain terms, the statute provided: "and the word 'author' shall include an employer in the case of works made for hire."[21] (Of this section, the House report says only, "Section 62 places an interpretation and construction upon the use of certain words.")

The reasons for the work-for-hire doctrine are not completely clear, but presumably Congress intended it as a matter of convenience for the purposes of renewal in the case of composite works. Section 23 of the act provided that in the case of such works, either a corporate body (other than as an assignee

or licensee of the individual author) or an employer for whom
such work was made for hire could renew the copyright—a
right otherwise limited to the author or his heirs. The House
report offered a partial explanation for this provision:

> In the case of composite or cyclopedic works, to which a
> great many authors contribute for hire and upon which
> the copyright was originally secured by the proprietor of
> the work, it was felt that the proprietor should have the
> exclusive right to apply for the renewal term. In some
> cases the contributors to such a work might number hun-
> dreds and be scattered over the world, and it would be
> impossible for the proprietor of the work to secure their
> cooperation in applying for the renewal.[22]

Despite this laudable motive, one could mount a good argument that the characterization of employers as authors is an
unconstitutional fiction, in view of the fact that the Constitution empowers Congress to grant copyright only to *authors*
and only for *their own* writings. The chances that the Supreme
Court will ever so hold, however, are slim. Much of the copyright industry is now based on corporate copyrights, and to
invalidate them (so the argument would doubtless be) would
create confusion in the industry and leave many works un-
protected. Such an argument, while not necessarily valid—
the result might well be simply to vest such copyrights in the
responsible hands of the authors who actually created the
works—is both venerable and effective. The booksellers in England, for example, used a similar plea to obtain passage of
the Statute of Anne—and then used it again to argue against
the enforcement of the resulting statute!

The troubling problem is that the reasons that make the
work-for-hire doctrine unconstitutional are the very reasons
that make it a convenient and powerful instrument of monopoly. Recall that under the copyright clause, copyright is the

grant of a limited monopoly to the author, not to the publisher. Given the history of copyright, we can reasonably assume that the framers purposely denied Congress the power to grant copyright to publishers. Paradoxically, the House report on the 1909 act (as discussed above) at one point recognized the central reason—that to grant the publisher a copyright would be to grant a corporate entity the rights intended to protect only the author, and that those rights could be used to form oppressive monopolies—but then overlooked its relevance to the work-for-hire doctrine.

One of the key protections ensuring a limited copyright monopoly is the division of labor, and therefore the division of rights, between the author and the publisher. The author creates the work; the publisher distributes it. While the author's assignment of the copyright could be used to defeat the division of rights, it nevertheless had an overall effect. The Statute of Anne, for example, limited the renewal term of copyright to the author—even then granting renewal only if the author was living. Under the work-for-hire doctrine, however, the division of labor was retained but not the division of rights. For example, only the copyright *owner* of a work made for hire (not the actual author) was empowered to renew the copyright.

Congress could not, in 1909, have foreseen the consequences of the work-for-hire doctrine which, with the rise of new communications technology, has resulted in a corporate copyright rather than an author's copyright. The disturbing similarity to the stationers' copyright—so effective as an instrument of monopoly and censorship—is too close to be ignored.

In sum, one provision of the 1909 act (the compulsory recording license) proved to be beneficial to both authors and the public; but two provisions (the right to copy and the work-for-hire doctrine) proved to be beneficial primarily to publishers and other copyright entrepreneurs. The losers under the latter two provisions were the public—because the changes diminished the rights of users *as well as* authors, who in many instances were denied even recognition for the creation of the work.

One further note: a complete assessment of copyright under the 1909 act requires a consideration of an additional development that is too seldom discussed—the trivialization of copyright. It was under the 1909 act that copyright protection was first extended to such "writings" as "statuettes, bookends, clocks, lamps, door knockers, candlesticks, inkstands, chandeliers, piggy banks, sundials, salt and pepper shakers, fish bowls, casseroles, and ash trays."[23] Compare these "copyrightable works" with newspapers—for which one court in the nineteenth century had actually refused to recognize copyright protection, on the grounds that they did not contribute to learning![24] That overly narrow ruling led to the 1909 act's designation of newspapers as being copyrightable, but in the process the fundamental intent of copyright was seriously compromised with the simultaneous inclusion of so much extraneous baggage.

A reasonable inference is that extending copyright protection to such items as fishbowls contributed to making more remote the relevance of both the constitutional policies of copyright and their implementing principles. And, indeed, as the century progressed, the regulatory aspects of copyright were increasingly subordinated to the proprietary aspects. In a case involving the infringement of a poster of the Dallas Cowboys cheerleaders by a poster of alumnae cheerleaders ("Texas Cowgirls," posed with breasts exposed), the court responded to the free-speech defense tersely: "The first amendment is not a license to trammel on legally recognized rights in intellectual property."[25] The inference was clear: copyright— at least in that court's jurisdiction—was now merely another species of property and not subject to free-speech concerns.

The nineteenth-century regulatory view of copyright was no longer ascendant.

In 1955, fifty years after Thorvald Solberg had asked for new copyright legislation to replace the 1870 Copyright Act, Congress commissioned copyright studies in preparation for a new revision act. The new statute, the 1976 Copyright Act, took more than twenty years to reach final form, but it eventually resulted in a new theory of copyright protection to accommodate new communications technology—and some important attempts to balance the regulatory/proprietary swings in copyright rulings.

Inconsistencies of opinion, arising from changes of
circumstances, are often justifiable.
—Daniel Webster

Certitude is not the test of uncertainty.
—Oliver Wendell Holmes, Jr.

Copyright in the Late
Twentieth Century
The 1976 Copyright Act

While the 1909 act was in force—for almost seventy years—
the rapid growth of motion pictures, phonorecords, radio,
television, photocopying machines, and computers combined
to produce a revolution in communications. In 1912 Congress
amended the 1909 act to provide copyright for motion pictures; but phonorecords continued without federal copyright
protection until 1972, and no amendment was ever passed
to accommodate radio—presumably because copyright pro-

tection for radio scripts protected the broadcasts. Television presented different problems. The camera could—without scripts—fill the television screen with programming such as live game shows, sporting events, and panel discussions. And during the twenty-one-year gestation period of the 1976 act, the photocopying machine and the computer emerged as major factors in the communication technology that created an information-oriented society.

The communications revolution necessitated changes in copyright, and Congress provided them in the 1976 act. On the surface these changes appeared to be no more than logical extensions of the old law (to which old precedents could still usefully be applied), but such appearances are deceiving. In fact, the 1976 act offers several key innovations of major significance. This was recognized immediately by Barbara Ringer, Register of Copyrights, who had played a prominent role in the revision process. In her words: "[T]he new statute makes a number of fundamental changes in the American copyright system, including some so profound that they may mark a shift in direction for the very philosophy of copyright itself." [1]

It is ironic that Ms. Ringer identified a shift in the philosophy of copyright as a likely result of the act, for that was almost certainly not the intent of those who shaped the legislation. Indeed, the fundamental nature of copyright—and the conflicts generated by the centuries-old debate over whether it is a natural-law property right or only a statutory grant of limited monopoly—were among the few topics not directly considered in the drafting of the act. During the twenty years prior to the new legislation, Congress and the Copyright Office apparently ignored Justice Oliver Wendell Holmes's dictum that we need study of the obvious more than investigation into the obscure. Of the thirty-four separate studies prepared under the supervision of the Copyright Office to provide necessary background for Congress, not one of them focused on either the history or the philosophy of copyright itself.[2]

Nevertheless, even though the action may have come as an unintended by-product of measures introduced to meet the needs of various vested-interest groups, the 1976 act clearly moves toward resolving the philosophical debate by strongly reflecting the statutory-grant theory of copyright and implicitly rejecting the natural-law property theory. A fuller analysis of this important point is reserved for the next chapter; for the present we will briefly summarize the 1976 act, identifying the four major changes it brings to U.S. copyright.

The pattern of the statute is traditional enough: chapter 1 defines the subject matter of copyright, makes the grant of rights, and states limitations on some of those rights (and the scope of others); chapter 2 deals with ownership and transfer of copyright; chapter 3, with the duration of copyright; chapter 4, with the formalities of copyright notice, deposit, and registration; and chapter 5, with copyright infringement and remedies.[3]

The pattern alone, however, does not reflect either the underlying premise of the statute or the revolutionary changes the statute wrought. We deal first with the underlying premise and then with four of the major changes: the abolition of the common-law copyright, the change in the concept of copyright protection, the creation of the electronic copyright as a companion to the print copyright, and the codification of the fair-use doctrine.

The Premise of the 1976 Act

The premise underlying the 1976 act is that its subject matter is the copyright of a work, not the work itself. The statute, in other words, reflects the distinction between the work and its copyright. In theory this has been true of all American copyright statutes since the 1790 act, and indeed the premise is mandated by the copyright clause, which empowers Congress to secure to authors for limited times the exclusive right to their writings. The exclusive right, of course, was the right of exclusive publication.

The narrow scope of copyright in previous statutes, however, meant that the premise was utilized but was unarticulated; and beyond the narrow scope of copyright the statutes themselves provided little internal evidence of it. The 1976 act, however, so enlarged the scope of copyright that the importance of the premise comes to the forefront, and evidence of the premise is abundant. Yet, the evidence is so obvious that it is easy to overlook.

Thus section 102(a) provides that "Copyright protection subsists . . . in original works of authorship fixed in any tangible medium of expression," but section 102(b) denies copyright protection for "any idea, procedure, process, system, method of operation, concept, principle, or discovery" even if embodied in an original work of authorship. Section 103 provides that copyright may be had for compilations, but protection extends only to the material contributed by the author, not to preexisting material that is used in the compilation. Further, section 105 denies copyright protection for any work of the United States government, and section 106 defines the exclusive rights in copyrighted works as follows:

> Subject to section 107 through 118, the owner of copyright under this title has the exclusive rights to do and to authorize any of the following:
> (1) to reproduce the copyrighted work in copies or phonorecords;
> (2) to prepare derivative works based upon the copyrighted work;
> (3) to distribute copies or phonorecords of the copy-

righted work to the public by sale or other transfer of
ownership, or by rental, lease, or lending;

(4) in the case of literary, dramatic, and choreographic
works, pantomimes, and motion pictures and other audiovisual works, to perform the copyrighted work publicly;
and

(5) in the case of literary, musical, dramatic, and choreographic works, pantomimes, and pictorial, graphic, or
sculptural works, including the individual images of a
motion picture or other audiovisual work, to display the
copyrighted work publicly.

These rights do not, however, prevent an assignee of the
copyright (or of one of the rights of copyright) from altering
the work or publishing it under a pseudonym contrary to the
author's wishes. Such matters, of course, may be taken care of
by contract, and, even if not, courts would probably grant an
injured author relief. Any relief granted, however, would not
be for infringement of copyright but for injury to the work or
the author as creator of the work. The point is simply that the
copyright statute deals only with the copyright, not the work
itself.

The major premise of the act is further substantiated by
those provisions dealing with the ownership of copyright.
Under section 201, copyright vests initially in the author of
a work, and that copyright may be transferred in whole or
in part, and any of the rights of copyright may be owned
separately. Section 202 makes a clear distinction between the
copyright of a work and a material object in which the work is
embodied. Thus transfer of ownership of the material object
(including the copy in which the work is first fixed) does not
convey the copyright, and vice versa: the transfer of the copyright does not convey property rights in any material object.

Further evidence of the fact that the statute deals only with the copyright and not the work itself is the author's termination right. This right empowers the author to terminate the assignment of copyright during a five-year period thirty-five years after the assignment has been made. The inference, of course, is that the author continues to own the work, since he or she may assign the different rights of copyright to different persons at different times.

Since the copyright act does not deal with the work itself, it leaves room for judicial development of rules dealing with ownership of the work, which by all reason should be vested in the author. We will deal further with this problem in Chapter 12, but it is worth noting at this point that section 301, the preemption section, does not alter this conclusion for two reasons. First, that section is also limited to the copyright and does not deal with the work; and second, the law preempted is state law, not federal law.

The Abolition of the Common-Law Copyright

The foundational change in the 1976 act occurred when Congress decreed that copyright came into existence as soon as a work is fixed in a tangible medium of expression—with no publication required—and thereby abolished the common-law copyright for such work. The common-law copyright was not in fact a copyright, since it protected a work only before publication, and it was governed by state rather than federal law. Thus, the existence of the common-law copyright had meant that the rights of authors were governed by the laws of two sovereigns—the dividing line being the publication of the work, at which point the federal law replaced the state law.

The practical problem under this dual arrangement had been that the development of the law of each sovereign, so to speak, was thwarted by the other. The common-law copyright could not provide protection after publication, and the statutory copyright could not provide protection before publication. The vice of this dichotomy was that it perpetuated the dual theoretical basis for copyright: the common-law copyright being based on the fact of creation, the statutory copyright on the fact of publication. Therefore, the abolition of the common-law copyright had significant consequences for copyright theory, a point we develop more fully in the next chapter.

The Change in the Concept of Copyright Protection

The elimination of the common-law copyright led to a change in the rules of copyright protection by clarifying precisely what copyright protects—an original work of authorship. While American copyright law has always required an original work of authorship as a condition for copyright, the terminology in prior acts created confusion as to the distinction between a work of authorship and its copy (that is, the material object in which it may be embodied). Thus under all U.S. copyright statutes prior to the 1976 act, copyright protected a work only as embodied in a material object (such as a book), which the statutes themselves identified as the subject of copyright. Consequently, the copyright for a particular book did not come into existence until that book was published with the appropriate copyright notice.[4] Since the book was only a copy of the manuscript (the original work of authorship), copyright protected not the work of authorship itself but the copy. There was, in short, a divergence between what copyright required and what copyright protected.

The 1976 act, however, defines the subject of copyright as an "original work of authorship" and recognizes copyright as coming into existence as soon as the work is "fixed in a tangible medium of expression." Thus, unlike those earlier statutes, under which only a published work was protected, the 1976

Copyright Act provides copyright protection for the newly created work itself—not for a copy of that work. The House report on the bill that became the 1976 act explains the point:

> "[C]opies" and "phonorecords" together will comprise all of the material objects in which copyrightable works are capable of being fixed. The definition of these terms . . . reflects a fundamental distinction between the "original work" which is the product of "authorship" and the multitude of material objects in which it can be embodied. Thus, . . . a "book" is not a work of authorship, but is a particular kind of "copy." Instead, the author may write a "literary work," which in turn can be embodied in a wide range of "copies" and "phonorecords," including books, periodicals, computer punch cards, microfilm, tape recordings, and so forth. It is possible to have an "original work of authorship" without having a "copy" or "phonorecord" embodying it, and it is also possible to have a "copy" or "phonorecord" embodying something that does not qualify as an "original work of authorship." The two essential elements—original work and tangible object—must merge through fixation in order to produce subject matter copyrightable under the statute.[5]

The clarification of the rule of copyright protection—from one that protects the copy (the material object in which a work of authorship is embodied) to one that protects the work of authorship itself—required further delineation of the nature of the works entitled to copyright, that is, what constitutes a work of authorship. The 1976 act provides copyright protection for only three kinds of original works of authorship: an imaginative work, such as a novel; a derivative work, such as a motion picture based on a novel; or a compilation, such as a telephone directory.

The important point to realize here is that, since only an

original work of authorship is entitled to copyright, only those
aspects of any derivative work or compilation that represent
original authorship are entitled to protection. This distintion
was also required under the 1909 act, but because the rules
were not clearly stated, the distinction often went unheeded.[6]
By limiting copyright protection to the elements of original
authorship, the 1976 act makes clear what earlier copyright
protection for the copy (for example, a book) had obscured:
there is a crucial difference between copyright protection for
a work and copyright protection for the contents of that work.

Thus, the 1976 act provides that copyright on a collective
work (a species of compilation) does not affect the copyright of
the material contained within the work. A collection of short
stories by different authors, for example, is entitled to copyright even if some of the stories may already be in the public
domain and the copyright of others owned by their individual
authors rather than the editor of the compilation. Therefore,
since it is the work as a whole that represents original authorship of a collective work, only the copying of the entire work
should constitute infringement of the compilation's copyright
(although copying an individual story may infringe the copyright of that story).

Although this change in the rule as to the nature of copyright protection is important for compilations and derivative
works, it has little impact on most imaginative works, and it
is instructive to understand why. In the case of works that
are a product of the author's imagination, the content of the
work itself is a product of original authorship. Copyrighted
compilations, however, often contain public-domain materials
(such as reports of judicial decisions, codes of statutes, listings
of names and addresses, or other factual data) that have no
author in the copyright sense of the term. Since only elements
of original authorship are protected, the copyright can protect
only the compilation as a whole; it cannot gain protection for

the components that are not the result of original authorship. The 1976 act, then, comes nearer than any of the prior statutes—in theory, at least—to implementing the constitutional policy of advancing the progress of knowledge by protecting authors. It requires an assessment of the elements of authorship (though not its quality) and provides copyright protection according to the presence of those elements.

The Print Copyright and the Electronic Copyright

A major innovation of the 1976 Copyright Act was the creation of an electronic copyright—provisions shaped specifically for television but also available for computers. The electronic copyright has received relatively little attention, however, since most people have assumed that the traditional rules of print copyright also apply to it. In fact, they do not, because the work is performed, not published; the electronic copyright is essentially a codification of the old common-law copyright for dramas now applied to the electronic media.

Just as the common-law copyright protected the performance of a drama on stage, the electronic copyright protects the transmission of a work over the public airwaves. But since that transmission may well be a live performance (for example, a National Football League game), copyright protection is now being given to a broadcast that may not be based on a writing, may have no author, and may never subsequently be available for learning—all conditions contrary to the copyright clause of the Constitution. Obviously, it was necessary for legislators to use legal fictions to overcome this obstacle, and they did.

Underlying the electronic copyright are three major fictions: the corporate-copyright fiction (the work-for-hire doctrine) by reason of which the employer of anyone who creates such a work is proclaimed the author; the fiction that the "fixation" of a work establishes it as a "writing," thereby making a transmission copyrightable if it is fixed even as it is being transmitted; and the fiction that a performance is equivalent to publication, thereby supposedly satisfying the promotion-of-learning condition required by the copyright clause.

The performance fiction is the only one of these unique to live television broadcasts, and it is the one that poses the greatest threat to copyright policies. This point becomes apparent when one compares the marketing differences between the print copyright and the electronic copyright. The print copyright requires publication (dissemination of the work in copies) in order for the copyright owner to earn a profit. The traditional requirement of publication before a copyright could be obtained (a necessity prior to the 1976 act) had assured not only the accessibility of all work for contemporary learning but also its eventual availability for the public domain after the copyright expired. Although copyright no longer requires publication, the marketing of printed materials continues to ensure public access to such copyrighted works.

The electronic copyright, in contrast, requires only the performance of a work over the public airwaves to obtain both copyright protection *and* a profit—whether that profit comes from advertising (for which the public pays indirectly) or from cable television fees (for which portions of the public pay directly). Although such a performed work may not be available to the general public for subsequent study or learning, the copyright owner profits from the initial performance and can still control any further access to it as if the copyright were a common-law copyright on an unpublished work. The electronic copyright, in short, empowers the copyright owner to receive all the benefits of copyright without any of the burdens.

The legal fiction that a work broadcast to millions over the public airwaves is merely performed—while a printed pamphlet is considered published even if no one purchases it—is nonsense that results from the unanalyzed use of an old common-law rule. The performance rule had its origin in an English case of the latter eighteenth century.[7] In that case, the court held that the performance of a drama on the stage did not constitute publication of the work—a holding necessary, in view of the particular facts of that case. The defendant had hired a person to transcribe the dialogue of a play as it was performed (on two successive evenings). The defense to the charge of infringement was that the author had not complied with the terms of the copyright act—the Statute of Anne—because he had not registered the title in the Stationers' Register.

The performance rule became a fixed part of the common law (American as well as English), but the rule that Congress enacted in 1976 was a different rule. The common-law performance rule had protected only the common-law copyright; the current performance rule applies to statutory copyright and serves essentially to protect the copyright owner's control of access to the work—an example of overkill, since the other incidents of statutory copyright already provide appropriate protection.

The real danger here, however, is the potential collateral effect of such excessive protection. If history is an accurate guide, any enhancement of the copyright monopoly to benefit entrepreneurs in the field of electronic communication will inevitably have a carry-over effect to benefit the owners of print copyrights. Note, for example, its role already in regard to current debates over the nature of the copyright owner's right to reproduce the work in copies. The issue is whether the right to copy is an independent or a dependent right, that is, whether it is absolute or relative. We will deal with this issue in detail later; for the present we use it only to make this point: if the copyright owner has only performed the work and has not reproduced it in copies, the inference is that he or she should have the right to reproduce the first copies. The argument that the copyright owner has an absolute right to make the first copies is persuasive. But since the copyright owner of a live television broadcast may never actually copy the performance, this would mean that the right of others to copy it (under the fair-use doctrine) is virtually eliminated. And, if the right to copy one kind of copyrighted work is legally curtailed, the argument becomes available that the right to copy other kinds is similarly limited. The fact that such an argument does not follow logically is irrelevant to the lawyer as advocate and is often unknown to the judge, whose knowledge of copyright law is usually limited to a reading of the current rules.

The Codification of the Fair-Use Doctrine

The above changes—the elimination of the common-law copyright, the change in the scope of protection, and the creation of the electronic copyright—essentially forced recognition of the need for another change: the codification of the fair-use doctrine. Congress did not elaborate on why it chose to incorporate in the statute material that had hitherto existed only as judicial law, but apparently they realized that, without a statement regarding fair use, the combined weight of the other changes constituted a very real threat to the constitutional purpose of copyright—the promotion of learning. Obviously, access to copyrighted materials is necessary if that fundamental goal is to be fulfilled. Yet the new statute granted copyright from the moment of creation, thereby eliminating the need for publication. And when copyright protection was granted to works that were performed, it made them available to users only at the will of the copyright owner (and even then usually for only a limited period within a rigid time frame).

Of the four major changes the 1976 act made, the codification of the fair-use doctrine is perhaps the least successful— in large part because its wording lacks the specificity generally present throughout the rest of the statute. Since we will analyze this crucial change more fully later (in both Chapter 10 and Chapter 14), we will limit our discussion here to an introduction of the issues it presents. Put most simply, section 107—the fair-use section—provides that the fair use of a copyrighted work "for purposes such as criticism, comment, news reporting, teaching . . ., scholarship, or research" is not an infringement of copyright. To determine whether the use made of a work in any particular case is a fair use, the statute lists four nonexclusive factors to be considered:

1. the purpose and character of the use, including whether such use is of a commercial nature or is for nonprofit educational purposes;
2. the nature of the copyrighted work;
3. the amount and substantiality of the portion used in relation to the copyrighted work as a whole; and
4. the effect of the use upon the potential market for or value of the copyrighted work.

The paradox of section 107 is that while it is intended as a limitation on the copyright monopoly, it in fact works to enhance that monopoly. There are three reasons for this: the factors of fair use are stated in terms of the interests of copyright owners; it fails to distinguish between users, who fall into two groups—competitors and consumers; and it provides the basis for an inference that the work and the copyright of the work are the same thing.

Consider first how the factors favor the copyright owner. The first factor will support an inference that if the use is commercial—or even if it is not for a nonprofit educational purpose—the use will be an infringing rather than a fair use. The second factor is a nullity because it does not state the relevancy of the nature of the work—a clear plus for the copyright owner. The third factor—implying that only a small portion may be used—is also a plus for the copyright owner.

The fourth factor—the effect of the use upon the value of or upon the *potential* market for the work—is sufficient almost to eviscerate the doctrine altogether, since any copyrighted work arguably has unrealized potential market value.

That the factors favor the copyright owner is no surprise, however, in light of the source for three of them—*Folsom v. Marsh,* the case in which Justice Joseph Story first articulated the fair-use doctrine.[8] The *Folsom* case did not include the nature of the use because it was unnecessary in view of the purpose of the doctrine. As discussed earlier, that purpose was to negate the fair-abridgment doctrine—under which one could abridge an author's copyrighted work and produce a new copyrightable work—and to do so it was necessary to state factors that favored the author. In this context, the factors are understandable because they are directed against a competing use. The rights of the copyright owner in 1841 (under the 1831 Copyright Act), however, were much more limited than under the 1976 act. They included only the right to print, reprint, publish, and vend.

As Justice Story set forth the fair-use doctrine, then, it was directed to those competitors who might abridge copyrighted works. But under the 1976 Copyright Act, the copyright owner has, among other rights, the exclusive right to reproduce the work in copies. Moreover, by including the purpose of the use, Congress codified a very different rule from the one Justice Story had propounded, since to consider the nature of the use as a factor is to consider the nature of the user. The result, of course, is to expand the fair-use doctrine to include all users, consumers as well as competitors. But to say that a consumer may make a fair use of the work is to say also that he or she may make an unfair use of the work. Therefore, any time a consumer's use entails copying—even incidental copying—that consumer may be subject to a charge of copyright infringement.

There is, of course, little danger that an individual is going to be sued for copying an article for his or her files—such an action would not be cost effective. The real danger is that copyright owners will organize and create a licensing system for the individual copying of copyrighted works—and such a licensing system is, in fact, now in its embryonic stage.[9] Copyright, in short, is already being used as the basis for a user's tax on published—and therefore public—information.

The basis for such a user's tax, of course, is the claim that the copyrighted work is the property of the copyright owners. Section 107—viewed in isolation—appears to support that claim. It is sufficiently ambiguous to support the erroneous inference that the work and the copyright are the same, and that when one uses the work, one uses the copyright. The conclusion that there is no reason to distinguish between a consumer's use of the work and a competitor's use of the work thus seems to follow naturally.

There are two things wrong with such a conclusion: it results in an unconstitutional use of copyright under both the copyright clause and the free-speech clause of the First Amendment, and it results in an unlawful use of copyright under the 1976 Copyright Act.

We will deal with copyright and free speech in greater detail in Chapter 9, so for the present it is necessary only to point out the following: under the language of the copyright clause, Congress can enact legislation dealing only with copyright, and only for the purpose of promoting learning. The exclusive right that Congress is empowered to grant is the right to publish the work, that is, to protect the work against use by competitors. While Congress has used fictions to expand its power under the copyright clause, arguably it cannot constitutionally empower the copyright owner to control any consumer's personal use of the work after it has been published.

That the power to license or not is the power to censor is

a proposition as self-evident as the truism that the power to tax is the power to destroy. The licensing of the copying of published materials is an exercise of both the power to license and to tax. That the authority used for this purpose is a federal statute should bring it within the proscription of the First Amendment. To make an unconstitutional use of a federal statute is as violative of First Amendment rights as an unconstitutional statute itself. Clearly, the government cannot sanction an unconstitutional use of a constitutional statute.

The fact is, however, that to treat the work and the copyright of the work as being the same thing is contrary to the 1976 act. Yet the change in the philosophy of copyright provided by the 1976 act has not yet been realized. There are many reasons to explain why: the many groups who wish to shape copyright to their special interests, the piecemeal interpretation that courts often give to the statute, the subtlety of some of the changes, and so forth. The root of all these reasons, however, is a failure to understand the nature of copyright and its relevance to such topics as free-speech rights, the role of fictions and fallacies in the law, and the scope of the right to copy. All these topics can best be analyzed in light of copyright history.

PART TWO

Copyright Issues

in Perspective

Nothing is so firmly believed as what we least know.

– Montaigne

One of the greatest pains to human nature is the pain of a
new idea.

– Walter Bagehot

8 The Nature of Copyright

As has been demonstrated throughout the historical survey
provided in the previous chapters, most of the major controversies dealing with copyright can be traced ultimately to the
basic debate over the nature of copyright itself. For over two
hundred years two conflicting theories of copyright have alter-
nated in ascendancy, one claiming that copyright is a natural-
law property right of the author by reason of creation (the
creative-work theory), the other asserting that copyright exists

only as a statutory grant of a limited monopoly by reason of legislation (the statutory-grant theory). Until 1976 both positions could cite supporting evidence, the former being a product of judicial decisions, the latter a product of previous legislation. It is our position that Congress (whether or not aware of all the implications) finally settled the nature of U.S. copyright in the 1976 Copyright Act, when it dissolved the legal barriers between the two theories and clearly selected a single theory on which to build the new law: the statutory-grant theory.

Although a rational analysis of the 1976 act clearly indicates that Congress has resolved this fundamental issue, it is not at all certain that copyright owners and the courts have recognized that solution—or, indeed, that they will accept it even upon recognition. Copyright owners have long tended to view copyright not in terms of what it has been or legally is, but rather in terms of what they would like it to be (that is, a property law, specifically a natural-law property right). And in many ways courts have reinforced that view, although they arrived there by viewing copyright in terms of precedent. Judicial decisions, the source of the natural-law theory of copyright, tend to be particularly persuasive because they provide flesh and blood for the statutory bones. Moreover, the theory that copyright is the property of the author is more appealing than the less personal theory that copyright exists as a necessary but limited monopoly.

This conflict in theories had its genesis in eighteenth-century England, when the booksellers first introduced the claim of an author's common-law copyright. The legacy of that period has been the dual and contradictory theoretical bases for copyright that have generated confusion in both the creation and application of copyright rules ever since. Perhaps the most unfortunate result of this duality is that it has obscured the crucial distinction between a work and the copyright for that work, since only the recognition of a single theoretical base can resolve this problem. Only a unified theory of copyright can ensure that the rules relate to each other and to the whole in a consistent way, which is to say that only a unified theory can provide the needed basis for integrity in the law of copyright.

As a practical matter, the dual theoretical base for American copyright has its source in three cases: *Millar v. Taylor* and *Donaldson v. Beckett* (the two major English cases—see Chapter 3)—and the majority and dissenting opinions in *Wheaton v. Peters* (the first major U.S. copyright decision confronting this issue—see Chapter 5). In scorecard terms, the result at first appears to be two for the creative-work theory of copyright (*Millar* and the dissent in *Wheaton*), and two for the statutory-grant theory (*Donaldson* and the majority in *Wheaton*). But a closer examination reveals that the issue is not so equally balanced.

Two of these cases purported to resolve the issue of authors' rights without hearing from an author—the authors were not parties in either *Millar* or *Donaldson*. While the authors were directly involved in *Wheaton,* the subject matter was not creative work but reports of Supreme Court opinions, which the Court eventually held were not subject to copyright.[1] The English cases thus involved not the rights of authors vis-à-vis booksellers, but the rights of booksellers inter se as assignees of authors. And the American case involved the rights of authors vis-à-vis each other—but over what turned out to be public-domain rather than creative material.

None of the three cases, then, had all the elements desirable for resolving the issue of literary property—author, bookseller, and a creative work. Therefore none of the cases contained issues for the court to determine the difference, if any, between rights conferred by ownership of the work by reason of the creative-work theory and rights conferred by ownership of the copyright by reason of the statutory-grant theory.

There was, in short, no question as to whether the ownership of work entailed ownership of the copyright. Counsel (and thus the courts) had no reason to assume that there was any distinction between the work and the copyright.

This last point is made apparent by the fact that the *proponents* of the author's perpetual common-law copyright in both *Millar* and *Donaldson* as well as in *Wheaton* claimed that the author owns the work he or she creates. *And the opponents of the common-law copyright agreed*. But did this mean that the author had a perpetual common-law copyright? The proponents said yes it does, while the opponents said no it doesn't, with both of them avoiding the real question: Is there a valid distinction between rights derived from the creation of a work (the common-law copyright) and rights derived from its publication (the statutory copyright)?

Since all the litigants in the English cases were booksellers, presumably neither side wanted this question before the courts because of the risk posed by a possible affirmative answer. Such an answer would have been to the advantage of all authors and the disadvantage of all booksellers. The custom in England had been for the bookseller to purchase an author's "copy" outright, and the trade apparently operated on the basis that ownership of the manuscript included ownership of the copyright. Thus, if the work and the copyright were ruled to be two different things, an author—by reason of his or her ownership of the work—would have gained significant rights.

For the plaintiff bookseller, this would mean that the author might be held to have a right to exercise control over the publication of a work even though the bookseller owned the copyright. For the defendant booksellers, it meant that even if the copyright had expired, a bookseller might be held responsible to an author. Obviously it was to the advantage of both sides in the case that ownership of the work and ownership of the copyright be treated as a single entity. Consequently neither presented the courts with an issue that would have enabled the judges to determine wherein the interests of the author and the bookseller might diverge. And since no author was represented in the cases, the judges treated the two interests as being the same.

Because the supply of arguments was limited, those made for and against the author's common-law copyright in all three cases were essentially the same. And what we here call the *Millar* error and the *Donaldson* error had the same basis: the failure to distinguish between the ownership of the work and the ownership of the copyright.

The *Millar* error was a failure in reasoning, and the route to the error was the treatment of the stationers' copyright as the exemplar of the common-law copyright. But the author's common-law copyright was based on the fact of creation, whereas a new work had not been necessary to obtain a stationers' copyright, which required only membership in the guild and ownership of a manuscript (the "copie"). Indeed, authors were not even eligible for that copyright, and entries in the Stationers' Register gave no indication as to how a stationer claiming copyright had obtained title to the copy presented. The creation of a new work did not become a condition for copyright until required by the Statute of Anne, and even then that condition was imposed primarily not to benefit authors but to create and protect the public domain against incursion by the booksellers' monopoly.

The error in analysis was an error as to the condition for copyright. The booksellers claimed that the author's creation of a work was a sufficient as well as necessary condition for the common-law copyright. For the stationers' copyright, however, ownership of the copy was a necessary but not sufficient condition, since the title of the copy had to be registered in order to obtain copyright. Similarly, for the statutory copyright, a *newly created* work was a necessary but not sufficient condition, as that copyright also required registration of the title.

The error in analysis, however, was obscured by the fact that the rights under statutory copyright were almost exactly the same as for the earlier stationers' copyright *and* the alleged common-law copyright—the exclusive right of printing and publishing. As Lord Mansfield in the *Millar* case said: "I use the word 'copy,' in the technical sense in which that name or term has been used for ages, to signify an incorporeal right to the sole printing and publishing of some[thing] intellectual, communicated by letters."[2] The only difference was that the statutory copyright was limited to a term of years, whereas the stationers' copyright had claimed to exist in perpetuity.

The *Donaldson* case also failed to distinguish between the work and the copyright, but the *Donaldson* error was, in a sense, the converse of the *Millar* error. *Donaldson* was deemed to have held that the replacement of the stationers' copyright by the statutory copyright meant that an author forfeited all ownership rights upon publication, except for those rights granted by the statute. This position, of course, is what one might expect counsel for Donaldson to urge—as in fact he apparently did. The evidence is in a note containing observations of arguments made by Donaldson's counsel "previous to assigning any reasons in support of [the] appeal," that Josiah Brown appended to his report of the case.[3] The question before the Court of Chancery, according to the note, was this:

> Whether the author having sold and delivered, for a competent price, one, or five hundred true copies of his work, retains in each of the copies so sold and delivered, by the true construction of such contract, the mere and absolute dominion and property, conveying to the vendee no more than a special limited use thereof: or *e converso*, whether

such vendee, or rather bailee, acquires by the true construction of the contract of sale and delivery, no absolute property to himself, but only a right of using, to a certain extent, the property of another?

To avoid the undesirable result of saying that one who has sold a chattel (book) retains control of the use of it, this idea was divided into two parts: the material part (the book itself) and the immaterial part (the doctrine contained in it, which is a product of the mind). In the ironic phrasing of Donaldson's counsel, this meant that "[t]he property in the material part [the book], passes according to the law in all other cases; but the property in the immaterial part [the copyright] remains to the author, which is about as intelligible as if one should state John to be the owner of the carcase and limbs of a horse, and Thomas the owner of the colour, shape, speed, and mettle."

In this summary, the counsel for Donaldson was indirectly recognizing (even as he ridiculed) the notion of a distinction between the work and the copyright. He then proceeded to argue that there can be no property in an idea, an argument to which the U.S. Supreme Court gave the force of law in *Baker v. Selden*, a little more than a hundred years later. Still, it did not follow from this conclusion that there was no distinction to be made between the ownership of the work and the ownership of the copyright.

The *Donaldson* error, however, was more in the reading given to the case than in its actual holding. The error was in concluding that the case meant an author forfeited all of his or her rights in a work upon publication except for those granted by the Statute of Anne. To reverse an injunction granted on the basis that the author had a common-law copyright, however, was merely to hold that the author did not have a common-law copyright (the right of exclusive publication) *in perpetuity*. It did not necessarily mean that the author no longer "owned" a work prior to publication, nor did it mean that the author had forfeited all of his or her interest in the work upon publication.

This error presumably had its genesis in the assumption that the Statute of Anne dealt with the author's entire interest in a work. But this would have been the case only if the author's entire interest had been the printing, reprinting, publishing and vending of the work. These were clearly the interests of the bookseller, but not necessarily all of the author's. As Lord Mansfield made clear in the *Millar* case, an author also has an interest in protecting both the integrity of the work and his or her name in connection with the use of that work.

Millar had created a true common-law copyright—the exclusive right of the author to publish his or her creation beyond its first publication. *Donaldson*'s overruling of *Millar*, however, made the common-law copyright a stillborn concept. After *Donaldson*, the common-law copyright was merely the exclusive right of first publication, not the right of continual publication. The common-law copyright thus presumably encompassed the author's entire property interest in his or her work, that is, it constituted ownership of the work. Although American courts did not deal with this issue satisfactorily, the conclusion follows from the fact that no one else had any basis to claim any rights in the work.[4] Presumably, for example, no one could even read the work without the author's consent prior to publication. To publish it with attribution was piracy; to publish it under another's name was plagiarism as well as piracy.

When the author published a work, however, he or she forfeited the common-law copyright because the author had then exercised the right the "common-law copyright" conferred: the right of first publication. The work either became subject to statutory copyright then or went into the public domain. If the author acquired the statutory copyright, the inference was that he or she had exchanged one copyright for another. Such inference, however, was not sound, since the common-law copyright is a copyright in name only, and the statutory copyright does not necessarily constitute ownership of the work. Statutory copyright is only a series of rights to which a work is subject—the right to print, reprint, publish and vend—but the right to vend is not the right to sell the *work*, only to sell a *copy* of the work.

This analysis was not made in England, probably because common-law copyright and statutory copyright were derived from different bodies of law—judicial decisions for the former, legislation for the latter. These dual sources for common-law and statutory copyright tended to preclude a recognition of the difference between the work and the copyright. And this failure of analysis was carried over to the United States, where the federal system made the different legal sources for the common-law and statutory copyright even more significant.

The reasoning in *Millar* and *Donaldson* was adopted by the justices in *Wheaton*, the creative-work theory by the dissenters, the statutory-grant theory by the majority. There was, however, a unique issue in *Wheaton*—a question as to the very existence of a common law of the United States, that is, a federal common law. Justice John McLean, writing for the majority, rejected the notion of federal common law and held that Congress had created the rights that comprised copyright solely as a statutory grant. The common-law copyright that the dissenting justices claimed to exist was left to the laws of the individual states.

In England, the common-law copyright and the statutory copyright were the products of two different bodies of law, but both were the law of the same sovereign. In the United States, these two bodies of law were the products of two different sovereigns—the state and the federal government—and thus produced a curious anomaly. Ownership of the work was vested in an author under state law by reason of creation, but as soon as the author published the work, he or she lost all rights under state law and had to comply with federal law (the copyright statute) in order to obtain a copyright. Thus one sovereign (the state) protected the work as a matter of natural law; another (the federal government) granted the copyright by positive law, that is, by statute.

This curious dichotomy may help to explain the judicial treatment of American copyright in the early nineteenth century. Copyright then was viewed as a monopoly to be construed as strictly as necessary to restrain the monopoly within reasonable bounds. Although the monopoly problem was a problem of publishers—not authors—the federal courts had no legal basis for separating the rights of publisher and author by reference to the author's natural-law rights, since that was a matter of state law. Moreover, the copyright clause of the Constitution empowered Congress to protect the rights of authors, and the constitutional provision was evidence that statutory copyright was the province solely of federal law.

In actual practice, the common-law copyright received no significant judicial development in either the federal or state courts. The continued existence of the common-law copyright as a natural-law property right of the author under state law, however, was not without its effect. Natural law can best be defined, perhaps, as a legal annotation of the Golden Rule, and as such it had a powerful emotional appeal. Federal judges were members of various state bars, of course, and state law was a part of their training. Inevitably, then, the existence of the common-law copyright influenced their thinking in the interpretation of the federal copyright statutes.

Consequently, the creative-work theory increasingly became accepted as a theoretical basis even for the statutory copyright, silently but effectively competing with and undermining the theoretical basis of the statutory-grant concept mandated by the *Wheaton* case. While Congress continued to legislate on the theory that copyright is a statutory grant, courts at various levels—beginning in the latter part of the nineteenth century—were starting to interpret the legislation on the creative-work theory, viewing copyright as a natural-law property right of the author.[5] The point is best made perhaps by Justice Oliver Wendell Holmes's famous comment in a case upholding copyright for advertisements: "Personality always contains something unique. It expresses its singularity even in handwriting, and a very modest grade of art has in it something irreducible, which is one man's alone. That something he may copyright unless there is a restriction in the limits of the act."[6]

In modern terms, the natural-law property theory of copyright is often referred to simply as the "author's property" theory. But the natural-law theory continues to have an impact on the judicial interpretation of a statute that clearly makes copyright a limited statutory grant. The question is why. There is no conclusive answer, but given the fact that decision makers, including judges, are often influenced by factors of which they themselves are unaware, and given the fact that the natural law is the ultimate source of the "author's property" concept, the following analysis may be useful.

As a general rule, property is a relative term, subject to many and varying limitations and constraints, and this is true also of copyright. But copyright is deemed to be more than a property right; it is a *natural-law* property, which gives rise to the idea that it is, or should be, an absolute right (that is, nothing is more one's own than that which an individual creates). Despite the statutory limitations imposed on copyright, then, the author is still generally thought by many to own a newly created work as a natural-law property.

To one unfamiliar with the history of copyright, the statutory copyright appears to be merely a codification of the common-law copyright with some limitations added. Thus it is easy to conclude that the statutory copyright is also ultimately grounded in natural law and is, therefore, a plenary property right of the author. From this, it would seem to follow that any limitation on the author's right is an incursion contrary to the dictates of equity.

The common-law copyright thus is the foundation for the natural-law theory of copyright. Herein lies the importance of the fact that the 1976 Copyright Act abolished the common-law copyright, for by doing so Congress accomplished two objectives. It eliminated the jurisprudential obstacle that for many years precluded courts from recognizing the distinction between the work and the copyright; and it eliminated the two-sovereign basis for copyright by making copyright solely a matter of federal law.

When the 1976 Copyright Act is carefully analyzed, it becomes clear that Congress enacted that legislation on the single theory that copyright is a statutory grant to—rather than a natural-law property right of—the author. The surprising point, however, is the extent to which the 1976 act implements the crucial distinction between the work and the copyright, a result consistent with its rejection of the common-law copyright.

To appreciate this point, one must recognize the fact that statutory copyright is no more than a series of rights to which a given work is subject—the right to reproduce in copies, the right to prepare derivative works, the right to distribute copies publicly, and the right to perform and display the work. The author may transfer each of these rights separately, because the copyright is divisible. But the transfer of title to the copyright does not constitute transfer of title to the work. In short, the 1976 act—consistent with prior statutes—does not deal with the ownership of the work, only with ownership of the copyright. The key difference now is that common-law copyright is no longer available to vest ownership of the work in the author.

The 1976 act vests copyright in the author of the work upon its creation, that is, upon its fixation in a tangible medium of expression. Unlike prior statutes, however, the 1976 act makes it clear that copyright is available only for a work of original authorship, and that the copyright of a collective work protects only those elements of the work that constitute original authorship. Consequently, before one can determine a possible infringement of a work consisting only partially of original authorship, one must distinguish the uncopyrightable components. There is, in short, a stated legal distinction now between a use of the copyright and use of the work. The use of the copyright may be infringement, but the mere use of the work—of, for instance, only its uncopyrightable contents—is certainly not.

The law abhors a vacuum, and it is reasonable to infer that the ownership of the work must vest in someone by reason of some law. The elimination of the two-sovereign basis for copyright means that the ownership must be determined by federal law, and the only logical candidate is the author who creates the work. While the 1976 act does not deal with the author's ownership of the work explicitly, it does so by implication in its innovative inclusion of an author's termination right. This new right—which is both inalienable and limited to the author (or heirs)—can be analogized to a reversionary interest in real property. Such an interest requires a proprietary basis other than the interest itself, and for copyright this proprietary basis has to be the work. Since a copyright is only a series of rights to which a given work is subject, the assignment of copyright (or any right of the copyright) should not

be held to be an assignment of the work itself. Thus, ownership of the work remains in the author, subject to the various
rights comprising copyright that the author assigns.

The utility of the statutory-grant theory, which requires a
distinction between the work and the copyright, becomes apparent when it is applied to practical problems. One of those
problems is the relationship of copyright and free speech;
another is how to understand (and limit) the fictions and fallacies that pervade the copyright statute; a third is the scope of
the right to copy. The satisfactory analysis of all these issues,
which are developed further in the next three chapters, depends upon the distinction between the ownership of the work
and the ownership of the copyright.

As we have demonstrated here, the unified theory of copyright informing the current statute is based on two elements:
(1) copyright is a statutory grant of rights to which a given
work is subject, and (2) the copyright of a work is distinct and
separate from the work itself. The rights to which authors are
entitled by reason of their creation of new work are independent of the copyright and therefore should not be treated as
a part of the copyright but in a companion body of law.

The justification for the statutory-grant theory of copyright,
finally, is simple. Copyright must accommodate the interests
of authors, entrepreneurs, and users. The accommodation can
be satisfactorily achieved only by legislation, and only if the
courts interpret that legislation in a manner consistent with
the theory upon which it is based.

The law hath not been dead, though it hath slept.
— William Shakespeare

Give me the liberty to know, to utter, and to argue freely
according to conscience, above all liberties.
— John Milton

Copyright and
Free-Speech
Rights

Copyright and free-speech rights (a phrase we use to encompass both the free-speech and free-press clauses of the First Amendment) can be viewed as opposite sides of the same coin. The former is a matter of proprietary rights, the latter of society's political rights. They are bonded because both deal with the flow of information, one in the interest of profit, the other in the interest of freedom. The profit motive, however, is not a wholly reliable monitor. Like the locks in a canal, it may facilitate the flow of information, or it may in fact serve to dam that flow. This explains why the regulatory aspects of copyright must govern the proprietary aspects, for the early history of copyright—which we ignore at our peril—demonstrates how closely copyright and free-speech values were (and are) connected.

The relationship between copyright and free-speech rights is a topic that has received relatively little close attention, perhaps because courts have not yet appeared to take it seriously. When the issue has been used as a defense in copyright infringement actions, for instance, the presumption consistently appears to be in favor of copyright. One explanation for this may be that copyright jurisprudence in the United States has had a much longer history than free-speech jurisprudence. Only in recent years, for example, has the Supreme Court begun developing the notion that free-speech rights encompass the right to *hear* as well as the right to *speak,* the right to *read* as well as the right to *print*—that is, *a right of access.*

Another explanation may be that as long as copyright required publication, the free-speech danger that it posed was minimal. This is because the point at which copyright and free-speech rights intersect is the right of public access, and the publication of the work ensured that access. But with the application of copyright to the unpublished materials of modern communication technology, the danger to the free-speech right of public access becomes more apparent.

The thesis of this chapter is threefold: first, because copyright had a major, if indirect, role in the development of the free-speech rights, the copyright clause encompasses free-speech values that merit recognition; second, because lawmakers (especially courts) have ignored those values, copyright today poses a significant danger to free-speech rights; and third, because both copyright and free-speech rights must be accommodated in a complimentary fashion, the proprietary aspects of copyright law must be recognized as being subordinate to the regulatory aspects of the statute.

The Role of Copyright in the Development of Free Speech

The historical origins of the relationship of copyright to free-speech rights have almost completely escaped scholarly attention—probably because the Statute of Anne, enacted some sixteen years after the end of the Licensing Act of 1662, is deemed to be the beginning of Anglo-American copyright.[1] Thus, the even earlier stationers' copyright and its role in governmental censorship have unfortunately become a mere footnote in copyright history. Ignorance as to what preceded a legal concept is ignorance of why it was created, and the cost of such lost perspective is confusion as to the significance of subsequent developments. This has been true, at least, in the case of copyright and free-speech rights.

We need to return to an obvious but fundamental point: both copyright and free-speech rights owe their origins to the advent of the printing press. Without the press there would have been neither a reason for copyright nor an occasion for press control. The presence of the press, however, coincided with religious fanaticism and political tyranny in England that caused the government to control and censor its output. It was the history of these events that caused the leaders of the former British colonies to establish free-speech rights as legal doctrine to forestall such happenings in their new nation. The freedoms protected by the First Amendment—freedom to establish and exercise religion, freedom of speech and of the press, and freedom to assemble and to petition the government for redress of grievances—are not a matter of coincidence, but history.

Prominent throughout the religious and political controversies in sixteenth- and seventeenth-century England was the stationers' copyright, which served as a tool of the censors. The role of copyright in censorship thus was instrumental, not substantive, in nature, for copyright was a private-property concept, created independently of political policies and only later pressed into governmental service. Its use as a device of governmental censorship has been forgotten since it lost its utility as such with the demise of the Licensing Act of 1662.

The end of the stationers' copyright inevitably meant there would be a new statute for the book trade. But since the new statutory copyright was to function in much the same way as the old copyright, one can also assume that Parliament, in creating it, was concerned with rendering copyright ineffective not only as an instrument of monopoly but also as a device of censorship. The Statute of Anne was thus directed to the monopoly of books per se as well as to the booksellers' control of the book trade.

Apart from the limited term for copyright that creates the public domain, three sections of that first English act suggest both a repudiation of censorship and an affirmative concern for the right of access to books: section 4 provided for price control of books, section 5 provided that copyrighted books were to be supplied to nine different libraries, and section 7 provided that the act was not to prevent the importation of, or apply to, books in foreign languages printed beyond the seas, which had previously required the licenser's imprimatur as part of the scheme of censorship. In short, the statute was intended not only to destroy the booksellers' monopoly but also to ensure what today we would call free-speech rights for the benefit of the public.

The drafters of the English copyright act took seriously its stated purpose—the encouragement of learning—a goal that required making books available to the public. The Statute of Anne thus created the rationale for the incorporation of free-speech values into the concept of copyright—values such as the right of access, which received expression also in the statute's creation of the public domain. The regulatory function of copyright to control publishers was thereby also utilized so as to benefit the public.

Whether or not the drafters of the U.S. Constitution fully comprehended the free-speech values in the provisions of the Statute of Anne we cannot know, but we do know that they made direct use of the wording of the statute's title, and it is clear that these words incorporate free-speech values. The three policies that the copyright clause mandates—the promotion of learning, the preservation of the public domain, and the protection of the author—are consistent with and essential to free-speech rights. Consider, for example, a society in which learning is suppressed, published material is subject to the control only of publishers, and authors have no rights. These were the conditions that had prevailed during the reign of the stationers' copyright, conditions that the Statute of Anne repudiated; because it did, the copyright clause of the U.S. Constitution contains free-speech values.

While these free-speech values of the copyright clause have received little, if any, recognition in copyright jurisprudence, their presence can be of considerable value in the administration of U.S. copyright law. Since the free-speech clauses of the First Amendment and the copyright clause deal in part with the same subject matter—writings—the fact that the copyright clause does contain free-speech values avoids a potential conflict between two provisions of the U.S. Constitution, with one denying a power that the other arguably grants.

In crucial ways, the free-speech values in the copyright clause can be said to complement the free-speech rights in the First Amendment. While Congress can make no law abridging the freedom of speech or the press, Congress can—to promote the progress of learning—make a law encouraging authors to disseminate their writings by giving them the exclusive right to publish for a limited period of time. The major rights of free speech in the First Amendment are the rights to speak and publish; the major free-speech value in the copyright clause is the public's right to hear and read.

Although the copyright clause incorporates free-speech values, it does not create free-speech rights. The major difference between the First Amendment and the copyright clause in terms of congressional power is that the first is a denial of power and the latter a grant of discretionary power with implied limitations—a situation that facilitates the use of fictions to expand the limited power. Since Congress has used fictions to expand its power, the problem now is essentially one of the administration and interpretation of the copyright act. For example, the copyright clause empowers Congress to grant copyright only to authors and only for their writings. Congress's creation of the corporate copyright is thus of questionable constitutionality, and if that copyright were to be used to inhibit public access, its use would surely be unconstitutional. Similarly, if the Copyright Office were to deny copyright registration for a writing based on its *content*, that action would surely violate the First Amendment. The First Amendment, in short, is a useful aid to the implementation of the free-speech values of the copyright clause without denying Congress the power to accommodate copyright to changing technology.

The Copyright Threat to Free-Speech Rights

The essential free-speech value in the copyright clause is the right of public access to copyrighted materials, and the remarkable aspect of copyright during the nineteenth century is the extent to which both Congress and the courts implemented this right. Congress did so by requiring publication of the work as a condition for copyright; the courts did so by developing the fundamental principles of copyright, the most important of which was the limited-protection principle.

The 1909 Copyright Act, however, provided a basis for the erosion of this principle with two innovations: the addition to the copyright owner's existing arsenal of the right to copy the work (which then provided a basis for the claim that the right to copy is an independent and absolute right) and the creation of the work-for-hire doctrine (which led to the corporate copyright, the basis of the electronic copyright).

The actual event that marks the beginning of the erosion of the limited-protection principle can be said to be the formation of the American Society of Composers, Authors, and Publishers (ASCAP) in 1914 by Victor Herbert and other outstanding figures. ASCAP is a musical performing-rights society, which licenses the *public* performance of musical compositions, the earliest example of a copyright user's tax. In this instance, however, the tax can be justified, as it was imposed on users-for-profit, the commercial exploiters of the music. Even so, the charge of a fee every time a work is performed or heard publicly is analogous to charging a fee every time a written work is read or copied for personal use—a point which is now being rapidly approached.

The 1909 innovations did not reach full fruition until the 1976 act, the drafting of which was influenced by the development of the new technology of communication—the photocopying machine, television, and the computer. Two of these machines—television and the computer—have made the *transmission* of information a separate industry. Consider, for example, the Westlaw and Lexis computer legal research services, which do not require the creation of writings but merely transmit public-domain materials via the computer and yet receive plenary copyright protection.[2] Consider also copyright protection for live television broadcasts, which has resulted in the electronic copyright, by reason of which the transmission itself is "copyrighted."

The third machine—the photocopier—has given rise to a copyright industry that engages in the licensing of the right to photocopy copyrighted materials for private use, thereby making the erosion of the limited-protection principle almost complete. The copyright user's fee has thus been extended from being a tax on commercial exploiters of musical compositions with statutory sanction, to being a tax on the individual user of copyrighted printed material without statutory sanction (and, at least in some cases, contrary to the user's right of fair use). An additional irony (and corruption of the intent of copyright) is that the Copyright Clearance Center—as its own literature indicates—imposes its user's tax to benefit not authors but publishers.

A copyright user's tax, of course, inhibits the right of public access to copyrighted materials. This problem is more important and the solution is less complex than most perceive it to be. It is important for two basic reasons. First, copyright law has been expanded to protect more than the creations of authors and artists. Probably the largest component of copyrighted works today is public-domain material—collective works that contain materials on which either the copyright has long expired or never existed. Newly "copyrighted" volumes regularly appear on the market containing judicial opinions, statutory codes, and classical literature (even the Bible, the Torah, and the Koran), as well as compilations of factual data (directories, catalogues, market reports, and so forth).

Second, copyrighted works no longer need be disseminated in copies as a condition for copyright protection, but may be only performed over the public airwaves. Television is the primary source for the political, economic, social, and scientific information most Americans receive, and such reports obviously shape opinions, attitudes, and decisions. To say that copyright gives the purveyors of this information a plenary right to control public access to it is not only nonsense, it is dangerous nonsense.

The central problem in copyright law today is that a constitutionally based statute is being given an unconstitutional interpretation by copyright owners—and worse, by courts. The copyright act should be interpreted in light of the policies of the copyright clause (which reflect its free-speech values) and the basic judicial principles of copyright that the current statute has codified. Herein lies the importance of a unified theory of copyright.

Free Speech and Proprietary Rights

The major flaw in the dual theoretical basis of copyright was that it encompassed both proprietary and political rights without any basis for subordinating one to the other. Proprietary rights, as the term is here used, are the individual's rights to control the products of his or her efforts for profit. Political rights, in contrast, belong to the members of the body politic and are related to self-governance—the right to vote, the right of due process, the right of free speech, and so forth.

Logically, political rights must be regarded as more important than proprietary rights, since the latter ultimately have to be both recognized and enforced by the government that is sustained by political rights. Proprietary rights tend to be concrete, however, whereas political rights are typically abstract, and in a one-to-one combat of ideas the concrete usually has the advantage over the abstract. In copyright litigation, for example, an accusation that a defendant has stolen the plaintiff's property is much more powerful than the claim that a defendant is exercising a free-speech right. The larger truth as to the importance of political rights is often lost in the legal melee.

If copyright were actually based on the creative-work theory, it would follow that copyright was primarily proprietary in nature, designed to protect one's property. And since free-speech rights deal with one's own speech, they would not—under that theory—extend to the transmitting or conveying of another's property. But once copyright is recognized as being based on the statutory-grant theory, it follows that copyright is primarily regulatory in nature. And since it is only a series of rights to which a given work is subject, copyright can now be construed in a manner consistent with free-speech rights.

The problem comes into focus when one recognizes that the subject matter of copyright and the essence of community rights are the same: information. The information may be cultural in nature (creative works) or political in nature (public-interest works). In either case, however, it is received information that not only shapes opinions and attitudes but also serves as the basis of action. Any legal instrument that enables one to control the flow of information poses censorship dangers.

The copyright statute curbs proprietary censorship in two ways. First, it limits the rights of copyright by defining those rights precisely. Second, it limits the scope of copyright protection for derivative works and compilations (which are most often public-interest works) as compared with the copyright protection offered for original creative works. Both of these features reflect the statutory-grant theory: the first by using the rules that grant the rights to limit them as well, the second by reducing the scope of copyright protection according to the nature of the author's efforts. The implicit lesson here is that the regulatory aspects of copyright, which serve the public purpose, must govern the proprietary aspects, which serve primarily a private purpose.

As the history of copyright demonstrates, this regulatory-proprietary pattern is neither accidental nor obscure, but it is often ignored. The reason can be traced ultimately to the failure to distinguish between the work and the copyright, for unless this distinction is made, there is no basis for distinguishing between the use of the work and the use of the copyright. The copyright statute governs only the use of the copyright, not the use of the work, but while Congress has legislated within the scope of its power (employing the aid of a few fictions), the statute is subject to interpretation by copyright owners as well as by courts. There is no constitutional restraint on the copyright owners as to either their proprietary interpretation or their power to sue alleged infringers who disagree with their interpretation. The binding interpretation of copyright is thus up to the courts. That interpretation should be made not only in terms of the wording of the statute, but also in light of the free-speech values of the copyright clause.

Copyright can be used either to control the flow of ideas, as in a totalitarian society, or to facilitate the flow of ideas within a free society. The use of copyright as an instrument of censorship during its early—and most proprietary—stage of development should not be forgotten. To facilitate the flow of ideas within society, copyright must be treated primarily as a regulatory concept. This is the command of both the copyright clause and the free-speech clause of the First Amendment. If one accepts the proposition that copyright must accommodate the interest of three groups—authors, entrepreneurs, and users— no other conclusion is available.

Recognizing the subordination of the proprietary aspects of copyright does not, of course, eliminate them. But it is important to keep in mind that even if copyright is a property, as the owners claim, that property is clearly limited to the copyright on the work and does not encompass the work itself. American copyright is only a series of rights to which a given work is subject: "Not primarily for the benefit of the author, but primarily for the benefit of the public such rights are given."[3]

Sin has many tools, but a lie is the handle which fits
them all.
—Oliver Wendell Holmes

In tragic life, God wot,
No villain need be! Passions spin the plot:
We are betrayed by what is false within.
—George Meredith

10 The Role of Fictions and Fallacies in Copyright Law

Since the Constitution specifically empowers Congress to grant
copyright only to authors, one might logically conclude that
Congress could not grant copyright to corporations. Yet all
Congress needed to do to circumvent the constitutional limitations was to enlarge the definition of *author* to include *employers*
(a class encompassing corporations). This is an example of a
legal fiction: a rule of law that as a proposition of fact would
be false; an agreement that, under certain circumstances, one

thing will be treated as another. The fiction that the employer is an author results in the corporate copyright—which, seen out of context, can lead to the fallacy that corporations, not people, create copyrighted works.

Copyright law is not unique in that it contains legal fictions, but it is certainly unusual in the number of legal fictions and fallacies it has accumulated. The major reason for this may have been the long-unperceived absence of a unified theory of copyright, since an ambivalent theoretical foundation provides leeway for interpretation and therefore leads to a malleable concept subject to opportunistic modification. Whatever the cause, however, the topic of copyright fictions and fallacies has received little attention, which accounts for much of the confusion that characterizes copyright. While it may be possible to understand what copyright rules say, it is difficult to comprehend what they actually mean without an understanding of the significant role that legal fictions and resulting fallacies have played in the way copyright operates in America today.

The prominence of legal fictions in copyright law is explained by the language of the copyright clause of the U.S. Constitution. Drafted at a time when the most advanced technology of communication consisted of the printing press, that clause is clearly a limitation on, as well as a grant of, congressional power. It empowers Congress to grant copyright *only* to authors, *only* for their writings, and *only* to promote learning.

The development of new communications technologies would eventually have forced Congress to employ legal fictions if it wanted to extend copyright protection to new media and remain—at least formally—within the bounds of its constitutional power. Congress did not wait on technology, however, using a fiction only twelve years after the enactment of the 1790 Copyright Act—a statute that protected only books, maps, and (marine) charts—to provide copyright protection for musical compositions in 1802.[1] And in the first copyright revision act in 1831, Congress brought etchings and engravings under the copyright umbrella.[2]

The first congressional use of fictions in copyright—recognizing musical compositions and etchings as "writings"—was justified by analogy. A musical composition is a form of writing, and etchings and engravings are reproduced by a process analogous to printing. But these early fictions prepared the way for giving the terms *authors* and *writings* the new meanings of "creators" and "works of authorship"—an exercise in etymology that proved useful as it became necessary to accommodate copyright to new technologies. Thus, in 1865, after photography had become commercially viable, Congress provided copyright protection for photographs, simply by legally designating photographers as authors and photographs as writings.[3]

The extension of copyright to the products of other new technologies followed in similar fashion. In 1909 Congress gave the copyright owners of musical compositions the right to record them—the first step that was to lead eventually to copyright protection for recordings. And in 1912 motion pictures were given copyright protection; from that point on, movies became "writings" and corporate studios were transformed into "authors."[4] By the time of the 1976 Copyright Act, television and the computer were prominent players in the communications industry, and their products were also given copyright protection. Live television broadcasts (recorded as they were broadcast), machine-readable computer chips, and "software" on floppy disks—all became copyrighted works of authorship, with their various corporate owners recognized as authors.

These extensions of copyright protection to products other than the actual writings of authors demonstrate the role of legal fictions in copyright law: to enlarge the copyright monopoly—sometimes for good, sometimes not. Generally, the fictions that have sound analogical bases (such as the term *author* with the meaning of "creator") serve a justifiable purpose. The fiction that a sculptor is an author and that his or her statue is a writing enlarges the copyright monopoly; but the reason for doing so is readily apparent, the result is limited to defined consequences, and the fiction arguably serves a good purpose.

When the fiction is without such an analogical base, however, the result is less sanguine—as is the fiction of an employer as author, which results in a corporate copyright as opposed to the constitutionally sanctioned author's copyright. Unlike the sculptor's copyright, the corporate copyright contains no valid analogy relating it to its paradigm: the sculptor, like an author, is genuinely a creator; the corporation is not. The reason for making an employer the author, then, is not apparent, and doing so entails ill-defined consequences for the whole of copyright law. Arguably the fiction is not warranted.

Although legal fictions are neither good nor bad in and of themselves, their use may present problems, partly because the use of one legal fiction tends to facilitate the use of yet others. The extension of copyright to photographs, for instance, made it easier for Congress subsequently to extend copyright to motion pictures, which in turn made it easier to extend copyright protection to live television broadcasts, which made it easier to extend copyright protection to computer-generated databases, and so on. Fictions thus move copyright further and further away from authors and their writings. The live telecast of terrorists holding a hijacked airplane hostage, whatever its intrinsic merits, is about as far from a writing of an author as one can get—yet it is protected by copyright.

One major problem is the threat that copyright fictions pose to the fundamental purpose of copyright: the promotion of learning. The further from actual authors and genuine writ-

ings that the fictions carry copyright, the more the basic policies and principles of copyright are obscured and the less the
general concern that copyright fulfill its basic purpose. If the
copyright of a work created by an employee belongs to his or
her employer, that copyright is not rewarding the real author;
if copyright protects a performance of a live television broadcast that may never be run again (or even saved), that copyright has not enriched the public domain; and if copyrights
are granted for fishbowls, door knobs, and salt-and-pepper
shakers, they do little if anything for the cause of learning.

Our point here is not that every copyrighted item must demonstrably promote learning, enrich the public domain, and
reward the author. But at the least, copyright law should not
be used so as actually to inhibit learning, to avoid the public
domain, or to deny the author a reward. We should never for-
get that copyright is not a right so much as it is a monopoly
privilege that is granted in return for a quid pro quo—the creation of a work of authorship to benefit the public. Copyright
can thus be viewed as being in the nature of a contract—a
bargain and sale—between the author (copyright owner) and
the public, represented by Congress. Without the copyright
statute, the author of a work would have no exclusive right of
publication and presumably less incentive either to create or
to publish more new work. Therefore, in exchange for the creation and dissemination of a work, the author is given certain
rights, monopolistic in nature. An implicit part of the copyright bargain is that the author will not use copyright to inhibit
learning or to defeat the public domain. By using the benefits to be obtained from copyright, the author (or copyright
owner) assumes certain obligations in return for the statutory
grant: to provide public access to the work and to preserve the
work for the public domain.

These obligations may seem minimal, but they are consistent with the author's self-interest: profit (because the author

can charge for a copy of the work) and an opportunity for lasting fame (because the work is preserved for posterity). Therefore, when the author eschews the obligations, one can assume that the self-interest factors inherent in copyright are not operative. The profit, for example, may come not from a distribution of copies but from an ephemeral electronic performance, and the copyright owner may be a corporation, to which fame is irrelevant. (The paradigmatic example is a local television newscast, the videotapes of which are regularly erased in order that the tape may be reused.) To the extent that those obligations are eschewed, then, copyright protection ought properly to be limited, so that the constitutional policies of copyright shall not be undermined—a particular danger when fictions are used to grant the copyright in the first place.

Fictions, of course, need not have the effect of undermining copyright policies; indeed, when limited to the functions for which they are intended, there is no reason for them to have that effect. The corporate copyright fiction, for example, is a product of the work-for-hire doctrine, which Congress put into the 1909 act to facilitate the administration of the copyright law. House Report 2222 (on the bill that became the 1909 Copyright Act) justifies that doctrine on the ground that treating the publisher as author would facilitate the renewal of the copyright for such works as encyclopedias and other compilations.[5] By the time the 1976 act was drafted, however, the corporate copyright had proved to be so beneficial to the copyright owners (but not to most authors) that it was continued as a matter of expediency.

So it is that legal fictions, once adopted, tend to assume a life of their own, a point that relates to the second major problem arising from their use: when employed out of historical context, legal fictions give rise to copyright fallacies. Two major copyright fallacies are grounded in legal fictions: first, that the author is the primary beneficiary of copyright; and second, that copyright is the private property of the author. The fallacies are reciprocal; one can argue either one in support of the other.

Since copyright is traditionally identified as an author's right, the fallacy that copyright exists primarily to benefit authors is easy to slip into. But even though the wording of the law states that copyright is an author's right, and even though that wording serves a valid purpose (to limit the availability of copyright to newly created works), the ultimate purpose is *not* primarily to benefit the author. By vesting copyright initially in the author, the law ensures that only authors who create new works are entitled to copyright, and that works already in the public domain are not subject to copyright. The true purposes of the rule, thus, are to encourage the creation of new works and to protect works in the public domain against capture or recapture by copyright. The primary beneficiary of copyright, in short, is intended to be the public.

Indeed, except for initial ownership, copyright statutes have always treated the author as only an incidental beneficiary of copyright. The one feature of the seminal Statute of Anne unique to the author—as opposed to the copyright owner—was that only the author was entitled to renew the term of copyright; in the 1976 Copyright Act, the major feature unique to the author is a specific termination right. Yet another indication of the subordinate role of the author in copyright is the fact that, beginning with the 1790 Copyright Act, American copyright statutes denied *foreign* authors *any* copyright protection for a century and more.

The second fallacy—that copyright is a private property of the author—is both a cause and a result of the continual expansion of the copyright monopoly through the device of legal fictions. Publishers and their lawyers regularly use this fallacy to expand the copyright monopoly, and the use of the legal fictions enhances the fallacy as the monopoly is enlarged. This is why the fallacy that copyright is the author's private property constitutes the greatest threat to copyright policies. Note the kinds of reasoning that illustrate this threat: if an individual is denied the right to make a copy of copyrighted material for study, copyright thwarts learning, *but this is necessary because no unpermitted use of another's property is ever justified;* if a television station regularly erases videotapes of its news broadcasts, the public domain is defeated, *but the station has a right to do with its property as it pleases;* and if a corporation owns the copyright, the actual author is denied the rewards of copyright, *but this is as it should be because the fruits of all employees' labor are the employer's property.* Underlying all these examples, alas, is the unexamined but increasingly common notion that copyright law imposes no affirmative duty on the copyright owner, *because copyright owners can do with their property as they wish.*

This kind of reasoning derives mainly from the two basic fictions in the 1976 Copyright Act: that any original work of authorship is a *writing,* and that a corporation as employer is an *author* when its employee creates a work of authorship. The fictions themselves prove the fallacy of the proposition that copyright is a private property of the author who creates the work, since neither of the fictions *requires* either a creative work or an author: the live broadcast of a National Football League game is the broadcast of an athletic contest, the author of which is the NFL (and/or broadcasting network). To put the point another way: only fictions can sustain the fallacy that copyright is an author's private property, or that a live television broadcast of a football game is a work of authorship and that the NFL and/or the broadcast network is an author.

Copyright fallacies, of course, can be used as premises to generate and regenerate other copyright fallacies, often characterized by incestuous reasoning. The fallacy that copyright is an author's private property, for example, gives rise to the following: (1) that copyright is a natural-law property (because an author creates the work); (2) that the primary purpose of copyright is to protect the author's property (because copyright is a natural-law property right); (3) that the author's right to reproduce the copyrighted work in copies is absolute and exclusive (because anyone can exclude others from the use of one's property); and (4) that copyright law does not entail a law of users' rights (because no one has a right to use another's property free of charge).

The dominant role of fictions and fallacies in copyright law is attributable to the fact that copyright law has historically been, and continues to be, shaped largely in response to claims by copyright entrepreneurs. These members of the industry constitute an unusually powerful special-interest group (because they control the media) and continually negotiate with lawmakers to obtain statutory benefits—often at the expense of the public interest. The entire history of copyright demonstrates the influence of these entrepreneurs, but it was never greater than in the shaping of the 1976 Copyright Act. As the Supreme Court has noted: "The [1976] Act . . . was the product of two decades of negotiation by representatives of creators and copyright-using industries, supervised by the Copyright Office and, to a lesser extent, by Congress."[6] The public interest, unfortunately, was not directly represented. As Congressman Robert Kastenmeier commented at the time, "Really, all interests in this bill are, in one form or another, special interests."[7]

The success of the information and entertainment industry in 1976, while not complete, was substantial. Copyright protection, for example, was extended specifically to *live* television broadcasts (even though copyright for any "writing" that is broadcast should have provided adequate protection). The 1976 Copyright Act thus represents the high-water mark in the use of copyright fictions: copyright protection is now available not only for writings but also for pictures, pantomimes, dances, sculptures, motion pictures, sound recordings, computer programs, and live television broadcasts—any of which may be "authored" by a corporation (as employer).

The primary role of fictions can thus be defined as that of enlarging the copyright monopoly. The danger is that they can be used to carry copyright beyond its constitutional boundaries—and, indeed, beyond its statutory limits. The danger is most prevalent when the fiction ceases to be recognized as a fiction, a possibility that increases with the passage of time. Familiarity breeds acceptance and thus obscures the most important point about copyright fictions: they must be applied in light of copyright policies and principles. A copyright fiction, in other words, should be limited to the reason for which it is employed. Otherwise it becomes a source of fallacies that may well result in corrupting the integrity of copyright itself.

The use of principles and policies to limit the effect of fictions is generally more important for arbitrary fictions than for those with an analogical base. Analogical fictions—such as defining a sculptor as an author—are usually consistent with the policies and principles of copyright, while such arbitrary fictions as the work-for-hire doctrine are not. The sculptor is an artist who produces a creative work that may contribute to learning and eventually enrich the public domain. The work-for-hire doctrine, on the other hand, results in a copyright for a corporation. The corporation is not a creator, its employees do not necessarily produce a creative work, the results may be only a minimal contribution to learning, and at least in some cases the work is destroyed before it could possibly enrich the public domain.

This occurs (as noted earlier) with copyrighted local television newscasts, for which employees prepare reports that are performed only momentarily over the public airwaves, with the videotapes usually being erased shortly thereafter. There are three fictions involved here: that the broadcaster (a corporation) is an author; that a live television broadcast is a writing (by virtue of being recorded as it is transmitted); and that a performance is the same as a publication for the purpose of promoting learning. Yet, the copyright for these corporate and ephemeral creations is legally distinguished from the copyright on the writings of a William Faulkner or Eudora Welty in only two small ways: the human author may eventually terminate the assignment of any copyright, and the corporate copyright has a fixed life of between seventy-five and a hundred years, while the author's copyright lasts fifty years beyond the life of the author.

Given the many and varied economic interests vested in copyright, it is not likely that Congress will or can eliminate fictions. Nevertheless, this should not at all exempt fictional copyrights from being interpreted in light of the principles and policies of copyright and narrowed accordingly. Two illustrations will suffice. Any corporation that subsequently fails to publish copies of a work that is performed over the public airwaves could be held to have forfeited its exclusive right to copy that work. And any corporation that destroys a work after it has been performed could be held to have forfeited its claim to copyright altogether.

The major difference between legal fictions in general and legal fictions for copyright is that the former tend to be procedural in nature, the latter substantive. The classic example of a procedural legal fiction is the presumption that an accused is innocent until proven guilty—the purpose of which is to ensure that the burden of proof remains on the prosecutor. Not coincidentally, the major fiction in copyright—the corporate copyright fiction—also began with a procedural purpose (to facilitate the renewal of copyright for encyclopedias and similar works). Yet the corporate copyright has subsequently become a major *substantive* part of copyright law.

Apart from the practical utility of legal fictions in copyright law, two factors help to explain their widespread and unquestioned acceptance. One, as mentioned earlier, is the conflicting duality of copyright's theoretical base. The other is the parochial and piecemeal nature of legal reasoning that advocacy of a predetermined conclusion demands. The art of advocacy increases both the burdens and responsibility of the courts. The judicial task is to discount the self-interest that dictates the legal arguments put forth in copyright litigation and to consider them in the context of the public interest.

The basic point here is that the remedy for the threat that copyright fictions pose to the fundamental policies and principles of copyright is to be found within those same policies and principles. It is necessary only to remember that law consists of three levels—policies, principles, and rules—and that the rules should never be analyzed in isolation from the fundamental concepts on which they are based.

Next to the originator of a good sentence is the first quoter of it.
— Ralph Waldo Emerson

Take the whole range of imaginative literature, and we are all wholesale borrowers. In every matter that relates to invention, to use, or beauty or form, we are borrowers.
— Wendell Phillips

 # The Scope
of the Right
to Copy

The scope of the copyright owner's right to copy the work determines the scope of the copyright monopoly of that work. It is surprising, therefore, that the legal contents of the verb "to copy" and the phrase "to reproduce . . . in copies" have been so casually assumed, so little analyzed.

There seem to be two meanings given to the verb "to copy" in copyright law: (1) to *duplicate* an original (for example, with a photocopying machine); and (2) to *imitate* an original (possibly incorporating portions from it) by using it as a model.[1] In a sense, this distinction hearkens back to the nineteenth century, when the rights of the copyright owner of a book were limited to the rights to print, reprint, publish, and vend, that is, to print it for the market. Another author could not duplicate the book for sale, but he or she could freely translate or abridge the work—imitate it, so to speak—without infringing the copyright. Most users, of course, had no interest in imitating a book, and the issue of duplicating it by copying was no problem in the prephotocopy era because it was cheaper to buy a book than to copy it. It is doubtful that any individual actually went to the trouble of duplicating a copy by hand, but even if an occasional eccentric had done so, there would have been no substantial threat to the marketing of the work.

In the nineteenth century, then, the right to copy by duplication—to print, reprint, and publish—was merely a function of the right to vend the copyrighted work. And because of the abridgment doctrine, the copyright owner did not have the exclusive right to copy by imitation, that is, to use the copyrighted work to create a new work. It was this second kind of copying that led to two of the major copyright decisions of the nineteenth century, *Folsom v. Marsh* and *Baker v. Selden*.[2] Justice Story in the *Folsom* case enhanced the copyright owner's right to prevent copying by imitation when he created the fair-use doctrine as a limit on the abridgment doctrine. In *Baker v. Selden,* the Supreme Court limited the copyright owner's right to prevent copying by imitation when it held that copyright protects the expression but not the idea.

The copyright owner's right to copy in the nineteenth century can thus be summarized as follows: The copyright gave the copyright owner the exclusive right to copy the work by duplication—to print, reprint, and publish—for the market. But this right, being directed to competitors, did not prevent an individual user from copying by duplication for his own personal use, a limitation that had little economic impact. The copyright also gave the copyright owner only a limited right to prevent another's copying by imitation. The owner could limit another's use of the work to a "fair use" but could not prevent another's use of the ideas to create a new work.

The scope of the copyright owner's right to copy was thus equitably, if only roughly, defined in a way that protected the public interest. The scheme, however, was brought into question by the 1909 act, which added the right to copy to the prior rights to print, reprint, publish, and vend. As we have demonstrated earlier, the addition of the right to copy was almost surely intended to apply only to artworks, but there is no definitive proof of this, so for present purposes we will deal with the issues only in analytical terms.

The problem with the addition of this new right to copy was that the verb "to copy" was a generic term now being incorporated within a series of expressions already accepted and used as "words of art," that is, as terms with clear, definite, and limited legal meanings. Logically, the right to copy should also have been read as similarly limited, but it was not. One reason it was not so read, apparently, can be traced to the dual theoretical base of copyright. Reference to the statutory-grant theory alone would probably have led to a restricted legal interpretation of the word *copy* as a word of art; the creative-work theory, however, justified its interpretation as a generic term, since the subject was the author's "property."

The present issue is whether the right to copy is a dependent or an independent right. If it is dependent, it must be seen as limited in nature; if it is independent, it would seem to be absolute in nature. Yet if the right to copy is independent in nature, copyright could be used to inhibit rather than to facilitate the flow of ideas in a free society. The issue is thus one that must be analyzed not merely in terms of what the current statute says but also in terms of what it means in light of copyright policies and principles.

Analysis of the Current Grant of Rights

One way to approach the problem is to examine the text of section 106, the grant of rights in the current copyright law. As that section makes apparent, the issue of the scope of the right to copy under the 1976 act is more complex than under prior statutes because of the expansion of the rights of the copyright owner. Section 106 gives the copyright owner the rights (1) to reproduce the work in copies; (2) to prepare derivative works; (3) to distribute the work in copies publicly; (4) to perform the work publicly; and (5) to display the work publicly. These rights are exclusive, and appear to be subject only to the limitations set out in the sections following section 106 in chapter 1 of the act. Except for section 107—which states that the fair use of a copyrighted work, including use by copying, is not an infringement of copyright—the limitations are fact specific (section 108, for example, deals with reproduction by libraries and archives). There is a plausible argument, then, that the right to copy is an independent right.

Indeed, this is the position taken in the House report on the bill that became the Copyright Act of 1976, which states that the rights granted in section 106 "though closely related, are independent. . . . Infringement takes place when any one of the rights is violated: where, for example, a printer reproduces copies without selling them or a retailer sells copies without having anything to do with their reproduction."[3] But this statement—which is not part of the law itself—is far too general to be accurate. A retailer of used books, for example, regularly "sells copies without having anything to do with their reproduction," and does so completely within the law: section

109 provides that "the owner of a particular copy . . . lawfully made under this title, . . . is entitled, without the authority of the copyright owner, to sell . . . that copy." And, of course, the fair use of a copyrighted work may involve copying without being an infringement of copyright.

The problem obviously is one that requires more study than it received in the nonbinding House report, and an analysis of section 106 strongly suggests a different conclusion: that the right to copy is a dependent right.

Section 106 is one rule with several parts that together constitute a statutory grant of rights. The section, in other words, creates rights that do not otherwise exist, and the central issue is the extent of the rights created. There are two points here. First, the rights granted are necessarily general in nature, for they are intended to encompass works of original authorship that take various forms. (Thus, the use of the term *phonorecords* as well as *copies*.) Second, while the core right is the right to reproduce the work in copies (or phonorecords), the rights taken together define the scope of a limited copyright monopoly. Logically, then, the parts of the rule should be interpreted to be consistent with each other in light of the limitations on that monopoly.

The right to copy has a unique status within the grant of rights because it is always appropriate, and in most instances necessary, to copy a work in order to implement the other four rights: to adapt it, distribute it to the public in copies, perform it publicly, or display it publicly. Thus the copyright owner can neither adapt the work without copying it by imitation nor distribute copies without copying the work by duplication. Similarly, if the work is to be available for repeated public performances, the copyright owner will surely have to reproduce it in copies (or phonorecords). The same is true of the display right if the display is to be widely replicated, as in the case of images of a motion picture.

The other four rights, in contrast, implement the function of copyright—the marketing of works. They are the rights that produce the income. A copyright owner could copy the work to his or her heart's content, but if there were no derivative work, no public distribution, no public performance, or no public display, there would be no source of income to make the copying profitable.

Clearly there are two kinds of exclusive rights involved in the section 106 grant of rights. The implementing rights of copyright owners (to adapt, to distribute, to perform, and to display) exist as *subject rights*—operating like the subject of a sentence in determining the scope of what follows. In significantly different fashion, the right to copy functions as a *predicate right,* necessary to make the subject rights operative. And, as we will demonstrate here, it is only as a predicate right that the copyright owner's right to copy is exclusive.

Since the copying of a work is often the most tangible evidence of copyright infringement, it might appear that one would have to violate the predicate right in order to infringe any other rights of the copyright owner. Most often this is true, but it is not always so: the performance right and the display right, for example, may be violated without copying the work. Thus, one may purchase a copy of a play and perform it publicly without violating the copyright owner's right to copy. Or one may purchase a copy of a graphic work and display it publicly without copying it.

Does the fact that one may infringe the copyright by performing or displaying the work without copying it mean that the right to copy is an independent right? The answer, of course, is no. It means only that the right to perform or display is an independent right. And, indeed, all the subject rights are independent in the sense that the various uses they entail may be exercised independently of each other. Thus one may infringe the work by violating one of the rights without violating any other right: setting aside temporarily the matter of fair use, no one other than the copyright owner has the right to prepare a derivative work, to distribute copies publicly, to perform the work publicly, or to display the work publicly.

There are four significant points here: (1) three of the subject rights are limited by the adverb *publicly;* (2) two of the subject rights—the performance and display rights—are limited to performance and display works, and thus do not apply to all copyrighted works; (3) another of the subject rights, the right to distribute copies publicly, is limited by the first-sale doctrine; (4) the fourth subject right, the adaptation right, is limited by the doctrine distinguishing the idea from its expression.

It is worth noting that these restraints apply only to the subject rights. Independent rights require limitation lest they become too expansive, but a dependent right needs no separate limitations because limitations already exist by reason of its dependent nature. A dependent right is a predicate right, and as such it is governed by the subject rights. The fact that Congress did not qualify the right to reproduce in copies, while it carefully qualified the independent rights, is further evidence that the right to copy is a predicate, or dependent, right.

To construe the predicate right—the right to copy—as being absolute, while recognizing all the subject rights as limited, would be to attribute to Congress either ignorance or guile, since such a construction would undermine the limitations on the copyright monopoly Congress so carefully crafted for the independent rights. The statutory scheme, however, is consistent with the fact that copyright is a limited monopoly. For in statutory construction, just as in grammar, the subject governs the predicate. The predicate right cannot logically override the limitations contained in the subject rights any more than a tail can wag a dog. The right to copy is a dependent right, given only to enable the copyright owner to exercise the other rights.

The reproduction right embodies *the right to copy by imitation* in order to adapt the work and *the right to copy by duplication* for public distribution, public performance, or public display— and no more. In the former case, the right to copy does not grant a monopoly of the ideas contained in the work; and in the latter, the right does not give the copyright owner the right to control the private use of the work.

If the above interpretation were not correct, *any* copying, even for private purposes, would be a copyright infringement. More specific limitations, such as the exclusive right to make a *public* distribution of copies of the work, would have no effect in limiting the scope of the copyright monopoly. If such were the case, in other words, one part of the rule would serve to negate the limitations on the copyright monopoly imposed by the other parts. Thus it is significant that it is not necessary that the right to copy be independent in order to protect the rights of the copyright owner to adapt (or to distribute, perform, or display the work publicly) because it is a predicate right. It is already clear in the law that if another party were to make copies so as to exercise any of the subject rights, that party has infringed the copyright.

Copying per se, either by duplication or imitation, may be an infringement, but only because of its relation to the subject rights. To use the example in the House report, if a printer were to reproduce copies *intended* for public distribution, it would not be necessary that the copies be distributed in order for the printer to be found guilty of copyright infringement. And if one were to create a derivative work intended for the market, that person would be guilty of copyright infringement. But neither of these means that the right to copy is an independent right, since in both situations the persons would clearly be exercising the right to copy as a predicate right—and it is the right to copy *as a predicate right* that is reserved exclusively to the copyright owner.

The Relevance of Copyright Principles and Policies

Since the textual complexity of section 106 means that reasonable persons may give it different interpretations, it is appropriate to weigh the ambiguities just revealed by considering the above analysis in light of copyright principles and policies.

Section 106 is derived from and reflects two basic copyright principles: the limited-monopoly principle and the market principle. This follows from the fact that the section defines, and thus limits, the copyright owner's rights. As the Supreme Court has said, copyright is "a series of carefully defined and carefully delineated interests to which the law affords correspondingly exact protections," by reason of which "the copyright holder's dominion is subjected to precisely defined limits."[4] The purpose of these limited monopoly rights can be inferred from their nature. The three expressly limited rights, being limited to *public* distribution, performance, and display, are obviously to enable the author to exploit his or her work commercially, as, of course, is the adaptation right. These rights are derived from, and reflect, the market principle. The four rights are thus a manifestation of the fact that American copyright law grants the copyright owner limited rights so as to protect the economic interest of the author in order to promote learning through the creation and distribution of new works. One can reasonably infer that the rights granted are limited to those acts necessary to the marketing of the works consistent with the market principle, but they are not so extensive as to inhibit the purpose of copyright—the promotion of learning.

Both of these relevant principles support the conclusion

that the right to copy—the reproduction right—is a predicate right, exclusive only for the adaptation of a work, or for its public distribution, performance, or display. The limited-monopoly principle and the market principle can, in turn, be viewed as the implementation of two constitutional policies: the policy that copyright promote learning and the policy that copyright protect the author's rights. If—as the Supreme Court has repeatedly said—copyright exists primarily to benefit the public and only secondarily to benefit the author, the dominant policy is the promotion of learning. But if there is to be material for learning, the policy of protecting the author becomes a part of the learning policy. The two policies, thus, may be complementary or in conflict. To complement each other, they must intersect at the proper point in the proper arena. Considering the proper relationship of the two policies, the copyright owner is entitled to be paid—and the user has a duty to pay—for copies of the work placed on the market. The proper arena, then, is the marketplace where the transaction takes place, and the proper point of intersection is a price that ensures the copyright owner's profit and yet is consistent with the consumer's willingness to pay for a copy of the work.

Economic Considerations

The copyright owner has two concerns in the marketplace: the competitor and the consumer. Clearly one of copyright's functions is to protect the copyright owner from piracy by a competitor. No competitor has a right to copy the work in order to place it on sale. To the extent this is so, the consumer may be harmed, of course, because copyright enables the copyright owner to charge a monopolistic price. But while copyrighted works theoretically are not fungible, the fact that there are many similar works usually provides the market discipline to keep the prices at a reasonable level.

The two policies—learning and the author's rights—can, however, easily come into conflict on the issue of the user's right to copy by duplication. If the copyright owner's right to copy is too broad, the user's right of use—and therefore the policy of learning—may be inhibited. But if the user's right to copy is too great, learning may also be inhibited, although perhaps at a more distant time, since the absence of a reasonable profit will almost surely diminish the future supply of copyrighted works.

Despite its importance, the answer to the problem of how to achieve a proper balance between the rights of copyright owners and the rights of users has escaped a rational solution, apparently because the issue has not been carefully analyzed. To do so one must first determine which factors need to intersect in order to achieve that balance. The general assumption seems to have been that intersection occurs only at the use of the work, that is, that both the copyright owner in selling and the consumer in buying are using the work. In fact, what intersects is the consumer's use of the *work* and the copyright owner's use of the *copyright*. The consumer's purchase is a use of the work that intersects with the copyright owner's use of the copyright in selling a copy of the work.

Copying may entail a use of the work or it may entail a use of the copyright. The former entails duplication copying by a user for personal use and is generally permissible; the latter entails illegal use of the copyright by a competitor (such as duplication copying for the market) or imitation copying, permissible under the fair-use doctrine. The property of the copyright owner that is protected, in other words, is the copyright, not the work. It is this point that explains why the copyright owner's right to copy is a predicate, not a subject right. The copyright owner's exclusive right to copy is limited to the uses protected by the copyright and does not extend to the consumer's subsequent use of the work. By the same token, the consumer's right to copy is limited to the use of the work and does not extend to the use of the copyright.

The objection to the above analysis, of course, is that it may well enable individuals to make copies of copyrighted works instead of purchasing them. The communications technology that has enlarged the market for copyrighted works, in short, is a two-edged sword. Technology facilitates private copying even as it has increased the profit potential for copyrighted works (for example, the sale of motion pictures on videocassettes).

There are three points to consider in dealing with this complex issue. The first is that to enlarge the copyright monopoly so as to prevent private copying could be viewed as a corruption of copyright policies. The purpose of statutory copyright, as manifested in the Statute of Anne and embodied in the copyright clause of the Constitution, was to limit the copyright monopoly, not to enhance it. But the elimination of the right of private copying would simply enable copyright owners to charge monopolistic prices—as they almost certainly would if their monopoly were to be enhanced in such a manner.

The problem, in other words, is one that should be left to the free market. Regardless of what the law says, the probability is that there will always be a group of persons who make private copies as an avocation, regardless of the cost. The probability also exists that most persons—in view of the fact that copying usually involves a loss of quality in transmission as well as expense in terms of money, effort, and time—will prefer to purchase authorized copies that are available at a reasonable price. The copyright owner can thus largely resolve the private copying problem by pricing his or her products for the market consistent with the function of copyright: to protect the copyright owner's right to obtain a profit in the marketplace.

Second, the problem takes on unusual dimensions in view of the increased subject matter of copyright: any original communication—regardless of content—fixed in a tangible medium of expression. A basic function of copyright is to protect copyright owners against piracy by competitors, not against the use of copyrighted materials by consumers. Yet to eliminate private copying would be to extend the copyright market into the home, the schoolroom, and the office by the imposition of a user's tax, which would almost surely constitute an impediment to the free flow of ideas that the Constitution guarantees. The fact that copyright owners could exact hundreds of millions of dollars in user fees (most of which would almost certainly not pass through to authors) does not mean they should be entitled to do so. Learning materials are no more a proper subject for a private user's tax than the right to vote is a proper subject for a poll tax.

Third, the above analysis is based on the premise that the work and the copyright are two different things—a key point relevant to an understanding of copyright in light of the copyright clause. It is worth noting again that the proper subject of copyright legislation is the copyright of works, not the works themselves. This is demonstrated by the fact that the copyright act deals with works only as a matter of form—literary works, musical works, dramatic works, and so forth. Indeed, if Congress were to enact a statute providing for a content-based copyright, it would probably be held to be an unconstitutional violation of the free-speech and free-press clauses of the First Amendment.

Since copyright legislation deals only with copyright, and since copyright is a series of rights to which a given work is subject, the issue as to whether a particular use is a use of the copyright or a use of the work should be determined accordingly. There are three types of works in terms of use—publication works (for example, a literary work), performance works (for example, an audiovisual work), and display works (for example, a graphic work). In general, copying a publication work for another publication is a use of the copyright and an infringement, unless it qualifies as a fair use; copying a performance work to perform it publicly is likewise an infringement—unless it is a fair use—and the same reasoning applies to a display work. It follows, then, that if the copying of a literary work is not for publication, the presumption should be that the use is either a personal use or a fair use; if the copying of a performance work or display work is not for public performance or display, the same reasoning should apply.

Of the many persistent fallacies that pervade copyright, none is more inimical to its fundamental purposes than the notion that the copyright owner's right to copy by duplication is independent and absolute. Copyright was intended as an economic incentive to create and distribute works for the purpose of promoting learning. But if the copyright owner's right to copy by duplication were to be made absolute, copyright would become an economic barrier to learning. Copyright was never intended to give the copyright owner an arbitrary power to control an individual's use of the copyrighted work—and it would be most damaging to the basic copyright policies and principles if copyright ever becomes so corrupted.

PART THREE

The Balance of Rights

In every man's writings, the character of the writer must be recorded.
— Thomas Carlyle

An author who gives a manager or publisher any rights in his work except those immediately and specifically required for its publication or performance is for business purposes an imbecile. As 99 per cent of English authors and 100 per cent of American ones are just such imbeciles, managers and publishers make a practice of asking for every right the author possesses.
— George Bernard Shaw

12 The Law of Authors' Rights
Moral Rights

There are two major aspects of the law of authors' rights: fair use and moral rights, but in this chapter we will focus primarily on moral rights. Although fair use was created as a right for authors—enabling one author to use another's work in the creation of his or her own work—it has largely lost its identity as such. Therefore, we have chosen to treat it in Chapter 14 as a component of the law of users' rights. Even so, it is important to appreciate the relevance of the author's right of fair use to the moral-rights doctrine, a point to which we will return at the end of this chapter.

The conventional view that copyright is primarily a law for authors is belied by the fact that the grant of rights in the copyright act is not to the author but to the copyright owner— whether creator or assignee. This is but one indicator of many that the law of authors' rights, as a visible and viable component of American copyright law, is sadly underdeveloped. The purpose of this chapter is to demonstrate how and why it should be developed further.

Before proceeding we make three preliminary points: First, for our purposes, we will ignore the corporate copyright fiction at this stage and deal only with the rights of the author/creator who is flesh and blood. Second, our concern is the author who is, in the true sense of the word, a creator—a limitation that the trivialization of copyright law makes necessary. The fact that any newly created work fixed in a tangible medium of expression is now entitled to copyright does not mean that all such work merits the protection of the law of authors' rights. The distinction, however, needs to be based on the nature of the effort, not the quality of the result. Third, our argument is not that the 1976 Copyright Act actually gives adequate recognition to the law of authors' rights as we treat it here, but that the provisions of the statute are consistent with the points discussed and that courts *could* develop the law of authors' rights with salutary effects.

There are many arguments to be made for and against the recognition of the author's moral rights in American law. Those arguments in favor will most likely be made by authors; those against, by publishers—consistent with the old saw that where one stands depends upon where one sits. Our concern, however, is whether or not the law as it exists justifies, or perhaps even requires courts to recognize, the author's moral rights.

The Common-Law Background

The concept of the author's moral right (*droit moral*) is a concept of French and German law, which can be viewed as the civil-law counterpart of what were seen as the author's natural-law rights in the common law. Recall that Lord Mansfield in *Millar v. Taylor* gave as good a definition of the author's moral rights as is to be found anywhere: the right to protect the integrity and the paternity of the work. And a large part of the history of Anglo-American copyright is the story of why Mansfield's theory of the author's moral rights proved to be a stillborn concept.

There are two levels to the story, narrative and analytical. The narrative portion we have already recounted; at this point it is necessary only to point out that the moral rights of the author were encased in the common-law copyright, which the House of Lords in the *Donaldson* case reduced to being merely the right of first publication. The destruction of the vessel for the author's moral rights essentially meant the death of the doctrine, at least for many years.

The analytical level is more complex. While the House of Lords was sympathetic to the rights of authors, its concern for the power of the booksellers overrode compassion. On this point, history is unusually illuminating, for had the lords been willing to distinguish between the work and the copyright, their ruling might well have been different. If the lords had separated the ownership of the work from ownership of the copyright, it would have been possible for them to have recognized the moral rights of the author as distinct from the economic rights of the bookseller.

The failure to make this distinction at the outset, however, almost inevitably precluded its development later because of the nature of moral rights and economic rights. Moral rights are personal in nature, whereas economic rights are essentially proprietary. The importance of this point is that property is a favored child of the common law, personal rights a stepchild. When there is a conflict between the two, the property rights almost invariably prevail. The point is best demonstrated by the fact that Lord Mansfield's definition of the author's personal moral rights was subsequently joined with the author's economic rights in the proprietary concept of the common-law copyright.

After the House of Lords scuttled the author's common-law copyright, it would have been an almost impossible task for common-law courts to have revived the author's moral rights separate and apart from statutory copyright. To have done so would have meant that personal rights—if the author chose to exercise them—would have been given priority over proprietary rights. The idea that an author, having assigned to a publisher the right to publish his or her book, might then override this proprietary right with a personal right to protect the integrity of the work was wholly foreign to the common-law way of thinking.

Moral Rights and the United States' Adherence to the Berne Convention

The Berne Convention (1887), the oldest and most important of the international copyright treaties, requires its adherents to recognize the author's moral rights and also eschews the imposition of formalities for copyright protection. These two Berne requirements explain why the United States, despite many earlier efforts, did not become a member of Berne until 1988. American copyright law had never had a moral-rights component, and it also imposed three major formalities for copyright protection—notice, registration, and deposit of copies in the Library of Congress.

The 1976 act took a step toward bringing the U.S. copyright law in line with Berne requirements by providing that registration and notice were no longer conditions for copyright protection. When these changes proved to be insufficient, Congress amended the 1976 act by enacting the Berne Convention Implementation Act of 1988, and that same year the United States became a member of the Berne Convention.

The Berne Convention Implementation Act, however, amended the 1976 act only in minimal fashion, primarily to remove the barrier that the requirement of formalities had posed. Congress, perhaps yielding to very strong opposition from publishing and broadcasting lobbies, was either unable or unwilling to include a moral-rights provision in the amendatory legislation. After an unsuccessful effort to do so, the lawmakers simply announced that the United States already recognizes the author's moral rights and that no change was needed.

That announcement was arguably a political use of a legal fiction. Moral rights are unique to the author, but there are only two rights in the copyright act that fall into this category: the right to own the copyright, which vests initially in the author upon the creation (in legal terms, upon "fixation") of the work, and the right to regain ownership of a copyright the author has assigned to another—the termination right, which may be exercised after a thirty-five-year period. Even so, the position that American law recognizes rights equivalent to the moral-rights doctrine was not wholly without foundation.

Moral Rights and the American Law

It is significant that Congress was not unaware of the moral-rights doctrine in preparing the bill that became the 1976 Copyright Act. One of the congressional studies prepared under the supervision of the Copyright Office was "The Moral Right of the Author," by William Strauss.[1] The author ended his study with the following comments:

> Judge Frank concluded in the case of *Granz v. Harris* [198 F.2d 585 (2d Cir. 1952), *concurring opinion*] that there were adequate grounds in the common law for enjoining distribution of a distorted version, and hence there was no need to resort to the doctrine of moral right as such. We believe that this is generally true for all aspects of the personal rights of authors, and that common law principles, if correctly applied, afford an adequate basis for protection of such rights. In our view, the contention that the author's rights of personality are not sufficiently protected in the United States, and the belief that there is an irreconcilable breach between European and American concepts of protection of authors' personal rights, seem to be dispelled by close scrutiny of the court decisions here and abroad.[2]

Presumably the above conclusion was influential in the decision to exclude moral rights from the 1976 act. The surprising thing, however, is that the conclusion supports our argument that the 1976 act provides a basis for judicial development of the moral-rights doctrine.

The inference to be derived from the congressional study is that moral rights—what Strauss calls personal rights—are a matter of common law. Since copyright is only a series of statutory rights to which a given work is subject, it follows that personal/moral rights relate only to that work. Thus, as Strauss states, "An author may prevent defamation of character (the 'excessive criticism' of the moral right doctrine), and unfair use or misuse of his work by action in tort, such as defamation, libel, slander, or unfair competition."[3]

Strauss clearly bases his conclusions on the distinction between the work and the copyright. In view of the fact that copyright is a matter of federal law, and the protection of the personal/moral right is at least in part a matter of state law, this distinction was necessary for him to reach his conclusion. Thus the personal/moral right is a law complementary to, but independent of, the law of copyright.

The question now, however, is whether the analysis stands up in view of the fact that the 1976 act preempts state law insofar as copyright remedies are concerned. The answer to this question is yes for two reasons. First, the 1976 act deals only with the copyright, not the work, and thus itself utilizes the distinction between the work and the copyright. Second, the statute by implication recognizes the author's ownership of the work by reason of the termination right: an inalienable right of the author to terminate the assignment of this copyright.[4]

The termination right is one of the few rights in the copyright act that is unique to the author (significantly, the corporate copyright is exempted from this provision of the law). An author who assigns the copyright under the 1976 act makes an assignment that can be analogized to the conveyance of a life estate in real property. Just as the grantor of the life estate retains a reversionary interest in the real property which is the subject of that estate, the author as assignor of the copyright can be said to retain a reversionary interest in the work. A reversionary interest requires ownership of something in which the interest exists, such as the real property that is the subject of the life estate or the work that is the subject of the copyright. And the author's termination right clearly implies ownership of the work.

One could argue, of course, that—given the brevity of human life—this special right of the author is virtually negated by the fact that the termination right does not begin until thirty-five years after assignment or actual publication (whichever term ends earlier). The influence of copyright entrepreneurs can certainly be seen in the time period specified, which is far longer than most authors would wish (or than most reasonable persons would have designated). Nevertheless, it stands as one of the author's few irrevocable rights—unassignable despite the customary intricacies of most publishing contracts—and it does indicate that Congress was not totally unsympathetic to authors' concerns.

The key question, however, is what does ownership of the work mean? Generally, the concept of ownership means the right to exclude others from the use of that which is owned, and these rights are usually designated as proprietary rights. But there is no reason to limit the concept of ownership so narrowly in view of the various kinds of things that one may own. A person's name and reputation are just as much the subject of ownership as his or her house or automobile or shares of stock in a corporation. The difference is that the latter are deemed to entail proprietary rights, while the former are labeled personal rights. (Proprietary rights, personal rights, and civil or political rights constitute the panoply of rights in our legal system.)

Our point here, however, is that whenever one owns *rights* to which something is subject, any physical object is merely a reification of the rights. But there are different types of ownership rights, and insofar as a copyrightable work is concerned, the ownership of the *work* could entail both personal and proprietary rights—unassignable personal rights against everyone, and assignable proprietary rights controlling the marketing of the work.

There is no logical reason why the personal rights could not be removed from the copyright and placed exclusively in the author as what are known as *moral rights:* the right to protect the integrity of the work and one's name in connection with its use—the integrity and the paternity rights. Moreover, whenever a copyright is lost—other than by expiration of its term—a limited proprietary right should (in contrast to current practice) return to the author as owner of the work, that being the right to royalties whenever the work is published.

Our primary concern at this point, however, is the author's moral rights; and the distinction between ownership of the work and ownership of the copyright is the key to how the law of authors' rights could and should be developed further. Clearly ownership of the work implies a right to protect the work itself against mutilation and to protect the creator's reputation in conjunction with the use of the work.

Policy Considerations

That courts may, consistent with the 1976 Copyright Act, develop the doctrine of moral rights more extensively is clear. That they will do so is not. The issue is one of policy, and apart from the fact that adherence to the Berne Convention implies a moral obligation to develop the law of moral rights, it is appropriate to discuss briefly the policy considerations.

The moral-rights doctrine is to the author what the fair-use doctrine is to the user—each being a limitation on the monopoly of copyright to benefit a class of persons favored by the constitutional copyright clause. That clause favors authors because it names them as the beneficiaries of copyright; and it favors users because it establishes the purpose of copyright to be the promotion of learning. As copyright law has developed, however, the rights of both authors and users have become tangential to the rights of intermediary publishers —mainly because publishers control the marketing of copyrighted works and consequently hold the economic power. It is axiomatic that legal rights tend to track economic power, often under the guise of benefiting others than the power holder—as in the case of copyright. (The fact that copyright is viewed as an author's right is actually beneficial to publishers, for despite the nomenclature, copyright continues to function as a publisher's right, being true to its origins in this respect.)

The vice of the copyright monopoly unlimited by the moral-rights doctrine (and barely limited by the fair-use doctrine) is that copyright ceases to be merely a monopoly for protection against competitors; it becomes a monopoly also against both authors and users. Thus, authors are severely restricted, not only in the right to protect their own products but also in the use they may make of the works of other authors to create new works (for example, in writing a biography or other scholarly work). And the monopoly against users inevitably inhibits the fulfillment of the constitutional purpose of copyright, the promotion of learning.

The lack of a moral-rights doctrine has had an even more subtle effect on copyright jurisprudence: it limits both authors and copyright owners to claiming copyright infringement as the only remedy for alleged wrongs (and, assuming a valid copyright, it limits alleged infringers to the defense of fair use). The absence of a moral-rights doctrine also encourages courts to view copyright essentially in terms of economic interests only, which means that judicial decisions in copyright cases tend to turn primarily, if not wholly, on economic considerations—even when the use entails no economic impact and even though copyright clearly involves considerations of larger moment than economic gain.

A classic illustration of this point is *Salinger v. Random House, Inc.*, a moral-rights case treated as one of copyright infringement, defended on the grounds of fair use.[5] In that case, the defendant intended to publish a biography of J. D. Salinger, a noted author with a passion for privacy. In the prepared biography, the biographer used excerpts from unpublished letters of Salinger available in the archives of various university libraries. Salinger sued for copyright infringement, the fair-use defense failed on appeal, and the publication of the biography was enjoined.

The court of appeals in its opinion concluded that unpublished works are subject to a narrower fair use than are published works, and in applying the four statutory factors of fair use, decided that the defendant author's use of the letters was not fair. Relying in part on the fourth fair-use factor—the effect on the market for the work—the court concluded that, even though the author had disavowed any intention of publishing his letters, he was "entitled to protect his *opportunity* to sell his letters"—an opportunity that was estimated to have a value in excess of $500,000.[6]

The soundness of the decision is certainly open to dispute, but the more significant point here is that the decision is one in which the author of the letters used copyright to protect his privacy, or—in terms of the moral right—to protect his reputation. Had the court decided the case on the basis of the author's moral rights, rather than economic considerations entailed in copyright, the decision might have been the same, but that is beside the point for present concerns. The effect of the decision as a copyright case, rather than a moral-rights case, has far-reaching consequences.

Moral rights are personal rights, limited to the creator and thus not assignable; the rights of copyright protect economic interests, are not limited to the author, and are assignable. The power that the *Salinger* decision vests in the author as copyright owner, therefore, is available to *all* copyright owners (for example, to publishers as assignees of the copyright, or to a widow or widower and heirs after an author's death). It is one thing to say that an author may personally prohibit the use of his or her unpublished letters even for a scholarly endeavor intended to promote the progress of learning; clearly it is another matter to say that his or her assignees, heirs, and so on, may prevent their use for the same purpose. While there may be merit in giving a person the right to protect his or her reputation (and the author the right to protect the integrity of his or her creations even for quixotic reasons), to give this right to third parties is to vest them with a power that yields no discernible benefit to them, even as it creates risks detrimental to the cause of learning. Such matters ultimately come down to a matter of judgment, and judgmental power is the most dangerous kind, for it inevitably reflects personal biases and prejudices. A surviving widow or widower may not wish an artist's creations to be subjected to *any* critical comment, even regarding early works that illustrate progress toward later achievements, and therefore may deny use of all works that were never published.

Surely the court did not realize the extent to which the *Salinger* decision, as a copyright infringement case, is likely to inhibit learning. Beguiled by the fact that the plaintiff was a noted author seeking to protect his letters, which allegedly have substantial market value, the court granted him protection. What the court failed to take into account is the salient fact that the 1976 Copyright Act makes authors of *all* letter writers, diarists, and note takers, thus subjecting every item of written material (that is not copied from another source) to the copyright monopoly—a monopoly that lasts for fifty years beyond the life of the author. If adhered to, this would mean that future scholars dealing with unpublished materials—whether found in the attic of an old house or the archives of a library—would be totally at the mercy of the law of copyright. The author of the letters, notes, or diaries, as the case may be, may or may not be concerned about their use, but the *Salinger* case makes copyright a loaded gun aimed at the scholar. The decision's greatest harm is in its *in terrorem* effect, since few publishers are willing to risk the cost of litigation for the cause of learning.

A moral-rights doctrine would, at the least, provide courts with the basis for rendering decisions involving the scholarly use of such materials on the merits of each case rather than on faulty logic. The 1976 act—by reason of the reversionary interest created by the termination right—provides a proprietary basis for the moral-rights doctrine. Therefore, to satisfy the common-law property bias, the moral right could be viewed as a personal-proprietary right, just as copyright itself carries a dual function as a regulatory-proprietary right. Certainly an author's reputation and the integrity of his or her work may well involve economic considerations no less than the copyright does.

To be sure, the moral-rights doctrine—if accepted—could also pose a threat of control that might be detrimental to the cause of learning, and because of that risk courts might continue to emphasize the proprietary rights over the personal rights. For that reason, moral rights ought to be explicitly limited to the individual creator as personal rights that cannot be assigned. The solution, of course, would entail compromise, but that is the essence of a sound copyright law. Indeed, it is the refusal to compromise—wittingly or unwittingly—that has prevented the development of the law of authors' rights to its proper place as a vital component of copyright law.

We return now to the problem of the relevance of fair use to moral rights. The justification for an author's right of fair use ultimately is the truism that all creative endeavors build on the efforts of others. But if, as we have suggested, an author owns the works he or she creates to the extent of having a right to protect the paternity and the integrity of the work, these rights may be used as an excuse to preclude another author's fair use of the work. Thus, *Salinger*, as a moral-rights case, could be used to inhibit the reasonable quotation of any author's letters in his or her biography. Indeed, if the parochial reasoning that has characterized the fair-use doctrine is allowed to infect the moral-rights doctrine, the same result will surely follow.

Therefore, it should be clearly understood that the moral-rights doctrine ought to serve the public interest in preference to the author. By protecting the paternity right, it could enable the public to identify the author of a work, and by protecting the integrity of a work, it could enable the public to benefit from the efforts of the author. This point is subtle, but important. The moral-rights doctrine should not be used promiscuously as a substitute for the law of privacy and defamation. Its purpose is not to protect the author's sensibilities but rather to protect an individual's legal rights to be known as the author of a work and to protect that work's integrity. The moral-rights doctrine should not, for example, be used—as fair use has been—to inhibit the genres of burlesque, parody, and satire. Much less should it be used to frustrate legitimate historians and biographers.

For that part which preserves justly every mans
Copy to himself . . . I touch not, only wish they be not
made pretense to abuse and persecute honest and
painfull Man.
—John Milton

Laws grind the poor, and rich men rule the law.
—Oliver Goldsmith

The Law of
Publishers' Rights
Monopoly Rights

Copyright began as a private monopoly right, granted by publishers to publishers, giving the exclusive right to sell books.
But while copyright's initial function was to protect the marketing of books, its purpose was profit. The success of the private copyright in terms of both function and purpose, however, resulted in an unacceptable monopoly of the book trade.
Therefore legislators intervened with the Statute of Anne and
replaced the private copyright with a statutory public copy-

right, retaining the function but changing the purpose. The public purpose of promoting learning was given priority over the private purpose of obtaining a profit.

That change alone, of course, would not have been sufficient to control the monopoly, so Parliament did more. It made the copyright statute a trade-regulation act of which authors were a beneficiary. To receive the statutory copyright an author was required to create a new work. A publisher could be a copyright owner only as assignee and could own the copyright for the second term only if the author were living to assign that term to him.

The first copyright act thus established the pattern for the publishers' component of copyright law by vesting the copyright in the author as an original right, while allowing the publisher to own copyright only as a derivative right. A part of the pattern of the statute as a trade-regulation act was the narrow rights contained in the copyright. The effect, intended or otherwise, was to limit the copyright to the primary, as opposed to the secondary, market. The success of this scheme, however, depended upon recognition of the fact that the work was distinct from the copyright and that the statute dealt not with the work but only with the copyright—a series of rights to which the work was subject. History, aided by the booksellers' efforts to override the Statute of Anne, confused this scheme by introducing what we have here called the creative-work theory of copyright.

Despite this history, however, the 1976 Copyright Act continues the long tradition of treating the publishers' component of copyright law as trade regulation. Yet the statute is so complex, judicial precedents so confusing, and an understanding of copyright history so rare that courts in recent years have tended to treat copyright as more proprietary than regulatory. And this development has tended to enhance the copyright monopoly beyond its statutory limits.

Copyright as Trade Regulation

Trade regulation is a body of law to ensure that markets are not dominated by monopolies, which would be detrimental to competitors (who might be forced out of the market) and harmful to consumers (who might be charged monopolistic prices or closed out of the market completely). The subject of statutes (for example, the Sherman Antitrust Act), trade regulation is also a matter of common law (for example, the law of unfair competition). The traditional basis of common-law unfair competition has been the "passing-off rationale," which makes it unlawful for a company to pass off its product as the product of another company. To do so might mislead members of the public into buying the product of a company different from the company whose product they intended to purchase. (Most people would assume, for example, that a Coca-Cola brand of powdered milk is produced by the Coca-Cola Company.)

The trade-regulation function of copyright law goes back to the Statute of Anne in England, which can be analogized to the Sherman Antitrust Act: it was designed to destroy and pre-vent the recurrence of the booksellers' monopoly of the book trade, which had been based on the perpetual stationers' copy-right limited to booksellers (as if they had entered into a trust agreement for this purpose). With the passage of time, how-ever, American copyright statutes lost their identity as anti-monopoly legislation, partly because they were so successful in preventing monopolies of the book trade; and copyright lost its identity as a trade-regulation concept, partly because in this respect copyright infringement had no recognized common-law counterpart. Copyright was usually infringed by copying, not by passing off the product as that of another (the rationale of common-law unfair competition).

Then in 1918, the Supreme Court had to deal with an unfair-competition case involving copyrightable material— news dispatches—that had not been copyrighted. The case, *International News Service v. Associated Press*, was an action between two news agencies that provided news reports to subscribing newspapers.[1] INS, whose correspondents had been barred from the war zone in World War I for violation of censorship regulations, had taken AP news dispatches for their own subscribers, and AP had sued to enjoin INS from doing so.

Had the news dispatches been copyrighted, INS would clearly have been guilty of copyright infringement, but they were not, and relief under the copyright statute was unavailable. On the other hand, the passing-off rationale of common-law unfair competition was inapplicable because the source of the news dispatches was irrelevant to the subscribing newspapers and their readers. Yet a competitor had clearly taken the work product of its rival, reaping where it had not sown. Since there was neither copyright nor passing off, the Court enjoined INS on the novel ground that it was *misappropriating* AP's work product and therefore was guilty of unlawfully copying AP's writings. The Court thus protected the writings against the competitor by creating the misappropriation rationale of unfair competition, which served as a substitute for copyright infringement. Both wrongs—common-law misappropriation and copyright infringement—involve copying another's work product.

While *INS* created a common-law counterpart to copyright infringement—providing us a better understanding of why copyright law is most usefully viewed as statutory unfair competition—it also had another, more subtle, effect. The rationale of *INS* was that it is unfair for anyone to appropriate someone else's work. Thus, it gave impetus to the idea that copyright is more proprietary than regulatory by providing courts a basis for incorporating common-law notions of fairness into copyright cases. In the years that followed, copyright infringement came to be viewed not merely as unpermitted copying but as the taking of another's property.

This importation of the common-law sense of fairness into statutory litigation had the effect of distorting the mandates of the statute. Such was particularly true of copyrighted works containing public-domain material—judicial decisions, telephone directories, catalogues, and so forth. The courts failed to realize that the copyright statute itself defined what constituted an unfair taking. For example, since copyright on a directory does not protect the factual data in the directory, it is not unfair for another to take and use the data—as the Supreme Court has just ruled in *Feist Publications, Inc. v. Rural Telephone Service Co., Inc.*[2] But until this recent decision, lower courts consistently held to the contrary as a result of the *INS* decision. Ultimately the continuing *INS* effect was a result of the natural-law creative-work theory of copyright, even though the 1976 act rejected that theory. Although the statute itself emphasizes the rights of the copyright owner, those rights—unless that owner is the author—are derivative, not original.

Original Rights and Derivative Rights

We use the term *original rights* as an analogical counterpart of natural-law rights. Both ideas are derived from the notion that an author, as a matter of fairness and justice, is entitled to ownership of rights in his or her works by reason of having created them. But copyright is a positive-law (statutory) concept, not a natural-law concept. "It is a right which could not be recognized or endured for more than a limited time, and therefore, . . . it is one which hardly can be conceived except as a product of statute, as the authorities now agree."[3] As its origin suggests, the right exists for marketing purposes and is therefore a right that is functionally for publishers as entrepreneurs. The goal of publishers historically, however, has been to make copyright a substantive right, by reason of which they would own any copyrighted works assigned to them.

The point is related to the fundamental question in dealing with copyright as trade regulation: What is being regulated— the work or the copyright? The answer, of course, is the copyright, which has its origin in the creation of a work by the author, the initial owner of the copyright. But if the author wishes to market the work, he or she must almost always assign the right to do so to a publisher. All of the publisher's rights of copyright thus are derivative in nature, even those of the corporate copyright. The only difference between the author's copyright and the corporate copyright is that the former is acquired by contract, the latter by law.

The derivative nature of the publishers' rights under copyright means that the copyright owner does not necessarily own the work, only the copyright. If copyright were intended to benefit just the author, the derivative nature of the copyright owned by the publisher would be of little consequence; only the rights of the author and publisher would be at issue. But copyright must accommodate not only the author and the publisher but also the user as consumer. The equities in copyright, in short, entail the public interest as well as the proprietary interest of the publisher and author, and recognizing the derivative nature of the publisher's interest helps keep the problem in proper perspective.

The problem boils down to one of control. What is the publisher to be allowed to control: the use of the copyright or the use of the work? To state the point another way: to what extent should the entrepreneur be allowed to treat a "publication" (both new work and public-domain material) as private property?

Publishers implicitly take the position that their right of control is plenary and absolute, apparently acting on a belief that any use of the work is the use of the copyright and vice versa. The clearest evidence of this may be seen in the increasingly common extended copyright notices, many of which claim to prohibit *any* reproduction of the work without written permission. Consider, for example, the following copyright notice that actually appeared in the quarterly *Granta* (Autumn 1989) for a seventeen-line poem by Salman Rushdie:

Copyright © 1989 Salman Rushdie and Granta Publications Limited. All rights reserved. No part of this poem may be reproduced, stored in a retrieval system or transmitted, in any form or by any means, electronic, mechanical, photocopying or otherwise without the prior written permission of the copyright owners. No part of this poem may be reproduced, whether for private research, study, criticism, review or the reporting of current events, without written permission of the publishers, Granta Publications Limited. Any unauthorized reproduction of any part of the poem may result in civil liability and criminal prosecution.

The most persuasive evidence of publishers' claims, however, is that of the Copyright Clearance Center, which (as discussed earlier) purports to license the personal use of published works by copying. Thus, publishers using the CCC provide notices such as the following, taken from the *ABA/BNA Lawyer's Manual on Professional Conduct* ("subscription rate $356.00 for the first year and $334.00 per year thereafter"):

Authorization to photocopy items for internal or personal use, or the internal or personal use of specific clients, is granted by The Bureau of National Affairs, Inc., for libraries or other users registered with the Copyright Clearance Center (CCC), provided that the base fee of $0.50 per page is paid directly to the Copyright Clear-

ance Center, 21 Congress St., Salem, Mass. 01970 or to
The Bureau of National Affairs, Inc.

Such a notice acts as if the provisions of fair use in section 107
simply did not exist. Furthermore, it shows equal disregard
for section 108—"Limitations on Exclusive Rights: Reproduction by Libraries and Archives"—which specifically authorizes
a library to make a single copy of a work for a user on request.
(What makes this particular situation even more egregious
is the fact that the *ABA/BNA Manual* includes much public-
domain material in the form of law!)

Unfortunately, the issue is not limited to published material
and the print copyright; it extends also to performance material and the electronic copyright. For example, the Public
Broadcasting System recently offered to educational institutions an "Educational License Agreement" to tape off-the-air
such programs as Bill Moyers's *The Public Mind.* The charge is
$125 for permission to make one set, $75 for each additional
set. The license reads: "Off-air Taping License provides institutions with audiovisual supplemental use rights for each set
of videotapes made under the license; playback and/or pro-
jection use; media resource use within the institutional community; closed-circuit within institution." This PBS "license,"
like the ABA/BNA "authorization," blithely ignores the fact
that both personal use and legitimate fair use of a work—
including use by copying for educational purposes—are not
infringements of copyright. Such misleading offers clearly require closer analysis.

We are not challenging the fact that publishers and other
copyright entrepreneurs have the exclusive right to distribute publicly and to perform publicly any copyrighted work
they control. But the license offered by members of the CCC
is not directed to publication (that is, the public distribution
of copies), and that offered by PBS is not directed to public

performance. In both instances, then, the licenses are clearly based on the copyright owner's assumption of an "exclusive" right to copy as an independent right—which it is not, as we have demonstrated in Chapter 11.

It is important to recognize what is happening here in terms of legal, practical, and policy considerations. From a legal standpoint, copyright holders like BNA and PBS are engaged in the time-honored practice of making private law in disregard of public law on the theory that what is not specifically forbidden is permitted. The copyright act does not forbid copyright owners to charge license fees for the use of copyrighted works—but neither does it authorize such by its terms. Indeed, under the fair-use doctrine, both the subscriber and the viewer may copy the work absent any license. In fact, the subscriber to a periodical owns the pages on which the work is printed, and such a dubious "license" being offered is an attempt to impose a restraint on one's use of his or her own chattel. The restraint has virtually the same effect as saying that a subscriber must destroy a periodical after reading it, cannot transfer title to it (either by gift or sale), or must return it to the "owner."

The situation with the televised material is somewhat different, because the copyright owner ordinarily does not provide the user with a copy. But since the user may (under section 107) make a lawful copy, then the same reasoning applies, and it involves an even larger consideration. Should a copyright owner be able to use the public airwaves to transmit material to influence the thinking of the viewers and yet retain control of access to the material? As the PBS journalist Bill Moyers has said: "Our public discourse and our ability as a political culture to face reality depend upon our information system."[4] To subject that vital information system to licensing by the informers is, of course, wholly and dangerously contrary to our political culture. For if the copyright owner has the power to grant a license to use the work, the copyright owner would then also have the power to deny the license completely—a matter of censorship in both instances, although for profit motives rather than political reasons.

The basic point is that publishers are attempting to transform their rights, which are derivative and thus only instrumental or procedural in nature, into original rights that are substantive in nature. Yet it seems clear that the purpose in giving the author the copyright as an original right was to avoid such a result—that is, to limit the publisher's proprietary interest to the copyright and not to extend it to the work.

Primary and Secondary Markets

The copyright entrepreneur's attempt to make copyright substantive in nature is a prelude to using copyright to control secondary as well as primary markets. The unarticulated premise they rely on for this purpose is that they *own* the copyrighted work, and to use the work is to use the copyright. But that premise is fallacious, since the copyright gives the copyright owner the legal right to control only *public* distribution of copies and *public* performance of the work (that is, control for the primary market). The basic issue, however, is whether copyright empowers the copyright holder to create a secondary market for the use of the work. And in terms of the copyright clause, judicial precedent, and the copyright statute, the answer is clearly *no*.

As we have demonstrated earlier, the exclusive right that the copyright clause empowers Congress to grant to the author is the right to publish his or her writings. The exclusive right to publish a book does not include the right to control the use of the book after it is published and sold, that is, to control the secondary market. This problem arose—apparently for the first time—when a copyright owner made the claim that the unqualified right to vend the copyrighted work in the copyright act included the right to resell the work after it had been purchased; in other words, the purchaser of the book could not resell it. The claim is analogous to the claim that only the copyright owner can make a personal copy.

The claim of the absolute right to vend resulted in the first-sale doctrine—specifying that the copyright owner's right to vend is exhausted with the first sale. The first-sale doctrine is now codified in section 109 of the 1976 Copyright Act as a limitation on the copyright monopoly, and in this regard, section 107, on fair use, serves the same purpose.

Control of the copyrighted work for the primary market, of course, is already a large reward in the form of a monopoly: justified protection against competitors in the marketplace. But to create a secondary market is to give any user—the target of the copyrighted work, whether published or performed—the status of a competitor who must pay a tax for using the work. The fact that copyright owners *can* obtain additional profits by creating a secondary market does not mean that they are or should be allowed by law to do so. There is little doubt, for example, that book publishers could have reaped additional profits by controlling the resale of books they published. But it was decided long ago by courts—and now by statute—that to give the publishers control of the secondary market would give them far too great a monopoly power.

From a policy standpoint, several considerations militate against allowing the use of copyright to create a secondary market for the work through the imposition of license fees for the individual use of copyrighted works. First, while the copyright act empowers the copyright owner to control the use of the copyright, this control does not extend to the use of the work per se. Second, the practice is contrary to almost every single principle of copyright law, especially the public-interest principle, the limited monopoly principle, the market principle, the right-of-access principle, the personal-use principle, and the fair-use principle. And, finally, such a practice would be contrary to the basic constitutional policy that copyright promote learning.

Serious damage would be done to the entire culture if the copyright monopoly were to be allowed to inhibit learning by controlling the secondary market merely to enhance the copyright owner's profit. Economic censorship has the potential of being every bit as harmful to the public interest as political censorship was centuries ago in England. And copyright censorship of meritorious works (such as *The Public Mind* series) for economic gain is just as dangerous as would be a reinstitution of censorship for allegedly "seditious, schismatical or heretical" works (such as Salman Rushdie's *Satanic Verses*).

The reason for recognizing the publisher's right as a component of copyright law should now be apparent. To do so enables one to deal with the monopoly issue of copyright in a perspective unwarped by the author's interest. The age-old argument is that it is the profit motive that encourages the author to create works, and that if an author were not entitled to copyright (and the profits resulting), he or she would not create. The fact is, however, that the publishers who wish to publish a work will pay an author for the right to do so. Thus, the argument that the author's copyright is *necessary* to encourage the creation of works is in fact an argument that the publisher wishes to have the strongest possible copyright in order to be able (or willing) to pay an author. (This point is demonstrated by the fact that stationers long ago made essentially the same argument—that copyright is necessary to encourage the creation of works—even before the right to copyright came to be vested initially in the author.)

Since copyright is the right to control the marketing of copies of a work, it theoretically makes no difference whether the copyright is owned by the author or the publisher, as is indicated by the custom that authors usually assign copyrights to the publishers. But the origin of copyright as a publishers' right, by reason of which *all* published works were under copyright, provided a very practical reason for Parliament in the Statute of Anne to give the author the initial ownership of the copyright by reason of its creation. This requirement meant that extant works could not be captured by copyright, and that works upon which the copyright had expired were not subject to recapture by copyright.

Since an author obviously owned the work he or she had created, however, the initial ownership of the copyright too easily came to be taken to mean that the assignment of the copyright meant also assignment of the work. The inference unfortunately gave credence to the old argument that copyright was primarily a property right of the author rather than just the grant of a limited statutory monopoly. Proponents of the limited statutory monopoly theory could never provide a satisfactory response to the argument that the author has a natural-law right of ownership to his or her own creation— mainly because those proponents also failed to distinguish the work from the copyright. This failure obscured the obvious: the statutory rules of copyright were directed not to (or against) the author's creation of the work but to the conduct of the publisher in the sale of the work in copies.

The publisher has an important role in copyright, but that role is, after all, only an instrumental one. To the extent that this role is exercised out of proportion, it becomes parasitic— and the host, even more than the author, is the public interest. The private interest of the publisher, if unchecked by the law, tends to consume the public interest that copyright is mandated to serve—in a manner not unlike that of the stationers in England, who continually supported laws of censorship in order to protect their monopoly.

Legitimate private interests and the public interest coexist in all endeavors, even though in copyright law the line dividing them has been ignored. That line, of course, is the one separating the copyright from the work—a division clear enough upon analysis. Unfortunately, as the political adage goes, all politics are local politics. In a similar manner, all reasoning is personal reasoning. Combine these points, realizing that there are many powerful but diverging economic interests, and one can easily understand why the Copyright Act of 1976 does not make the dividing line clear: it would have been uniformly rejected by the diverse interests.

In fact, "most of the statutory language was not drafted by members of Congress or their staffs at all. Instead, the language evolved through a process of negotiation among authors, publishers, and other parties with economic interests in the property rights the statute defines."[5] Yet, for all their efforts, the vested interests could not completely erase the dividing line between the work and the copyright. Although somewhat obscured, that line continues to exist—and it remains there for courts to employ in their interpretation of the copyright statute. If copyright is to be kept within its constitutional boundaries, eventually the courts will have no choice but to recognize the crucial distinction between a work and its copyright—and to apply it in their rulings.

Users have no rights.
—ASCAP Lobbyist, 31 January 1990

If the law supposes that, . . . the law is a ass, a idiot.
—Charles Dickens

 **The Law of Users' Rights**

Personal Use and Fair Use

The constitutional scheme of copyright—to promote learning by granting to authors the exclusive right to publish their writings—presupposes the right of other citizens to make personal use of copyrighted works. Yet the law of users' rights is perhaps the least understood component of copyright law. Perhaps it would be clearer if more people realized that the whole concept of copyright is built around the use of the work—with copyright owners being granted special rights of use for a limited period of time. Thus, a copyright owner may use a copyrighted work by reproducing it in copies, by making a derivative work, by distributing copies of it to the public, and by performing or displaying it publicly. In theory, the statutory grant of these rights is to encourage authors to create new works that can be distributed for use by others—books and periodicals to read, motion pictures and television programs to view, computer programs to employ, and so forth.

A common presumption seems to be that, without copyright, authors would not create and publishers would not disseminate works—a presumption whose logic fails in the face of reality. Thousands of books consisting of public-domain works —including works by Chaucer, Shakespeare, Milton, Pope, Swift, Austen, Dickens, Melville, Hawthorne, George Eliot, and so forth—are published now without copyright protection. And both radio and television were born, prospered, and passed through their golden years without the benefit of copyright protection for live broadcasts. Even so, the vested interests composing the copyright industry take the view that only absolute copyright protection can prevent a return to the Dark Ages for our culture.

In truth, the only protection that copyright owners need is protection against the piracy of their works by competitors in the marketplace. A copyrighted work reproduced in thousands of copies, or broadcast over the airwaves to be seen or heard by millions of people, needs no protection against the individual user. The market success of such works is determined not by the presence or absence of copyright but by the marketing mechanism. An individual who videotapes a broadcast off the airwaves possesses no television station to rebroadcast it. Furthermore, if the market success is affected by individuals' making copies, the reason is almost sure to be a monopolistic price. The law of users' rights, in other words, serves a socially desirable purpose in that it promotes market discipline by allowing market forces to determine prices. To deny the right of individual use would be to employ copyright to control the conduct of countless citizens for the alleged financial benefit of a few. But contrary to the claims of the industry, copyright was never intended to create and guarantee profit, only to protect the work in the marketplace. Users also have rights.

As an essential component of copyright law, the law of users' rights consists of two branches: the law of personal use and the law of fair use. The law of fair use is a well-recognized and highly visible part of the current copyright act, a matter of frequent litigation. In contrast, the law of personal use is neither codified nor litigated as such. Preliminarily, then, it should be noted that personal use by a consumer and fair use by a competitor are two different concepts. While a personal use should always be fair in a generic sense, it is not a "fair use" in a technical sense and should not be subject to fair-use restraints.

Personal Use

A personal use can be defined as the private use of a work for one's own learning, enjoyment, or sharing with a colleague or friend—without any motive for profit. Obviously there is no infringement of copyright when one reads a copyrighted book, sings a copyrighted song in the shower, watches a copyrighted movie on television, and so on. Only when one wishes to make a copy of such a work for personal use does the issue begin to take focus.

The problem with the law of personal use derives in part from the design of the 1976 act—exclusive rights subject to limitations—which *appears* to abrogate the law of personal use. Moreover, the law of personal use exists not in an explicit statutory rule but rather by virtue of the policies and principles of copyright. Since the particular is nearly always more persuasive than the general, the conclusion follows all too easily that the law of personal use must be limited to the specified exceptions to the exclusive rights.

This conclusion, however, overlooks the fact that the statute must be interpreted as an integrated whole—not in piecemeal fashion—a fact to which three points are relevant. First, the specific exceptions to a copyright owner's exclusive rights are directed for the most part to the commercial use or marketing of copyrighted works (for example, the four compulsory licenses). Second, all rules of law have implied limitations and extensions (for example, the right to vend does not mean the right to resell). And third, these implied limitations and extensions must be determined in light of the principles and policies from which the rules are derived. When the last two points are applied to the interpretation of section 106, the grant of rights, it becomes apparent that they must be construed in light of the fact that copyright is the grant of a limited monopoly in order to promote learning, even as it protects the rights of copyright owners.

All these elements taken together suggest that a reasonable statement of the rule of personal use is as follows: *An individual's use of a copyrighted work for his or her own private use is a personal use, not subject to fair-use restraints. Such use includes use by copying, provided that the copy is neither for public distribution or sale to others nor a functional substitute for a copyrighted work currently available on the market at a reasonable price.*

One key point here is that personal use is not subject to length restrictions, but it is limited to a single copy not intended for distribution. The user who goes beyond these limitations must resort to fair-use criteria to determine the appropriateness of the use.

Another point is that the rule of personal use has less application if the copyrighted work being used has a functional purpose other than the dissemination of knowledge. For example, a copyrighted work could be designed to operate a machine (such as a computer program), or it could be the architectural plans for the construction of a building. Such works are less amenable to the rule of personal use because their primary purpose is not to advance the cause of learning, so the probability exists that one will not make copies of such works without also making a functional use of them. For this kind of work, the rules of fair use would ordinarily have to be applied. The rule of personal use is appropriate only when the motivation for the use is learning (in the constitutional use of the term), not the avoidance of a purchase that would otherwise be made.

Nevertheless, it is significant that the 1976 Copyright Act, unlike its predecessor, utilizes the rule of personal use. Indeed, two of the paradigmatic fair uses stated in the first paragraph of section 107 are for scholarship and research, exemplars of personal use. Moreover, under section 108, a library is expressly permitted to make a copy of a work for a patron's personal use—and because a library does so only as an agent, the logical inference is that the patron can make the copy for himself or herself. This personal application of fair use, or personal use, is thus exemplified in the provisions of section 108(d) and (e) of the copyright act, since the classic illustration of personal use is the photocopying for one's file (and self-education) of a passage or an article from a periodical that is to be returned to the library shelf or that one no longer wishes to retain in its full context.

Despite the fact that the rule of personal use was not employed in copyright statutes until the 1976 Copyright Act, it has been a part of American copyright law from the beginning. Presumably, Congress did not articulate the rule earlier because there was no need to do so, but the need arose after two hundred years as a result of the enhancement of the copyright monopoly in the 1976 act. Indeed, arguably, Congress would have exceeded its authority under the copyright clause had they failed then to recognize the rule of personal use. To subject to restraints the use that an individual may make of a copyrighted work after it has been publicly disseminated would be contrary to the basic purpose of copyright, which is intended to facilitate the learning process.

Fair Use

The role of the fair-use doctrine in copyright is to ensure that copyright does not become an undue obstacle to learning. Originally promulgated to permit a second author to make a fair use of another's copyrighted work (that is, to exercise a right otherwise reserved to the copyright owner), the principle continues to be sound and necessary, but it is also the most complex and difficult concept in copyright law—and the basis for many misconceptions.

The relevant passage in the copyright act reads as follows:

Section 107. Limitations on exclusive rights: Fair use
Notwithstanding the provisions of section 106 ["Exclusive rights in copyrighted works"], the fair use of a copyrighted work, including such use by reproduction in copies or phonorecords or by any other means specified by that section, for purposes such as criticism, comment, news reporting, teaching (including multiple copies for classroom use), scholarship, or research, is not an infringement of copyright. In determining whether the use made of a work in any particular case is a fair use the factors to be considered shall include—

(1) the purpose and character of the use, including whether such use is of a commercial nature or is for non-profit educational purposes;

(2) the nature of the copyrighted work;

(3) the amount and substantiality of the portion used in relation to the copyrighted work as a whole; and

(4) the effect of the use upon the potential market for or value of the copyrighted work.

Among the larger legal issues fair use raises in regard to users' rights are two that are interrelated. First, does fair use constitute a limitation on the right of personal use? Second, does fair use apply to the use of the work or only to the use of the copyright?

The answer to the first question need not long detain us. There are only two arguments for the position that fair use restrains the personal use of copyrighted materials: one is that the copyright owner's right to copy is independent and absolute; the other is the purpose-of-the-use factor in section 107. We have dealt with the first issue in detail (see Chapter 11), and the conclusion that the right to copy is not absolute stands as being derived from the premise that copyright is more regulatory than proprietary in nature. Moreover, the very wording of the purpose-of-the-use factor in section 107— including whether it is of a commercial nature or for non-profit educational purposes—provides a sound basis for concluding that personal use lies outside the boundaries of use being addressed there. Even more persuasive, perhaps, is the common-sense proposition that to employ the fair-use doctrine to inhibit personal use would be to take the very doctrine intended to limit the copyright monopoly and use it instead to enhance that monopoly beyond all reason.

The more interesting problem is whether fair use applies to the use of the work or the use of the copyright. This issue should not be confused by the fact that the use of the copyright necessarily entails the use of the work. The key point is that the use of the work does not necessarily entail the use of the copyright.

To use a copyright is to exercise one of the rights reserved to the copyright owner (for example, to use a copyrighted play as the basis for making a motion picture). If such a use is made without permission, it constitutes copyright infringement—unless the use is fair use. But it must be conceded that section 107 is at best a murky guide as to what should or should not be a fair use. The basic problems with that section are that it is a principle disguised (and therefore treated) as a rule, and that its wording is ambiguous as to whether fair use applies to the use of a work as well as the use of a copyright of the work.

As a principle, the fair-use doctrine implies a rule, but one needs to determine precisely what the rule is. The fair-use doctrine is a formulation of the limited-protection principle of copyright, and as such it is an implementation of the constitutional policies that copyright promote learning and also protect the author's right. Learning is acquired by use of the work, and the author's right to be protected is the copyright. It is reasonable to infer, then, that the proper statement of fair use as a rule is this: *One may make a use of the copyright of a work to the extent that such use does not unduly harm the copyright owner.*

This direct statement of the rule assumes, of course, that it is the copyright, not the work, that is subject to fair use, and that one may make a use of the work itself without either infringing a copyright or resorting to fair-use guidelines. Whether or not this is correct depends upon what the law protects. Does it protect the work or the copyright? The answer becomes apparent when one realizes that only the copyright can be infringed, not the work itself. The law, that is, protects a given work only to the extent of its copyright, because there is a distinction between the work and the copyright.

We acknowledge that section 107 seems to ignore this basic distinction by saying it is the use of the "copyrighted work" that may be fair, but this statement contains a latent ambiguity which needs to be clarified. Because any use of a copyright necessarily entails a use of the work, the phrase "copyrighted work" is justified. Nevertheless, just as the transfer of title to a copy of a work does not entail a transfer of title to the copyright of that work (or vice versa), the use of a work does not necessarily entail a use of its copyright. (One may, for example, sell his or her copy of a book without infringing the copyright owner's right to sell the work.) Therefore, it follows that an infringer infringes only the copyright, not the work, and that one can use the work without infringing the copyright. As Benjamin Kaplan has emphasized, it is "fundamental that 'use' is not the same thing as infringement."[1]

Given the fact that the subject of fair use is the use of the copyright, it follows that fair use is concerned with competitive—or quasi-competitive—uses. This explains why most courts interpret fair-use issues in favor of the copyright owner, usually considering the fourth factor—the effect of the use upon the economic value of a potential market for the work—to be the most important. One probable reason for this weighting is that the other three factors are relatively empty propositions, providing no guidance for implementation. Judges—like everyone else—tend to ignore what does not make sense to them, and although the other factors are given boilerplate recitation, they are seldom taken seriously. Yet another reason is that most judges still view copyright as property, and the economic value of (or the market for) property has meaning for them.

The result is confusion as to the meaning of fair use, because it has been treated as a narrow—and to some extent inflexible—doctrine. Paradoxically, a doctrine of equitable reason has tended to become a doctrine of inequitable reasoning because the focus has been on the rights of the copyright owner, not the public interest. Ultimately, however, the fair-use doctrine should entail a consideration of its factors not only in relation to the established principles of copyright but also to the basic copyright policies.

The Rules of Fair Use

Section 107 lists four nonexclusive factors that courts may use in determining whether a particular use of copyrighted materials is fair: the purpose of the use, the nature of the work, the amount used, and the effect on the economic value of (or potential market for) the work. As formulated, however, the four factors have no substantive content. The first, for example, implies that a nonprofit educational use is more likely than a commercial use to qualify as fair use, although the wording in no way excludes commercial fair use. The second factor—the nature of the work—does not even imply what kind of work is relevant for fair-use purposes, and the third and fourth factors appear to be similarly devoid of any guidance for their application.

Even though the fair-use doctrine is "an equitable rule of reason," there is still a need for agreement as to the content of the factors in order to determine the equities. In the absence of any statement to the contrary, it seems clear that the intention of Congress was that the four statutory factors be given content within the context of, and consistent with, the policies, principles, and rules of copyright. The general factors, in short, imply specific factors, providing a basis for translating them into rules of fair use which can be applied with a reasonable measure of consistency.

We have already proposed a general rule of fair use: *One may make a use of the copyright of a work to the extent that such use does not unduly harm the copyright owner.* The subordinate rules, and their justification, follow.

1. *The purpose and character of the use:*
   The fair-use standard as to the purpose and character of the use is satisfied if that use is (1) for a non-
   profit educational purpose; (2) to make critical, social,
   or political commentary; or (3) to further the cause of
   learning.

The operative element in this factor is "purpose and character." The exclusion of personal use—which does not violate
the right of the copyright owner—leaves four other kinds of
uses relevant to copyright: educational use, creative use, commercial use, and competitive use. (These uses, of course, are
not necessarily discrete—a single use may be two or more of
them—but in most instances one use will predominate and
can be treated as the governing purpose.)

As copyright exists primarily to benefit the public and only
secondarily to benefit the author, the purpose of the use should
be viewed in terms of its relevance to the public welfare. From
this perspective, there are three activities involved—learning,
free speech, and the advancement of knowledge. Therefore,
to the extent that the use furthers learning, involves the exercise of free-speech rights, or advances knowledge, the presumption is that the use is fair—even though the use may be
commercial or competitive.

As to learning, one can reasonably infer that the language of
section 107 is intended to create a presumption of fair use for
educational purposes, especially in view of the designation of
teaching, scholarship, and research as paradigmatic examples
of fair use in the first paragraph of section 107. Congress
clearly did not intend for copyright to create a bottleneck for
the classroom.

Similarly, Congress did not intend for copyright to super-
sede free-speech rights or to constitute a roadblock to the ad-

vancement of knowledge. The risk, however, is that the right of free speech and the cause of learning may be used as excuses rather than bona fide reasons. If the user's motive in this regard is suspect, further guidance is provided by the other factors.

2. *The nature of the copyrighted work:*
The fair-use standard as to the nature of the copyrighted work is satisfied to the extent that the work is vested with a public interest. Works containing public-domain materials or informational materials relevant for an informed citizenry are vested with a public interest.

The nature of the work as a fair-use factor is confusing because the phrase can refer either to form or to content. The copyright act, of course, has only one content requirement—it must be an original work of authorship fixed in a tangible medium of expression—and classifies works as to form primarily for administrative convenience. In using the nature of the work as a fair-use factor, however, one must view the work in terms of content. Thus, whatever form it may take, the nature of the work satisfies fair-use standards if the content of the work consists in part of public-domain materials or is vested with a public interest. For this purpose, public interest in the materials is measured by their relevance to an informed citizenry. This means, of course, that some works (for example, a novel or a poem) are unlikely to satisfy the "nature of the work" criterion for fair-use purposes. This does not mean that such works are not subject to fair use; it means only that one must look to the other factors.

Three kinds of material are clearly vested with a large public interest: governmental material (including law), informational material of public concern (for example, newscasts, public-affairs materials, or a report on the discovery of a cure for cancer), and the major creative work of the past. While some of these materials are not entitled to copyright as a matter of content (such as U.S. government publications), and others are now out of copyright and in the public domain, all of them appear within copyrighted volumes on a regular basis. A copyrighted anthology, for example, may contain both newly copyrighted work *and* a U.S. government work (a statute or the report of a court decision) or other public-domain materials (Shakespeare's plays).

In view of these complexities, when one considers the nature of the work for fair-use purposes, it is useful to think in terms not of the work itself but of the material contained in the work. For example, one can copy *Hamlet* (or any other play) from a copyrighted anthology of Elizabethan and Jacobean dramas without infringing the copyright on the anthology; fair use becomes relevant only when one also copies the copyrighted commentary and critical annotations to the plays.

The governing fair-use element as to the nature of the work, then, is the public interest vested in the materials contained therein. Governmental works, news and public-affairs reports, and public-domain materials all fall into this category. While the nature of the work is of minimal importance as a fair-use factor in regard to some works, it is the most important factor in regard to the categories mentioned. This is because such works involve free-speech concerns, and the copyright clause itself embodies free-speech protections.

3. *The amount used of the copyrighted work:*
   The fair-use standard as to the amount used is satisfied if that amount is reasonable in both qualitative and quantitative terms. Whether the amount used is reasonable must be determined in light of the size of both the copyrighted work and the work in which it is used, and the economic effect of the portion taken to both works.

This factor is the most difficult to parse, since it is a function of the other three factors: the purpose of the use, the nature of the work, and the effect upon the value of the copyrighted work. To use a minimal portion of a work (such as the quotation of a sentence from a short essay, a paragraph from an article, or even a page from a multivolume treatise) would be a fair use. Obviously, absent other factors, one cannot use a half or a third of a book and claim fair use; yet some works (such as short poems) are so brief that it is difficult to quote any of them without using the whole work. In such cases, the purpose of the use is probably the most reliable factor in assessing the amount used for fair-use purposes. One may copy an entire poem for use in the classroom, for instance, but without the permission of the copyright owner one should not copy the same poem—regardless of how short—for an anthology to be published.

The purpose of this factor is to prevent an exploitative use of the copyrighted work without inhibiting fair use. Therefore, one must consider the amount used in relation to the size of the copyrighted work and the size of the new work, as well as the significance of the portion used to both the works. With these factors in mind, one should resort to the fourth factor.

4. *The effect of the use upon the value of, or potential market for, the work:*
   The fair-use standard as to the effect upon the value of, or potential market for, the existing copyrighted work is satisfied if the use does not have an adverse impact on the marketing of the work in light of one or more of the following factors:
   a. Accessibility of the work.
   b. Date of the work.
   c. Economic life of the work.
   d. Availability of copies on the market.

e. Price of the work.

f. Evidence of abandonment.

Courts generally consider this factor the most important. Their emphasis on it, however, must be balanced by a recognition that any copyright owner who does not make or keep a work accessible has essentially failed to maintain his or her part of the copyright bargain. To the extent this is so, the right of fair use is enlarged.

Accessibility of the work is relevant particularly to the electronic media, as such works are normally not available in published form. Videotapes of the president's State of the Union message, for example, are generally not accessible to the public after the initial broadcast, nor are television broadcasts of congressional hearings or of past newscasts. Yet, significantly, most such works are clearly of major public interest.

The date of the work is evidence of its accessibility, especially for educators. A fifty-year-old text, a seven-month-old weekly magazine, a three-week-old newspaper—all are examples of materials that a teacher could probably reproduce substantial portions of for a class. In most cases a publisher would neither keep such materials available nor reprint them for this purpose. (When the classroom use is planned in advance, however, users should still check on availability—regardless of the age of the work. Some magazine and journal publishers maintain extensive inventories of individual-article offprints and back issues for single-copy and classroom sales.)

The economic life of a work is relevant in the case of newspapers, television newscasts, the broadcast of sporting events, and so forth. Yesterday's newspaper provides little profit to the publisher, although it may be very valuable to the historian. Such ephemeral works are subject to a very broad application of fair use, because the use is seldom harmful to the economic interest of the copyright owner.

Availability on the market, of course, is related to accessibility. If a work is publicly disseminated in copies but then disappears from the market, the argument that a use of the material is a fair use is considerably strengthened—especially for teachers who have immediate instructional needs. Indeed, in some instances the work is no longer available through purchase because a publisher has remaindered copies or (especially in the electronic media) actually destroyed the original, and only personal copies continue to exist. (Those who plan extended instructional or competitive uses should realize, however, that temporary nonavailability of a work does not necessarily mean that copyright has been abandoned. Individual authors, for instance, seldom have control over the remaindering of their copyrighted works.)

Price of the work is relevant because a quid pro quo for the copyright monopoly is that copyrighted works be available at a reasonable cost to the public. In other words, a part of the copyright bargain is that the copyright owner shall not abuse the monopoly rights granted.

If there is *evidence of abandonment* of the copyright, use of the work is almost sure to be held to be a fair use. If, for example, a demonstrably reasonable effort to obtain consent fails to yield anyone authorized to give consent, abandonment may be inferred. Similarly, one may infer abandonment if the work is systematically remaindered or destroyed by a corporate copyright holder, whose action may be viewed as an admission of the exhaustion of the profit potential.

In this regard, more needs to be said about the "potential market" for a work. Presumably, any copyrighted work can be said to have a potential market in relation to which another's use would be adverse. Therefore, if read literally, this single condition would effectively do away with fair use. But Congress cannot have meant that a copyright owner could continue to control access to a copyrighted work on the basis

of a self-serving assertion of unformulated plans for marketing at some indefinite date, for to do so would be contrary
to the copyright bargain—especially in view of the fact that
economic harm resulting from fair use is minimal at most
and is more likely to be imaginary. Consequently, in applying
this element of the fourth factor as evidence of infringement,
the courts should require the copyright owner to present substantial evidence supporting any claim that a potential market
would be adversely affected.

The Application of the Rules of Fair Use

The purpose of recasting the section 107 fair-use factors here
as rules has been to facilitate their future application. But fair
use makes sense only within the history and context of copyright as a grant of a *limited* monopoly in order to promote
learning. This context means that to serve the public welfare
copyright must accommodate two often conflicting, private
interests—the copyright owner's right to economic rewards
for disseminating a work to the public, and the user's right to
employ those copyrighted materials for the advancement of
knowledge.

It is not in the public interest, for example, for the copyright
owner to retain absolute control of the use of copyrighted
works after they have been publicly disseminated, since that
would clearly be a derogation of the public's right to use the
material for learning. By the same token, it is not in the public
interest for a user to employ copyrighted works at will in disregard of the copyright owner's economic rights. These two
private rights, in short, must be weighed and balanced against
each other—which is the province of fair use.

By and large, however, recent court decisions have not manifested the balanced view that the fair-use doctrine requires.
No one, of course, can know the precise causes for this bias,

but there is reason to suspect that ownership of copyright has mistakenly been taken to mean ownership of the copyrighted work. That unfortunately common notion is based on a specious logic, for—as the copyright act makes clear—copyright is distinct from the copyrighted work: copyright is only a series of statutory rights to which the work is subject. The copyright act does not vest ownership in the work itself; it simply grants copyright to those who create, thereby implying ownership of the work under the common law by reason of creation. Even the loss of copyright through some technicality would not mean that the author has to forfeit his or her right to be known as the author, but that is a matter separate from the economic interests which copyright protects. The copyright act merely creates rights to control the use of the work *for the market* (primarily to reproduce the work in copies for public distribution). The right to market the work, however, does not logically extend to the right to control the use of a copy of the work after that copy is sold.

A related error has been an increasing tendency of the courts to confuse a *condition* for the grant of copyright (the creation of a new work) with the *function* of the grant (to encourage dissemination). The creation requirement as a condition for copyright was not designed to encourage the creation of works (although that may be a collateral consequence) but to protect works already in the public domain from falling back under the copyright monopoly. (Absent the condition of creation, there would be nothing to prevent a new claim of copyright for such classics as Shakespeare's plays whenever they were republished.) The purpose of copyright is to promote learning, and its main function is to encourage distribution of works, without which they would not be available for learning.

By treating copyright's function as encouraging the creation (rather than the distribution) of works, courts have increased the difficulty of equating the user's interest in having access to the work for learning with the copyright owner's interest in protecting the right to profit. The difficulty is compounded because the claim of profit is a concrete right with an equitable basis (creation and distribution of the work), whereas learning is only an abstract right with no equitable basis. Yet the fallacy that copyright is intended to encourage the creation of works has been a prime cause of the copyright-is-the-ownership-of-the-work fallacy. And given this latter fallacy, it takes judges with vision to balance the right of learning with the right to profit, as did the framers of the copyright clause. For some judges, unfortunately, fair use has become an aberration barely to be tolerated.

In the proper context, however, fair use stands as a rational and necessary doctrine, and two points become apparent: (1) the section 107 factors are the elements to be placed on the public-interest scale; and (2) not all the factors have the same weight. The major factor in favor of the user is the nature of the work; the major factor in favor of the copyright owner is the economic impact of the use. The amount used is a function of the economic impact of the use, the relevance of which should be governed primarily by the nature of the work.

The remaining factor—the purpose of the use—is something of an anomaly. In origin, the primary intent of fair use was to permit a fair *competitive use* (that is, to allow one author to make use of another author's work). In codifying the fair-use doctrine, however, Congress added the purpose of the use to the three more established factors. And since the language in the statute can be read as creating a presumption that a noncompetitive use is a fair use, while making no mention of competitive use, the purpose of the use requires closer examination.

For our analysis here, let us say that there are two major kinds of use, competitive and noncompetitive; and there are two kinds of works, those that inform and instruct, and those that entertain (that is, didactic and creative works). This means that there are two general tracks that fair use may follow as determined by the nature of the work. Typically, the use of a didactic work will be an educational, noncompetitive use, which will have minimal impact on the copyright owner. In contrast, the use of a creative work will typically be a noneducational, competitive use, which may well have a significant economic impact on the copyrighted work.

One need not look far, however, to find variations on the typical situations: a didactic-work-noncompetitive track (the teacher copies a scholarly article for members of the class); a didactic-work-competitive track (a publisher copies a substantial portion of the article to reprint); a creative-work-noncompetitive track (a teacher videotapes a motion picture off the air to show to a sociology class); and a creative-work-competitive track (a publisher reproduces a poem in an anthology).

The starting point for determining the relevance of the fair-use factors in all these situations is the nature of the copyrighted work. Because the constitutional purpose of copyright is to promote learning, it is the nature of the work that determines whether the use of the work is consistent with this goal. A didactic work is given preference over a creative work for fair use, because—in fair-use terms—it is vested with a public interest. But there are varying degrees of public interest. Abraham Zapruder's fortuitous filming of President Kennedy's assassination, for instance, is vested with so much public interest that almost any use of it will be fair. On the other hand, the novel *Gone With the Wind*, despite its popularity, is a creative work that is not vested with significant public interest as defined in this larger sense; therefore its use must normally comply with a strict standard as to the amount used. A paradox results: the less the value of the work to society, the greater the copyright protection it receives (for example, Betty Boop and Cabbage Patch Kids dolls receive more protection than a Pulitzer Prize–winning history of the United States). But there is a compelling reason. The author— or copyright owner—who influences or seeks to influence the course of events by shaping ideas with a new work cannot claim such a proprietary interest that he or she monopolizes its use in the marketplace of ideas. That is why "the copyright holder's dominion is subjected to precisely defined limits."

Still, the amount used can be identified as the factor to prevent one from abusing the fair-use doctrine in an exploitative manner. When the work is didactic in nature and the purpose is noncompetitive, the amount used can be much greater without being exploitative than if the work is creative and the purpose is competitive. The same is true as to the noncompetitive use of a creative work as opposed to a competitive use. So important is the learning goal of copyright that the amount of a didactic work used competitively may be greater than the amount of a creative work used noncompetitively.

Whether or not a use is competitive, however, depends upon the conduct of the copyright owner as well as the conduct of the user. Among the factors to consider, therefore, is whether a given work is actually available on the market (which is often not the case with ephemeral products such as a week-old newspaper, a six-month-old magazine, or a television broadcast not reproduced in copies for purchase). If a copyright owner limits his or her use of the work to the primary market, the use of the work by others for the secondary market may not be competitive and may be a fair use in light of all the section 107 factors.

The rules of fair use provided in this study, by giving content to the section 107 factors, are intended to provide flesh for such analytical bones. The rules attempt to make clear that the purpose and character of the use should, in generic terms, promote learning; that the work most amenable to fair use is one of learning; that the amount used must be reasonable in light of the purpose of the use; and, most significantly, that the economic impact of the use should be considered not only in terms of the conduct of the user but also in terms of the conduct of the copyright owner.

The section 107 factors are neither immutable nor fixed: they are, by design, flexible and functional, their relevance being determined by the facts of the particular situation. This means that whether a particular use is a fair use is to a large extent a matter of judgment. While there can be no warranty that one's judgment, regardless of how sound, will be concurred in by the courts if litigation occurs, it is well to remember that judicial decisions result in rules of law for particular litigants so as to resolve a conflict arising out of a particular set of facts. Most, if not all, fair-use litigation thus far has been between competitors and, not surprisingly, has produced restrictive interpretations of fair use. While it does not follow that the same restrictive rules should apply to noncompetitors, there is a transference factor at work of which copyright owners have already made use—and which has remained unrebutted because thus far they have not sued individuals making a noncompetitive use of their work.

Relevant to this last point—and particularly important for educators—is section 504(c)(2) of the 1976 Copyright Act. That provision requires courts to remit (that is, to refrain from enforcing, to pardon) statutory damages "in any case where an infringer believed *and had reasonable grounds for believing* that his or her use of the copyrighted work was a fair use under section 107, *if the infringer was* . . . *an employee or agent of a nonprofit educational institution, library or archives acting within the scope of his or her employment* who . . . infringed by reproducing the work in copies or phonorecords" (emphasis added). This little-known protection for educational users no doubt helps to explain why noncompetitive fair use has received so little direct challenge from copyright owners thus far.

The blame for a corrupt fair-use doctrine, however, is not limited to the courts. Judges are capable of learning, and part of their problem is that previous commentary on copyright has not provided them with learning material as to the fair-use doctrine. For the most part, copyright scholars—who should provide courts with the deeper perspective their busy schedule otherwise denies them the opportunity to obtain—have merely reported what the courts do, not why they should have done it differently. Consequently, courts in fair-use cases too often view copyright as a plenary property right rather than a limited statutory right based on venerable policies, principles, and rules of its own.

The Fair-Use Doctrine and Unpublished Material

The section 107 factors—and the rules derived therefrom—do not distinguish between published and unpublished materials. Yet the issue as to whether or not fair use applies to unpublished materials is of crucial importance for biographers, scholars, and their publishers—as well as for librarians whose archives contain a substantial number of letters, journals, diaries, and papers of noted persons. Since courts have not dealt with this issue definitively, the following analysis is based on the copyright policies and principles identified in earlier chapters.[2]

The problem arises because the fair-use doctrine as originally promulgated was applicable only to published material protected by statutory copyright. Until 1976, unpublished materials were protected by the common-law copyright and presumably were not subject to fair use. This is because the common-law copyright, unlike the statutory copyright, was a plenary proprietary right that protected the author's right of first publication. If the author did not publish the material, no one had any right to use that material in any manner. The 1976 Copyright Act effectively eliminates the common-law copyright. Statutory copyright now exists from the moment an original work of authorship is fixed in a tangible medium of expression, with copyright protection being granted whether or not the work is published. This development suggests that the distinction between published and unpublished works is no longer useful for the application of the fair-use doctrine. Rather, the test should be whether the material has been made accessible to the public.[3]

For present purposes, there are four categories of unpublished copyrighted material: (1) material intended for publication (for example, a manuscript in preparation); (2) material intended to be performed rather than published (for example, a drama or a motion-picture or television script); (3) professional material originally intended for public consumption but which, for various reasons, was not made public (such as early drafts of novels or plays that subsequently appeared in different versions); and (4) private or personal material (primarily letters, diaries, journals, and so forth).

As to the first category—materials that can be characterized as works-in-process—there should be no fair-use issue. An author has the exclusive right of first publication, and there is no logical reason to dilute this right by subjecting such works to the fair-use doctrine until after they have been published.

The second category, works to be performed, likewise presents little problem. Although they are to be performed, they must be fixed in a tangible medium of expression for statutory copyright to attach. The fact that they are performance works rather than publication works is no reason to treat them differently from works-in-process. Prior to its first public performance, the work should not be subject to fair use; after public performance, it should be.

The third and fourth categories, professional and private or personal materials, present the most complex issues. There are two conflicting policies involved: the author's right of privacy and the public's interest in learning. Both policies rank very high in our scale of values, but in view of the importance our society attaches to the dignity of the individual, the right of privacy probably ranks higher with regard to personal material, whether professional or otherwise.

The presumption, then, has been that neither professional nor personal materials are subject to use by others and therefore are not subject to the fair-use doctrine. That presumption, however, is rebuttable. If the author makes private materials accessible to the public by donating or selling them to a library without stipulating restrictions on public access, they cease to be private. In such cases the right of privacy is no longer an issue, and it follows that the materials should be subject to fair use.

The ultimate policy issue—whether an author may use the law of copyright to prevent, rather than to promote, learning—involves policy considerations of substantial moment on both sides. To place the matter in perspective, it should be noted that the right of an author to make fair use of another author's work does not mean the right to publish the work in full. It means only the right to make fair use of the work, a use that is not harmful to the author's economic interest. This, in part at least, explains why fair use does not require permission of the copyright owner. If the use is so extensive that permission is required, the use is no longer fair use, but use with permission.

In favor of the author is the argument that writings are an extension of personality, and the right to protect one's personality and reputation is inherent in the tradition of a free society. Therefore, apart from economic rights, we should recognize that the author has a moral right to protect the privacy of his or her work. Given the emphasis that our society places on the dignity of the individual, the argument has a powerful appeal. But in this case the appeal is misplaced. The issue is not really whether the author has a moral right to protect the privacy of his or her works. The issue is whether the author has a right to use the benefits of copyright but reject its burdens. Our position here is that, for the reasons set out below, the author should not have this right.

The basic argument in support of fair use of private materials placed in libraries is that to deny the use of copyright to protect the author's privacy does not deny the author the right of privacy. The author may, for example, retain possession of the materials, present them to a library with time restrictions to prevent public access for a period of years, or even destroy them. The choice, in other words, is that of the author, and it is not necessary to corrupt the law of copyright to accommodate what often may be an idiosyncratic whim.

A second argument is that the author who presents his or her papers to a library obviously does so in the interest of posterity. Having sought posterity, the author should hardly be able to use the law of copyright to manipulate the judgment of posterity. Furthermore, such presentations to libraries often result in either monetary reimbursement or income-tax write-offs for the author—benefits that need not be pursued but, once accepted, carry responsibilities to society.

A third argument is that the U.S. law of copyright is not as protective of the right of privacy as it may first appear. Copyright does not protect ideas, so copyright cannot preclude the communication of ideas or opinions contained in unpublished or unperformed material. Thus, before copyright could be used to provide privacy protection for publicly accessible materials it would be necessary to alter basic copyright doctrine.

The final argument, however, is the most persuasive. The private papers of authors and artists are important to the cause of learning. At one level, creative genius remains a mystery, and any material that sheds light on the creative process and its development is treasured by scholars as a means to a greater understanding of the minds contributing to our cultural heritage. At another level, the private papers of authors whose works reflect and shape our understanding of life and society are a part of our cultural heritage. They are a source of influence; to the extent that they remain hidden from public view they constitute a secret influence in our cultural life. Although it is easy to agree with those who bemoan the ways in which the American media devour celebrities—often focusing more on physical qualities and sensational behavior than on an artist's creative work—it is fallacious to assume that interest in an author's secrets has no relevance to interest in the author's work. Perhaps this is so for the small- and prurient-minded, but for others the interest is the same as in any learning endeavor: a search for understanding. And it is critically important that law not be shaped merely to frustrate small minds at the expense of the larger public interest.

There is, of course, the counterargument that distinctions should be made between professional efforts and personal writings, and there is also the issue of the right of privacy of those whose affairs are discussed in personal writings (for example, one author writing to another about a third party). With this problem, however, the law of copyright and fair use should not be concerned. The First Amendment precludes both a content-based copyright and a content-based fair-use doctrine. The fair-use doctrine should not be made available as a censorship device for copyright holders any more than copyright itself should be.

The above analysis assumes that the author of the materi-

als made the presentation to the library while living. When
the presentation is made after the author's death (by an heir
or literary executor), different considerations come into play.
The literary executor, seeking "to protect" the author's reputation, may claim that the author's private papers are not subject to fair use. At this point, however, not even the right-of-
privacy argument has much merit. Since the author is dead,
the author's right of privacy, being a personal right, is no
longer a relevant principle. If the materials are in a library,
the literary executor should have no more control over the
fair use of the materials than the author would have if living.
To do otherwise is to give the literary executor the right of
censorship by copyright.

How courts will respond to the various considerations involved, one cannot know. Probably different courts will respond differently until the Supreme Court decides the issue.
One point, however, seems clear. The librarian faced with deciding whether or not to provide access to, and/or copying of,
the material should be able to do so, limited only by the conditions of the grant under which the material was received. If
private papers are presented to the library on condition that
they not be available for public access for a certain period of
years, obviously that condition must be adhered to. If there
are no such limitations on public access, however, the librarian
may provide access to and, upon request, provide copies of the
material for the requester's personal use, research, or scholarship. The responsibility for the subsequent use of the material
falls not on the library but on the person who uses it.

The Fair-Use Doctrine and
New Communications Technology

According to the copyright act, the fair-use doctrine applies
to all copyrighted works without exception. Therefore, it fol-

lows that fair use applies to copyrighted works of new communications technology—television broadcasts, sound recordings, computer software, computer databases, and so on. Yet there are those who ignore this basic proposition, most notably EDUCOM (self-styled as "a non-profit consortium of over 450 colleges and universities committed to the use and management of information technology in higher education") and ADAPSO ("the computer software and services industry association"). These two organizations have published a 1987 brochure entitled *Using Software: A Guide to the Ethical and Legal Use of Software for Members of the Academic Community,* which announces that:

> (1)*Unauthorized copying* is illegal. Copyright law protects software authors and publishers, just as patent law protects inventors.
>
> (2) *Unauthorized copying* of software by individuals can harm the entire academic community. . . .
>
> (3) *Unauthorized copying* of software can deprive developers of a fair return for their work, increase prices, reduce the level of future support, and inhibit the development of new software products. [emphasis added]

The implied equation of copyright law with patent law reflected here is a common error, though a bit disconcerting when it comes from a professional association that ought to know better. More troubling, however, is the brochure's failure to mention that copying is permitted under the fair-use doctrine (which, of course, does not require authorization).

This official-sounding document is thus incomplete—and dangerously one-sided in its emphasis, particularly for those who are ignorant of the rights they legally possess under the fair-use provisions of the current statute. And the fair-use doctrine does indeed have applicability to the products of new technology—regardless of whether those products are sold or "leased."

A common practice of the producers of computer programs has been to distribute them with shrink-wrapped "licenses." These self-proclaimed licenses purport to bind the purchaser (upon opening the package) to the copyright owner's terms—which invariably restrict the use the purchaser may make of the work. Such licenses are almost surely against public policy as unilateral attempts to override public law with private law in an adhesion contract. One can be sure that to the extent the provisions of such licenses preclude the fair use of the work, they have no legal effect, although their *in terrorem* effect may be substantial. In our opinion, users would be well within their rights to ignore such unlawful terms and to comply instead with the law of fair use.

In this regard it is worth recalling a perceptive observation from a Supreme Court opinion in *Sony Corp. v. Universal City Studios, Inc.*, a case dealing with the fair use of copyrighted movies broadcast on television: "While the law has never recognized the author's right to absolute control of his work, the natural tendency of legal rights to express themselves in absolute terms to the exclusion of all else is particularly pronounced in the constitutionally sanctioned monopolies of the copyright and the patent."[4] This is particularly true when the copyright monopoly is extended to the products of new technology. Thus, in the *Sony* case the copyright owners were seeking to negate the fair-use doctrine for motion pictures broadcast on television (a recent development in terms of copyright law), just as EDUCOM and ADAPSO now seek through their brochure to negate fair use for computer software. Significantly, the Court in *Sony* ruled decisively against the owners.

The patina of rationality that makes such claims seductive derives from a complex set of facts. The fair-use doctrine

Congress codified is essentially a nineteenth-century doctrine, intended to protect a copyright owner against competitors and therefore primarily a concept to protect the marketing of books. Because the marketing of books involves considerations different from those involved in marketing such products as television broadcasts, computer software, and computer databases, it has been all too easy for such entrepreneurs to argue that the fair-use doctrine does not fit the travails of marketing such works and therefore should not apply to them. Fair use does not normally entail the copying of an entire book, the copyright owners argue, but most uses of computer software would require such extensive copying. Furthermore, they insist, special protection is needed because of the ease with which such works can be copied.

Such arguments, however, miss the mark. Copyright is the grant of a limited monopoly, and the fact that copyright is extended to products of new technology is not an occasion for making it an absolute monopoly. The essential point such arguments try to ignore is that Congress has made *all* copyrighted works—including television broadcasts, sound recordings, computer software, and computer databases—subject to fair use.

Copyright owners of such works are much too modest when they claim that the ease of copying entitles them to greater protection than the copyright act allows. They denigrate their marketing skills, but their claim is not without guile. The greater the protection they can obtain, of course, the less their competition—and the higher the price they can charge. The less their protection, the more competitive their prices must be.

The ultimate goal of such copyright owners, it appears, is to transmute copyright from a device to protect the work for the market (a limited monopoly) into a device for guaranteeing a profit (an absolute monopoly). In other words, they want copyright to protect the work not only against the competitor but also against the customer. Conveniently ignored is the fact that market forces and economics will ultimately determine whether or not people will engage in copying alleged to be harmful to the copyright owner. Copying a work involves expense—in time, effort, and money. The copyright owner's remedy, then, is to make the purchase of the product a more attractive alternative than the copying of it. Copyright, in short, was never intended to be a substitute for market discipline. Yet if the fair-use doctrine does not apply to these works, this is a function that copyright will be used to fulfill. It is not without reason that Congress made fair use applicable to all copyrighted works—and what Congress has given the public, copyright owners cannot lawfully take away by unilateral pronouncement.

PART FOUR

Conclusions

Truth and understanding are not such wares as to be
monopoliz'd and traded in by tickets and statutes,
and standards. We must not think to make a staple
commodity of all the knowledge in the Land, to mark
and licence it like our broad cloth, and our wooll packs.
— John Milton

15 The Future of American Copyright

Confusion in the law of copyright is not the fault of the stars
but of ourselves. The very factor that makes copyright so important in the life of our nation is the same factor that causes
the confusion: the value of learning. The difficulties arose
as soon as the printing press made the transmission of information a profitable enterprise for entrepreneurs. Within
some sixty years after the arrival of the printing press in England, the political conditions created by Henry VIII's break

with Rome caused the government to accept printers and publishers as allies in controlling the dissemination of information. The result of this censorship arrangement was an infamous monopoly of books, of knowledge, of learning.

The Statute of Anne, as we have seen, was designed to destroy that monopoly with a rule that bespoke the simplicity characteristic of genius: the learning subject to the monopoly of copyright had to be *new* learning and was to be monopolized only while it was new. The author was to be rewarded, the transmission of new learning to the public was assured, and existing learning was removed from the perpetual control of copyright monopoly.

The implementation of these basic propositions was formidable enough in those simpler times, but this century's new technology of communication has made the pursuit of such ideas similar to a quest for the Holy Grail. Today we have not one but many different kinds of copyright: a print copyright and an electronic copyright; a creator's copyright and a corporate copyright; a copyright for copies and a copyright for phonorecords; and a copyright for "original works of authorship," which can be an imaginative copyright, a derivative copyright, or a compilation copyright—all governed by the same law.

In retrospect, it is clear that the process giving rise to distinct kinds of copyright began as early as 1802, when the first amendment to the 1790 U.S. Copyright Act extended copyright to musical compositions. The changes are there for all to see: prints and etchings in 1831, dramas in 1856, photographs in 1865, the entire panoply of artworks in 1870, the performance right for musical compositions in 1897, motion pictures in 1912, and sound recordings in 1972. A reasonable conjecture, then, is that in the future, various kinds of other copyrights will continue to emerge to accommodate the new markets that technology will produce (and the entrepreneurs who will inevitably step forward to help market those new technologies).

Despite the different copyrights in the 1976 act, however, one familiar with copyright history could have predicted what was likely to occur after 1978 (the effective date of the 1976 act): that courts would initially ignore the existence of different types of copyright; that, for a time at least, courts would even continue to use the old precedents rather than read the new statute; that judicial precedents decided under old statutes would be applied to the new statute, and the copyright monopoly would be expanded, usually needlessly and sometimes mindlessly; and that the mesmerizing effect of new technology—especially computers—would be such that many decisions would enhance the monopolistic position of industry leaders. This is precisely what happened.

But if history is a reliable guide, our 1978 seer could also have foreseen further change, albeit at a greater distance. Generally, old learning that no longer has a sound basis tends to fade as truth emerges (few persons today, for example, belong to the Flat Earth Society). But in law this function of truth is sometimes slow to be served, since law tends to be precedent driven, and courts often treat the holdings of their predecessors as being immune to reason and logic. Yet law is a matter of statute as well as judicial decision, and reason commands that new statutes be interpreted in light of the language they contain rather than prior precedent decided under discarded language. Such a command needs to be trumpeted anew for the benefit of courts applying the 1976 Copyright Act.

Old precedents applied to the current statute tend to undermine the basic principles—and therefore the constitutional policies—of copyright. The truth now emerging is that no change in the *rules* of copyright alters either the *principles* or the *policies* of copyright—nor did Congress intend that the 1976 Copyright Act have that effect. Once courts stop reading that statute piecemeal and begin to recognize it as an integrated whole, they will realize that Congress may have legislated better than it knew (and surely better than most special-interest groups either hoped or thought), because the basic principles of copyright have all found expression in rules of the 1976 act, sometimes in more than one.

Consider these examples: section 102(a), providing copyright protection only for original works of authorship, is a manifestation of the limited-protection principle; section 102(b), denying copyright protection to ideas, is a manifestation of both the limited-protection and the statutory-monopoly principles; section 103(b), limiting copyright protection for derivative works and compilations, is a manifestation of the same two principles; section 106, the grant-of-rights section, again manifests the limited-protection and statutory-monopoly principles, as well as the market principle; section 107, fair use, reflects the above-cited principles and also the right-of-access principle; and section 202, distinguishing between the ownership of the copyright and the physical object in which the work is embodied, reflects the personal-use principle.

If the courts were to relate the fundamental principles to the policies of copyright, they would find a basis for limiting copyright protection any time the rule—as governed by a principle—frustrated those constitutional policies: the promotion of learning, the protection of the public domain, and the protection of the author (though not necessarily the publisher). But to achieve this goal, courts dealing with copyright issues should—indeed, *must*—begin with the right question, a truism that is sometimes lost in dealing with the complexity of the 1976 act. Much of the confusion in copyright law arises from the fact that courts—especially at the lower levels—tend to provide answers without knowing the question.

The ultimate issue is integrity in the law of copyright: the proper relationship of the parts to each other and to the whole. By this measure, it is clear that integrity is not yet a fixture of copyright law. The law of authors' rights and the law of users' rights are both currently underdeveloped, while the law of publishers' rights is overdeveloped—primarily because of the courts' emphasis on economic rights. To achieve the desired integrity in copyright law it is crucial that courts be reminded of two fundamental points: first, that there is a distinction between a work and its copyright; and second, that copyright must accommodate the interests of three groups —authors, entrepreneurs, and users. The questions, then, are these: What rights are unique to the author as creator (and thus owner) of the work? What rights should the monopoly of copyright encompass? What rights should the user have in relation to the work? As we have attempted to show in this book, the answers are remarkably uncomplicated: moral rights for the author, marketing rights for the entrepreneur, and learning rights for the user. Yet the importance of these goals merits additional consideration here, even at the risk of some repetition.

Moral Rights of the Author

An anomaly of American copyright law is that it is a law governing artistic culture but limited in its concern to the protection of the economic interest of the copyright owner—whether author or entrepreneur. This means that copyright does not protect the work per se for the benefit of the creator. Instead, it protects the work for the market to the benefit of the entrepreneur—and by so doing, American copyright law had essentially excluded the moral right of the author from its jurisdiction.[1] Moral rights, a product of the civil law, are the rights of an author—independent of copyright ownership— to protect the integrity and paternity of his or her work. All

moral rights, thus, are based on the assumption that a work
has merit warranting protection regardless of the economic
return to the copyright owner that any alteration may bring.
The economic right involves no such assumption.

In most cases it is inordinately difficult to prove the effect
of what does not exist. But in this instance, one can make a
reasonable case that the absence of the author's moral right
in American copyright law helps significantly to explain the
common perception that copyright is irrelevant to free-speech
rights, the misconception regarding the scope of the copyright
owner's right to copy, and the copyright industry's alleged
limitations on the fair-use doctrine.

One's premise, of course, determines one's conclusion. If
the general premise is that copyright protects only economic
rights, it follows that only the economic interests of the copyright owner will be protected. At that point it becomes irrelevant whether copyright ownership is by reason of creation,
by assignment of the copyright itself, or by the work-for-hire
doctrine: the copyright owner's economic interest requires the
right to copy. Consequently, to the extent that fair-use copying
is perceived to harm the copyright owner's economic interest,
fair use will be limited, and the copyright owner's exercise of
the right to exclude others from copying will be seen as irrelevant to free-speech concerns because the issue involves only
property, not politics.

Arguably, the major theoretical deficiency in American
copyright law is the absence of consideration for the author's
moral right. Yet one could make a case that the moral right
is implied in the copyright clause of the Constitution, which
provides the authority for Congress to enact legislation giving
authors the exclusive right to their writings in order to promote learning. As the right is to be exclusive to—and exclusively for—*authors,* one could argue that a part of that exclu-

sive right is the right of the author to protect the integrity of the work and his or her reputation in connection therewith.

Admittedly, this reading is a gloss that is not entirely consistent with historical developments; but the historical development of copyright in England was in large part a reaction against the efforts of publishers to enhance their monopoly of the book trade. And, indeed, except for that concern, the common law would almost surely have recognized the author's moral right, although not necessarily under that term. In the case of *Millar v. Taylor,* that is precisely what the English court did in 1769.[2]

The issue in *Millar* was whether, despite the Statute of Anne, the author had a common-law right in his works. Lord Mansfield (holding that he did) explained that, without the common-law right,

> The author may not only be deprived of any profit, but lose the expense he has been at. He is no more master of the use of his own name. He has no control over the correctness of his own work. He can not prevent additions. He can not retract errors. He can not amend; or cancel a faulty edition. Any one may print, pirate, and perpetuate the imperfections, to the disgrace and against the will of the author; may propagate sentiments under his name, which he disapproves, repents and is ashamed of. He can exercise no discretion as to the manner in which, or the persons by whom his work shall be published.[3]

This was then, and continues to be, a fine definition of the author's moral rights. There was only one problem: the court in *Millar* treated the right as assignable to a publisher, and such an assignment, of course, defeats the protection that the moral right provides the author. This was the fatal flaw that subsequently led the House of Lords in *Donaldson v. Beckett* to limit the author's common-law copyright to unpublished works. In Anglo-American law, then, the moral-rights doctrine was accepted but limited to unpublished works in the guise of the common-law copyright.

The 1976 Copyright Act eliminates the common-law copyright for any new works that are fixed in a tangible medium of expression. Yet, although Congress did not give explicit statutory recognition of moral rights, the statute does contain one provision that *could* serve as the basis for judicial development of the doctrine: the termination right. Although many authors may be unaware of this provision in the 1976 act, an author may, after thirty-five years, terminate the assignment of his or her copyright, and that right to terminate is inalienable. The author thus retains a reversionary interest in his or her work. Any conduct of the copyright owner that affects either the integrity of the work or the author's reputation thus potentially has a direct impact on the author's economic interest. Paradoxically, the moral-rights doctrine in American copyright law may well be developed on the basis of economic rights.

The development of the moral-rights doctrine will almost certainly have implications for the future use of copyrighted works by both users and competitors. Whether the use is a personal or a fair use, users in the years to come are likely to have a legal responsibility to consider not only the economic interest but also the moral rights of the author. In many respects, of course, anyone who uses a copyrighted work already has a moral responsibility to do so with regard for the integrity of the work as well as the reputation of the author.

Marketing Rights of the Entrepreneur

Marketing rights are the core concern of entrepreneurs, and since they took an active role in drafting the legislation, it is not surprising that the publishers' component of copyright law is overdeveloped. At first glance it appears that Congress is at fault for allowing this to occur. As Jessica D. Litman observes in her article, "Copyright, Compromise, and Legislative History": "One can choose a statutory provision almost at random; a review of the provision's legislative history will show that credit for its substance belongs more to the representatives of interested parties negotiating among themselves than to the member of Congress who sponsored, reported, or debated the bill."[4]

Closer analysis, however, reveals that this occurred not so much because Congress abdicated its responsibility as because Congress faced political reality: "The incessant pressure to achieve agreement among industry representatives was deliberate and planned in advance."[5] Such was acknowledged in the 1965 testimony of Abraham Kaminstein to the Senate Subcommittee on Patents, Copyrights, and Trademarks, when he responded to a question as to why there had not been more frequent revisions of the copyright law:

> If there is a single answer to this question, I believe it is that there are so many interrelated creator-user interests in the copyright field, and they present such sharp conflicts on individual issues, that the consensus necessary for any general revision is extremely difficult to achieve. Examples of this difficulty are found throughout the concentrated efforts to revise the 1909 act which went on continuously between 1924 and 1940 and which all ended in failure and futility. Realizing fully what copyright law revision is up against, Arthur Fisher, my predecessor as Register of Copyrights, planned a program that would be based on a thorough knowledge of all the issues and a painstaking effort to resolve as many disputes as possible before a bill reached the stage of congressional hearings.

It took us 10 years, but the program he planned has been carried out to the best of our ability.[6]

The strategy that Register Fisher chose resulted in a new copyright statute, but it also had three effects that one suspects were unintended. First, it made easier the use of questionable copyright fictions. Agreement among the affected parties as to what they wanted often resulted in compromise, which gave their wishes the aura of reasonableness (and what seems reasonable is easily rationalized as constitutional).

Second, the strategy resulted in a basic structure for the copyright act which—contrary to all prior statutes—implied that copyright is property rather than the grant of a regulated monopoly. That structure, of course, was the granting of exclusive rights subject mainly to fact-specific limitations.

Third, the structure resulting from the strategy served to obscure the existence of the various kinds of copyright, giving all copyright owners a distinct advantage insofar as the judicial interpretation of the statute is concerned. Since copyright is a uniform concept, any rights that accrue to the owner of one kind of copyright accrue to the owners of all kinds of copyright by reason of a cross-pollination effect. Consider, for example, the exclusive right to copy a book and that same right as applied to a live television broadcast. The right is treated as identical, even though the right to copy the book serves functionally to implement the right of public distribution, while the live television broadcast is only performed, not published.

Yet if fault is to be found with the end result, the process must shoulder the blame. Contrary to the assumption of many "that Congress is in the business of devising wise solutions to copyright dilemmas based solely on considerations of good public policy," as Thomas P. Olson points out, the fact is that "Congress is an intensely political body, loath to impose one-sided losses on legitimate interest groups."[7]

Given the nature of the political process, the suprising thing is not that the 1976 Copyright Act is imperfect but that it ended up as strong as it did—a tribute to the legislators and staff members involved. To infer that the copyright industry coopted Congress is to get things backward. Actually, Congress coopted the industry, as even critics such as Jessica D. Litman admit:

> Congress consistently resisted lobbying over substantial issues, insisting instead that would-be lobbyists sit down with their opponents and seek mutually acceptable solutions. Nor did Congress pass the 21 years of copyright revision waiting idly for industry representatives to do its work. Members of Congress worked very hard on the copyright revision bill. They held repeated, lengthy subcommittee hearings, attended numerous executive sessions, and drafted a flood of committee reports. More important, they encouraged, cajoled, bullied, and threatened the parties through continuing negotiations. They mediated disputes and demanded that combative interests seek common ground. Viable compromises emerged from the interminable negotiations largely because of congressional midwifery.[8]

The fact of the matter is that copyright entrepreneurs have generally had more success in the courts than in Congress. It appears that most lower courts are not very knowledgeable about copyright, are too overburdened to learn, tend to rely on faulty precedent, and too often consult only portions of the copyright statute rather than reading it entire. Only the Supreme Court of the United States can be counted on to render copyright decisions that take into account copyright policies and principles as well as rules, but unfortunately few copyright cases reach the high court.[9] The danger that the copyright monopoly will exceed constitutional bounds, then, rests more in the courtroom than in the legislative chamber, because "the scope of copyright protection is ultimately defined by litigation." [10]

Most problems contain their own solution. To bring the publishers' component back within the confines of constitutional limitations, courts need only return to the constitutional policies of copyright and accept three premises: (1) there is a crucial difference between the ownership of a work and the ownership of its copyright (and thus between the use of one or the other); (2) the copyright act governs only the use of the copyright; and (3) copyright is the grant of a limited statutory monopoly, the regulatory aspects of which are more important than its proprietary aspects. In other words, once the courts adjust their premises to acknowledge the fact that the grant of copyright by Congress is not a right but a privilege, they will begin to recognize that those who accept this privilege assume an obligation to fulfill the constitutional purpose of copyright, the promotion of learning. And this recognition, in turn, should result in a loss or reduction of owners' rights in those cases where an owner has asserted a right of use beyond those granted by the statute or has used copyright protection to frustrate the learning process by inhibiting public access to a copyrighted work—thus violating his or her bargain with society.

The jurisprudential problem that courts face in this context appears to be more complex than it need be. Simply stated, the problem is how to vindicate the public interest without destroying the private incentive. Working from the old premises, courts dealing with infringement cases have usually delivered all-or-nothing judgments for the copyright owner—even in cases where the copyright appeared to be abused—because the only alternative was deemed to be an invalidation of the copyright. Given the correct premises, however, courts may well choose to deal with the problem by employing one of two little-known doctrines already available, albeit in inchoate form: *copyright misuse* (based on the patent-misuse doctrine) or *copyright estoppel*. The paucity of judicial precedent means that both of these doctrines remain undeveloped, but they clearly offer applicability and potential utility.

Generally, the misuse doctrine would seem to be appropriate for conduct that affects all potential users of a work—for example, an owner's employment of an overreaching copyright notice proclaiming that no one may copy any portion of the work by any means for any reason without the written consent of the copyright owner. Copyright estoppel, on the other hand, would seem to be most appropriate for conduct that affects the defendant individually (as when a copyright owner makes no objection to a defendant's use of a copyrighted work for an extended period and then, for whatever reason, sues for infringement, or when an owner fails to make copies of a copyrighted work accessible to the public but then sues for infringement if someone makes use of a privately obtained copy of the work).

The utility of such doctrines should be apparent. They would enable courts to limit the scope of the copyright monopoly without imposing the forfeiture of copyright itself (that is, they can fit the punishment to the crime, because the particular wrong will receive a particular, rather than a general, sanction). The copyright owner who uses the overreaching notice loses that case but may then correct the notice—repair the copyright, so to speak—with no further harm. Similarly, the copyright owner who is estopped for failing to act sooner against a particular defendant, or for failing to make a copyrighted work accessible to the public, need not lose his or her cause of action against other potential defendants unless the conduct is repeated. In any of these cases, copyright owners who abuse their monopoly privileges would have no basis to complain about the loss of those privileges.

This is not the place to suggest the content of the law of copyright misuse and copyright estoppel, only the principle underlying them—namely that copyright, being the statutory grant of a limited monopoly privilege, requires that copyright owners recognize their duties even as they exercise the rights the statute grants. The two doctrines are thus an answer to the dilemma posed by the grant of the copyright privilege: how to serve consistently the often conflicting interests of the copyright owner and the public. The best course of action may be to let the copyright owner decide whether the minimal burdens that the copyright act imposes are worth the substantial benefits it grants. To the extent that copyright owners decide to eschew the burdens or to claim rights beyond those the statute allows, their conduct would determine the application of the doctrines in any given case.[11]

Learning Rights of the User

The factor that separates men and women from the beasts in the jungle is learning, and to subject learning to the proprietary control of entrepreneurs is to demean its importance. It has always been difficult to subdue the primeval urgings of the darker recesses of the mind, but to make information—the basis of learning—merely another commodity in the marketplace would be to burden the effort severely. Charity is not an inborn trait, and the fact that a free-market system makes a virtue of necessity is no cause for society to forfeit the purpose of copyright (the promotion of learning) in favor of its function (to protect the author's right to publish). There is a line beyond which the claims of monopolists must not be allowed to extend. For, as in all endeavors, too much reward in copyright monopoly will set in motion the law of diminishing returns, resulting ultimately in excessive private control over the learning that each generation must acquire anew.

The current term of copyright—either life of the author plus fifty years, or up to one hundred years for corporate copyrights—encompasses at least three and often four or more generations. This is a major expansion from the two terms of the 1790 act (fourteen years each) that covered at most a little more than one generation. To encase all new learning in the straitjacket of copyright for a period of time that exceeds the normal life span can hardly be said to be consistent with the constitutional policy of promoting learning or protecting the public domain. (Consider the historian in 2025 who wishes to make a study of the news media's impact on the Reagan administration in the 1980s. His or her efforts will almost surely be entangled in, and possibly frustrated by, the current law of copyright.)

On the surface it appears that the extension of the copyright term was made primarily to benefit the author, but that turns out to be a charade. The users who benefit most are those who secured its enactment—the members of the industry who own the corporate copyrights. The notion that copyright is an author's property right has proved to be a useful fiction in more ways than one. The facile claim that only profit for the author will induce the creation and dissemination of learning is in fact a claim that only a guaranteed profit will achieve the desired result. Thus the members of the copyright industry are implicitly arguing that the law must indemnify the author (by which they mean "publisher") and guarantee his or her profit for controlling the dissemination and use of information. Their premise seems to be that it is the law's duty not only to protect their right to earn a profit but also to *create* a profit for copyright owners by empowering them to impose a user's tax on learning materials.

The danger that the copyrightists will succeed in this regard is more real than fanciful, for the industry's strong involvement in the legislative process means that the effort to eliminate the right of personal use altogether is continuing.[12] And should the user's tax rationale prevail, we may be sure that never in the history of mankind will so many have to pay so much to so few for the exercise of what was previously recognized as the natural-law right of learning.

In practical terms, the major hope appears to be the courts —particularly the Supreme Court—which are protected from industry lobbyists. Yet the fact-bound conflicts that come to courts are not conducive to dealing with the law in terms of its broader reach. A crucial point frequently overlooked is that the narrow ruling judges give in a specific case, theoretically binding only the parties involved in that litigation, serves subsequently as precedent, which in turn too often serves as a substitute for analysis and reason. Courts need to bear in mind that the copyright act must be continually interpreted in light of the copyright clause, and that the copyright clause embodies free-speech values—values that are as important as they are fragile.

The copyright task facing the courts now and in the early twenty-first century will be similar to that which confronted the courts in the nineteenth century. That task is to apply the basic principles of copyright in the interpretation of the rules of the new copyrights in order to ensure that the copyright policies of the Constitution are continued. Whatever form copyright takes, and however far copyright is extended, it remains a law dealing with the control of information and knowledge. The words of President George Washington to Congress on 8 January 1790 that led to the enactment of the 1790 Copyright Act are as true today as they were then:

Fellow Citizens of the Senate and House of Representatives: . . .
Nor am I less persuaded that you will agree with me in

opinion, that there is nothing which can better deserve your patronage than the promotion of science and literature. Knowledge is, in every country, the surest basis of public happiness. In one in which the measures of government receive their impression so immediately from the sense of the community as in ours, it is proportionably essential. To the security of a free constitution it contributes in various ways: By convincing those who are intrusted with the public administration that every valuable end of government is best answered by the enlightened confidence of the public; and by teaching the people themselves to know and to value their own rights; to discern and provide against invasions of them; to distinguish between oppression and the necessary exercise of lawful authority; between burthens proceeding from a disregard to their convenience, and those resulting from the inevitable exigencies of society; to discriminate the spirit of liberty from that of licentiousness, cherishing the first, avoiding the last, and uniting a speedy but temperate vigilance against encroachments, with an inviolable respect to the laws.[13]

Truth and understanding are difficult enough to come by under the best of circumstances, but if we allow knowledge to be monopolized by copyright as merely another species of private property, we will dispense with an enlightened and confident public. Not without cause and good reason did George Washington's colleagues provide the security of a free constitution by denying Congress the power to make knowledge the "staple commodity" that John Milton decried. Truth and understanding cannot become wares to be traded in the marketplace, not least because such trade would be unconstitutional. There is a vital link between liberty and learning. Preserving the integrity of copyright law—including its law of users' rights—is critical to our free society.

Notes

Chapter 1. The Role of Copyright in American Life

1. David A. Kaplan, "The End of History?" *Newsweek*, 25 Dec. 1989, p. 80.

2. Jacques Barzun, *On Writing, Editing, and Publishing*, 2d ed. (Chicago: University of Chicago Press, 1986), pp. 128–29. The full context of Barzun's statement makes it clear that his irritation is directed not against the law but rather (as partially signaled by his ironic acknowledgment to Dickens's heirs) against the common practice of publishers to force their authors to chase down permissions for the use of all quoted work, regardless of whether or not it might qualify as fair use. Barzun's eloquent protest, first published as "Quote 'em Is Taboo," *Saturday Review of Literature*, 22 Sept. 1945, remains timely almost a half century later, for the publishers' practice is still well entrenched.

3. The best brief analysis of the current judicial confusion over the fair-use doctrine is offered by Pierre N. Leval, "Fair Use or Foul?" *Journal of the Copyright Society of the U.S.A.* 36 (1989), 167–81. As U.S. District Judge in the Southern District of New York, Judge Leval presided in two controversial fair-use cases, *Salinger v. Random House, Inc.* (1986) and *New Era Pub. Int. v. Henry Holt & Co.* (1988). His findings of fair use in both cases were overturned by the Second Circuit Court of Appeals, leading to Judge Leval's wry appraisal: "It has been exhilarating to find myself present at the cutting edge of the law, even though in the role of the salami" (p. 168).

See also Pierre N. Leval, "Toward a Fair Use Standard," *Harvard Law Review* 103 (1989), 1105–36, which develops further the concept that fair use must be interpreted in light of basic copyright principles. For an opposing viewpoint, see Lloyd L. Weinreb, "Fair's Fair: A Comment on the Fair Use Doctrine,"

Harvard Law Review 103 (1989), 1137–61; Weinreb argues for a principle-free, precedent-driven concept of fair use.

4. Both the "Agreement on Guidelines for Classroom Copying in Not-for-Profit Educational Institutions with Respect to Books and Periodicals" and the "Guidelines for Educational Uses of Music" appear in H. R. Rep. No. 1476, 94th Cong., 2d Sess., 68–71. The first of these is often circulated in selectively edited form by the vested interests, most recently in 1989 by the Association of American Publishers and the National Association of College Stores, Inc. (528 E. Lorain St., Oberlin, Ohio 44074) under the title *Questions and Answers on Copyright for the Campus Community.* In this publication readers are advised that "some limited copying which does not fall within these guidelines (*and* which is not expressly prohibited . . .) may still qualify as permissible conduct under the copyright law"—an insidious distortion of what the House Report had expressly labeled "*minimum standards . . . not intended to limit the types of copying permitted under the standards of fair use.*"

The "Guidelines for Off-Air Recording of Broadcast Programming for Educational Purposes" may be found in the *Congressional Record,* 14 Oct. 1981, pp. 24,048–49. And *Using Software: A Guide to the Ethical and Legal Use of Software for Members of the Academic Community* (1987) is produced by ADAPSO, the computer software and services industry association, through EDUCOM, which describes itself as "a nonprofit consortium of over 450 colleges and universities" (c/o Software Initiative, P.O. Box 364, Princeton, N.J. 08540).

Chapter 2. Copyright in the Beginning: A Publisher's Right

1. Edward Arber, ed., *A Transcript of the Registers of the Company of Stationers of London 1554–1640 A.D.,* 5 vols. (London: Privately printed, 1875–94), 2:11.

2. For historical and critical analysis, see esp. W. W. Greg, *London Publishing between 1550 and 1650* (Oxford: Clarendon Press,

1956); Cyprian Blagden, *The Stationers' Company: A History,
1403–1959* (Cambridge: Harvard University Press, 1960); and
Lyman Ray Patterson, *Copyright in Historical Perspective* (Nashville:
Vanderbilt University Press, 1968).

In addition to Arber, the most valuable primary source materials include: *A Transcript of the Registers of the Worshipful Company of Stationers; from 1640–1708 A.D.* [no editor named; Eyre & Rivington listed on the spine], 3 vols. (London: Privately printed, 1913–14); W. W. Greg and E. Boswell, eds., *Records of the Court of the Stationers' Company, 1576 to 1602* (London: Bibliographical Society, 1930); and William A. Jackson, ed., *Records of the Court of the Stationers' Company, 1602 to 1640* (London: Bibliographical Society, 1957).

3. Although the printing patent suggests a common source for the idea of exclusivity in the manufacture and sale of products—the basis of both the patent and copyright—it has more relevance to patent law than to copyright law. The direct source of American patent law was the British Statute of Monopolies enacted in 1624. That statute can be viewed as the point at which patent and copyright law were bifurcated, for it limited the royal power to grant letters patent, but it excluded printing patents from its operation. Even so, the royal use of the printing patent diminished: the last one is said to have been granted by William and Mary in the late seventeenth century, some twenty years before the Statute of Anne was enacted.

4. This point is demonstrated by the provisions in section 5 of Company Ordinance of 1681, which provided:

And whereas several members of this Company have great part of their Estates in Copies; and by ancient Usage of this Company, when any Book or Copy is duly Entred in the Register Book of this Company, to any Member or Members of this Company, such Person to whom such Entry is made, is, and always hath been reputed and taken to be Proprietor of such Book or Copy, and ought to have the sole Printing thereof; which Priviledg and Interest is now of late often violated and abused:

It is therefore Ordained, That where any Entry or Entries, is, or are, or hereafter shall be duly made of any Book or Copy in the said Register-Book of this Company, by, or for any Member or Members of this Company; That in such case, if any other Member or Members of this Company shall then after, without the License or Consent of such Member or Members of this Company, for whom such Entry is duly made in the Register Book of this Company, or his or their Assignee or Assigns, Print, or cause to be Printed, Import or cause to be Imported from beyond the Seas, or elsewhere, any such Copy or Copies, Book or Books, or any part of any such Copy or Copies, Book or Books, or shall sell, bind, stitch, or expose the same, or any part or parts thereof to sale, That then such Member or Members so offending, shall forfeit to the Master and Keepers, or Wardens and Commonalty of the Mystery or Art of *Stationers* of the City of *London,* the sum of *Twelve Pence* for every such Copy or Copies, Book or Books, or any part of such Copy or Copies, Book or Books Imprinted, Imported, sold, bound stitcht, and exposed to sale contrary hereunto. (Arber 1:22–23)

5. Arber 3:45.

6. Arber 1:xl. An ordinance of 1678 provided: "And be it further Ordained, That when any difference or differences shall here-after arise between any member and members of this Company for any Copy, Right, or any thing relating to Printing, Book-selling or Book-binding, That then before any Action or suit be commenced, they shall first make their application to the Master, Wardens and Assistants in a Court of Assistants, and give them true information of the ground and occasion of such Difference or controversie; which said Master, Wardens and Assistants, in a Court of Assistants, are hereby authorized to hear all parties concerned, and to use their utmost Endeavours to compose such Difference and Differences without the trouble and charge of going to Law; upon pain that every member that shall for any of the Causes aforesaid commence any Suit or Suits, without application made as aforesaid, shall forfeit and pay to the Master

and Keepers or Wardens and Comminalty of the Mystery or Art of *Stationers* of the City of *London*, the summe of *Ten pounds*" (Arber 1:14).

7. Thus, item 7 of the Star Chamber Decree of 1637 provided "That no person or persons shall . . . imprint . . . any Copy, book or books, or parts of any book or books . . . which the said company of Stationers, or any person or persons have or shall [have] by any . . . Entrance in their Register book . . . [upon pain of forfeiture and a fine or other punishment]" (Arber 4:531).

8. "The heretical doctrines of Luther were, it is true, spread by word of mouth; but printed books and pamphlets could be produced and distributed in their hundreds—secretly; they did not disappear but remained for second readings and for passing on to friends; they were difficult to answer back. Closely related to the fear of theological heterodoxy in the printed word went fear of criticism of the Government; the adjectives heretical and seditious appear over and over again in official pronouncements up to the beginning of the eighteenth century" (Blagden, p. 29).

9. The charter (reprinted in Arber 1:xxviii–xxxii), which was confirmed by Elizabeth I on 10 Nov. 1559, authorized "[T]he Master and Keepers or Wardens . . . to make search whenever it shall please them in any place, shop, house, chamber, or building of any printer, binder or bookseller whatever within our kingdom of England or the dominions of the same of or for any books or things printed, or to be printed, and to seize, take, hold, burn, or turn to the proper use of the foresaid community, all and several those books and things which are or shall be printed contrary to the form of any statute, act, or proclamation, made or to be made; and that if any person shall practise or exercise the foresaid art or mistery contrary to the foresaid form, or shall disturb, refuse, or hinder the foresaid Master or Keepers or Wardens for the time being or any one of them for the time being, in making the foresaid search or in seizing, taking, or burning the foresaid books or things, or any of them printed or to be printed contrary to the form of any statute, act, or proclamation, that then the foresaid Master and Keepers or Wardens for the time being shall

imprison or commit to jail any such person so practising or exercising the foresaid art or mistery contrary to the foresaid form,
or as is stated above, disturbing, refusing or hindering, there to
remain without bail for the space of three months; and that the
same person so practising or exercising the foresaid art or mistery
contrary to the aforesaid form, or so, as is above stated, disturbing, refusing or hindering, shall forfeit for each such practising
or exercising aforesaid against the form aforesaid and for each
such disturbance, refusal or hindrance a *hundred shillings* of lawful
money of England, one half thereof to us, the heirs and successors of us the foresaid Queen, and the other half thereof to the
foresaid Master, Keepers or Wardens and community."

10. Reproduced in Arber 1:322, 2:807–12, 4:528–56.
11. Charles Firth and Robert Rait, eds., *Acts and Ordinances of the Inter-
    regnum*, 3 vols. (London: H.M. Stationery Office, 1911), 1:184–
    87, 1021–23; 2:245–54. In addition, Orders of the Lord Protec-
    tor regulating printing were issued on 28 Aug. 1655 (reprinted
    in William Clyde, *The Struggle for Freedom of the Press from Claxton
    to Cromwell* [New York: B. Franklin, 1934], app. E, pp. 323–537).
12. The Licensing Act of 1662 was renewed (16 Car. 2, cap. 7; 17
    Car. 2, cap. 4) until the dissolution of the Cavalier Parliament in
    1678, and was revived again for seven years in 1685 (1 Jac. 2,
    cap. 17) and renewed for the last time in 1692 (4 & 5 William &
    Mary, cap. 24).
13. Blagden, p. 172.
14. Blagden, p. 120.
15. Blagden, p. 118.
16. "Even if we did not know that the drafters of the 1662 Bill had
    been referred back to the wording of 1637, it would have been
    possible to deduce the reference from similarity in phraseology
    and from the fact that two dozen of the clauses in the Decree
    found places in the Act" (Blagden, p. 153).
17. Blagden, p. 173.
18. 17 U.S.C. § 503.
19. The Congers were "joint-copyright-owning and joint-distributing
    groups of booksellers," whose main purpose was the protection
    of copyright through control of wholesaling (Blagden, p. 175).

20. The House of Commons stated eighteen reasons for refusing to renew the Licensing Act, among which were the fact that books were required to be entered in the register of the Stationers' Company. The stationers are "empowered to hinder the printing [of] all innocent and useful Books; and have an Opportunity to enter a Title for themselves, and their Friends, for what belongs to, and is the Labour and Right of, others." See 11 H.C. Jour. 305–6.

21. For a fuller account of these efforts, see Patterson, *Copyright in Historical Perspective*, pp. 138–42.

22. 8 Anne, cap. 19. This celebrated statute is best identified, as here, by the regnal year of Queen Anne, since some historical references date it in 1709, others in 1710. The confusion results from England's long delay in standardizing calendars. Although the general public had long considered years to begin on 1 January, the official legal method of dating—from the Middle Ages until 1751—marked the year as beginning on the Feast of the Annunciation (25 March). This resulted in many English writers using double year–dates (such as the Statute of Anne's 1709/10) for events occurring between 1 January and 24 March. The practice continued until the Gregorian (New Style) calendar was adopted (24 Geo. 2, cap. 23) in 1751. Since the effective date of the Statute of Anne was 10 April 1710, safely within that year by either calendar, we let that date stand alone here.

23. The copyright in the Statute of Anne was available to the author *or* proprietor. As Robert Maugham states in his 1828 argument for the author's perpetual right in his or her property: "The bill on which the act [the Statute of Anne] was founded, went to the committee as a bill to *secure* the undoubted property of copies *for ever.* It seems objections arose in the committee to the *generality* of the proposition; and that the debate ended in securing properties for a term—without prejudice to either side of the question upon the general claim as to the *right*" (Robert Maugham, *A Treatise on the Laws of Literary Property* [London: 1828], p. 26).

24. The Licensing Act, for example, had named various officials as licensers for books to be published and had prevented the importation of books from beyond the seas. The Statute of Anne

introduced price-control provisions, but the officials to whom complaint could be made were those named as licensers in the Licensing Act; and the Statute of Anne specifically permitted the importation of books from beyond the seas.

Chapter 3. Copyright Changes: An Author's Right?

1. 22 H.C. Jour. 400; see Patterson, *Copyright in Historical Perspective*, pp. 54–158.
2. *Millar v. Taylor* in 4 Burr. 2303; 98 Eng. Rep. 201 (1769). *Donaldson v. Beckett* in 4 Burr. 2408; 98 Eng. Rep. 257; 2 Brown's Parl. Cases 129; 1 Eng. Rep. 837 (1774); 17 Cobbett's Parl. Hist. 953 (1813).
3. 4 Burr. at 2338; 98 Eng. Rep. at 220.
4. 4 Burr. at 2345; 98 Eng. Rep. at 224.
5. 4 Burr. at 2398; 98 Eng. Rep. at 252.
6. 4 Burr. at 2405; 98 Eng. Rep. at 256.
7. 4 Burr. at 2386; 98 Eng. Rep. at 245.
8. As Donaldson's counsel argued, "The bill in this cause was penned by the respondents [Beckett et al.] with extreme caution. . . . It might therefore be inferred, that the present attempt was an experiment, to try how far the doctrine of [*Millar v. Taylor*] may be extended beyond the case itself" (2 Brown's Parl. Cases at 132; 1 Eng. Rep. at 847).
9. 4 Burr. at 2408–9; 98 Eng. Rep. at 257–58.
10. In *The Federalist* No. 43, the following statement appears: "The copyright of authors has been solemnly adjudged, in Great Britain, to be a right of common law."
11. Howard B. Abrams, "The Historic Foundation of American Copyright Law: Exploding the Myth of Common Law Copyright," *Wayne Law Review* 29 (1983), 1119.
12. 17 Cobbett's Parl. Hist. at 1003.
13. See Abrams at 1164, n. 189.
14. Abrams at 1159.
15. 17 Cobbett's Parl. Hist. at 962.
16. 17 Cobbett's Parl. Hist. at 965.

17. 17 Cobbett's Parl. Hist. at 975–76.
18. 17 Cobbett's Parl. Hist. at 992.
19. 17 Cobbett's Parl. Hist. at 971.
20. 17 Cobbett's Parl. Hist. at 991.
21. 17 Cobbett's Parl. Hist. at 999.
22. 17 Cobbett's Parl. Hist. at 1002.
23. 17 Cobbett's Parl. Hist. at 1003.
24. 4 Burr. at 2417; 98 Eng. Rep. at 262.
25. 34 H.C. Jour. 100.
26. A. S. Collins, *Authorship in the Days of Johnson* (London, 1927), p. 100. Collins continues: "We find petitions of the booksellers and printers of Edinburgh; of sundry booksellers in London and Westminster on behalf of themselves and their brethern in the country; of the printers and booksellers of the city and University of Glasgow; of the Committee of the Royal Boroughs of Scotland; of the booksellers, printers, and bookbinders of York; and of Donaldson himself."
27. 17 Cobbett's Parl. Hist. at 1090.
28. 17 Cobbett's Parl. Hist. at 1400–2.
29. Lord Chief Justice De Grey, with whom Lord Camden agreed, said: "With respect to the first question, there can be no doubt that an author has the sole right to dispose of his manuscript as he thinks proper; it is his property, and, till he parts with it, he can maintain an action of trover, trespass, or upon the case, against any man who shall convert that property to his own use: but the right now claimed at the bar, is not a title to the manuscript, but to something after the owner has parted with, or published his manuscript; to some interest in right of authorship, to more than the materials, or manuscript, on which his thoughts are displayed; which is termed literary property, or an exclusive privilege of multiplying copies of the manuscript, or book which right is the subject of the second question posed to us" (17 Cobbett's Parl. Hist. at 988).
30. *Boswell's Life of Johnson*, Oxford Standard Authors Edition, ed. R. W. Chapman (London: Oxford University Press, 1953), pp. 1008–9.

Chapter 4. Copyright in the U.S. Constitution: Policies

1. 8 Anne, cap. 19; 1 Stat. 124, 1st Cong., 2d Sess., ch. 15.
2. U.S. Const. art. 1, § 8, cl. 8.
3. Berne Convention Implementation Act of 1988, H.R. Rep. No. 609, 100 Cong., 2d Sess. 23 (1988).
4. Robert Maugham, *A Treatise of the Laws of Literary Property* (London, 1828), p. 1. In support of his conclusion, the author cites Lord Mansfield's definition of *copy* from *Millar v. Taylor:* "an *incorporeal right* to the *sole* printing and publishing of something intellectual, communicated by letters."
5. See L. R. Patterson and Craig Joyce, "Monopolizing the Law: The Scope of Copyright Protection for Law Reports and Statutory Compilations," *UCLA Law Review* 36 (1989), 719, 787–90; see also L. R. Patterson, "Free Speech, Copyright, and Fair Use," *Vanderbilt Law Review* 40 (1987), 1, 13–19.
6. The state statutes are printed in *Copyright Enactments, Laws Passed in the United States Since 1783 Relating to Copyright,* Copyright Office Bulletin No. 3 (rev. ed. 1973).
7. *Copyright Enactments,* p. 1.

Chapter 5. Copyright in the Nineteenth Century: Principles and Rules

1. Thus, in 1894, the court in *Harrison v. Maynard, Merrill & Co.*, 61 F. 689, 691 (2d Cir. 1894), said: "But the right to restrain the sale of a particular copy of the book by virtue of the copyright statutes has gone when the owner of the copyright and of that copy has parted with all his title to it, and has conferred an absolute title to the copy upon a purchaser, although with an agreement for a restricted use. The exclusive right to vend the particular copy no longer remains in the owner of the copyright by the copyright statutes. The new purchaser cannot reprint the copy. He cannot print or publish a new edition of the book; but, *the copy having been absolutely sold to him, the ordinary incidents of ownership in personal property, among which is the right of alienation, attach*

to it. . . . Clemens v. Estes, C.C., 22 Fed. 899" (emphasis added). Subsequent codification: 17 U.S.C. § 109.

2. "Abridgements of books, translations, notes, as effectually deprive the original author of the fruit of his labours, as direct particular copies, yet they are allowable" (Lord Chief Justice De Grey, *Donaldson v. Beckett*, 17 Cobbett's Parl. Hist. at 990).

3. 101 U.S. 99 (1879).

4. 101 U.S. at 103.

5. 33 U.S. (8 Pet.) 591 (1834). For the definitive study of this case, see Craig Joyce, "The Rise of the Supreme Court Reporter: An Institutional Perspective on Marshall Court Ascendancy," *Michigan Law Review* 83 (1985), 1291.

6. 33 U.S. at 596.

7. 33 U.S. at 599.

8. 33 U.S. at 603.

9. 33 U.S. at 657 (emphasis added).

10. For a discussion of the printer's right, see Patterson, *Copyright in Historical Perspective*, pp. 49–51.

11. See, e.g., Arber 2:608, Thomas Scarlet to print books he and William Wright sold to Thomas Mann; Arber 2:650, John Danter to print works he sold to Cuthbert Burbye; Arber 3:289, Simon Stafford to print works he sold to John Wright.

12. Eaton S. Drone, "The Law of Property in Intellectual Productions," *Drone on Copyright* (Boston: Little, Brown, 1879), p. 386.

13. See *Drone on Copyright*, chap. 9. Drone, citing cases to the contrary, took the position that such conduct was piratical.

14. 9 F. Cas. (No. 4901) 342 (C.C.D. Mass. 1841).

15. 9 F. Cas. at 348.

16. "Not primarily for the benefit of the author, but primarily for the benefit of the public, such rights are given" (H.R. Rep. No. 2222, 60th Cong., 2d Sess. 7 [1909]). Similar language occurs in Sen. Rep. No. 1108, 60th Cong., 2d Sess. 7 (1909). The House statement of 1909 was reaffirmed by Congress in 1988, when it was quoted and endorsed ("This statement still rings true today") in the Berne Convention Implementation Act of 1988, H.R. Rep. No. 609, 100 Cong., 2d Sess. 23 (1988).

17. *Harper & Row Publishers, Inc. v. Nation Enterprises*, 471 U.S. 539

(1985); *Sony Corp. v. Universal City Studios*, 464 U.S. 417 (1984); *Twentieth Century Music Corp. v. Aiken*, 422 U.S. 151 (1975); *Mazer v. Stein*, 347 U.S. 201 (1954).

18. *Stover v. Lathrop*, 33 F. 348, 349 (C.C.D. Colo. 1888).

19. *Stowe v. Thomas*, 23 F. Cas. (No. 13,514) 201, 207 (C.C.E.D. Pa. 1853).

20. The courts' failure to articulate the distinction between the work and the copyright led to their failure to distinguish between the original rights of authors and the derivative rights of publishers. Since all statutory rights in copyright originate with the author by reason of creation, any rights the publisher obtains must be derived from the author (i.e., as an assignee). There is no constitutional basis for Congress to grant copyright to publishers, only to authors. The question the courts should have confronted (but did not deal with) was this: Should an assignee's loss of derivative rights by reason of his or her own conduct result in the assignor's loss of original rights? The issue remains unexamined and therefore unanswered.

Chapter 6. Copyright in the Early Twentieth Century: The 1909 Copyright Act

1. T. Solberg, ed., *Copyright in Congress, 1789–1904*, Copyright Office Bulletin No. 8 (1905), p. 7.

2. 209 U.S. 1 (1908).

3. 209 U.S. at 13–14, quoting *Boosey v. Whight* (1899), 1 Ch. 122; 81 L.T.R. 265 (1900).

4. 23 F. Cas. 201.

5. 2 Stat. 171–72 (1845); 4 Stat. 436–39 (1845); 16 Stat. 212–17 (1871); *The Revised Statutes of the United States*, 43d Cong., 1st Sess., 1873–74, 959–60 (1878).

6. 17 U.S.C. § 1 *et seq.* (1909 act).

7. 13 Stat. 540–41.

8. *Burrow-Giles Lithographic Co. v. Sarony*, 111 U.S. 53, 4 S. Ct. 279 (1884).

9. Edison also invented the motion picture before the 1909 act, but Congress did not provide copyright for motion pictures at that time. The oversight was cured with an amendment in 1912 (37 Stat. 488–90 [1913]).

10. *White-Smith Music Pub. Co. v. Apollo Co.*, 209 U.S. 1 (1908).

11. H.R. Rep. No. 2222, 60th Cong., 2d Sess. 7 (1909).

12. 4 Burr. 2303; 98 Eng. Rep. 201 (1769).

13. 4 Burr. 2408; 98 Eng. Rep. 257 (1774).

14. 33 U.S. (8 Pet.) 591 (1834).

15. H.R. Rep. No. 2222 at 4 (emphasis added).

16. 2 Stat. 171–72. See also sections 6 and 7 of the 1831 Revision Act, 4 Stat. 436–39, which maintain the distinction.

17. 1 Stat. 124–26 (1845).

18. The language and punctuation of the 1790 act were retained in the 1802 amendment, which made prints and engravings copyrightable. In the 1831 Copyright Revision Act, however, the language in section 1 was "the sole right and liberty of printing, reprinting, publishing, and vending," i.e., a comma was added after publishing, giving a basis for arguing that the right to vend was an independent right. It is difficult to believe, however, that the change in punctuation was intended to have a substantive effect, since the use of the disjunctive *or* would have been the more conventional and more appropriate way to signal such a purpose. (Stat. 436–39 [1846]). Thus section 2 of the 1790 act provided that one who "shall print, reprint, publish, *or* import" the copyrighted work infringed the copyright (1 Stat. 124–26 [1845]).

19. The reference is to the statute as it was enacted. See *Copyright Enactments*, p. 64 *et seq.*

20. H.R. Rep. No. 2222 at 13–25.

21. The reference is to the statute as it was enacted. See *Copyright Enactments*.

22. H.R. Rep. No. 2222 at 13–20.

23. *Mazer v. Stein*, 347 U.S. 201, 221 (1954) (Douglas, J., concurring). After listing the above items, Douglas commented, "Perhaps these are all 'writings' in the constitutional sense. But for me, at least, they are not obviously so."

24. *Clayton v. Stone*, 5 F. Cas. (No. 2,872) 999 (C.C.S.D.N.Y. 1829).
25. *Dallas Cowboys Cheerleaders, Inc. v. Scoreboard Posters, Inc.*, 600 F.2d 1184, 1188 (1979).

Chapter 7. Copyright in the Late Twentieth Century: The 1976 Copyright Act

1. Barbara Ringer, "First Thoughts on the Copyright Act of 1976," *New York Law School Law Review* 22 (1977), 477, 479.
2. The studies were published as a series of ten committee prints in 1960–61, during the 86th Congress, 1st and 2d sessions, under the title *Copyright Law Revision, Studies Prepared for the Subcommittee on Patents, Trademarks, and Copyrights of the Committee on the Judiciary.* The complete series of studies has also been privately published: *Omnibus Copyright Revision Legislative History*, vols. 1 & 2, (Buffalo, N.Y.: William S. Hein & Co., 1960–61).
3. The statute as enacted contains eight chapters, but the last three are irrelevant to the discussion. They are chap. 6, "Manufacturing Requirements and Importation"; chap. 7, "Copyright Office"; chap. 8, "Copyright Royalty Tribunal."
4. See, e.g., 17 U.S.C. § 10 (1909 act).
5. H.R. Rep. No. 1476, 94th Cong., 2d Sess., 53 (1976).
6. See Justice Sandra Day O'Connor's discussion of sections 3 and 7 of the 1909 act in *Stewart v. Abend*, ___ U.S. ___ (1990); compare the dissent of Justice John Paul Stevens discussing the same provisions. See also Justice O'Connor's opinion in *Feist Publications, Inc. v. Rural Telephone Service Co., Inc.*, ___ U.S. ___ (1991), discussed in n. 9 for ch. 15, below.
7. *Macklin v. Richardson*, Amb. 644, 27 Eng. Rep. 451 (1770).
8. 9 F. Cas. 342.
9. The organization is the Copyright Clearance Center. Some quotes from its brochure, "Income from Copyrights" (1990), describes how it operates:

   Collecting Royalty Payments from Users
       CCC tracks and collects royalty income in several ways.
   One source of income is from a broad base of users—the

TRANSACTIONAL REPORTING SERVICE. Market segments include: document suppliers; higher education; federal, state and local government agencies; and large service corporations.

A second way to collect royalty payments is from corporations under a photocopy license—the ANNUAL AUTHORIZATIONS SERVICE—through which the corporate user makes a single payment to CCC for an annual license. Current corporate licenses number nearly 100 and include many Business Week 1000 and Fortune 500 companies.

How CCC's Programs Work

CCC's services require two agreements: one with the publisher, which empowers CCC to act as its agent to authorize users to photocopy its works, and one with the user, establishing the terms and conditions for those authorizations.

In the Annual Authorizations Service

Royalties are paid by U.S. corporations based on sample projections of use. Authorizations are granted for U.S. employees and internal use only.

In the Transactional Reporting Service

Royalties are paid on an item-by-item basis.

In its 1989 Annual Review (March, 1990), the Copyright Clearance Center states:

UNIVERSITY LICENSING. After years of planning and preparation, 1989 saw the beginning of the first CCC pilot programs to license photocopying in universities. Agreements were executed with 29 U.S. publishers and the Copyright Licensing Agency in Great Britain, collectively authorizing over 1,000,000 titles. The initial university participants in the two-year pilot include Northeastern, Columbia, and Stanford Universities; an additional two or three universities are expected to enter into the program in 1990.

The pilot is designed to collect and provide data on photocopying in universities, so that CCC, rightsholders and universities can attempt to craft a nationwide licensing program. In addition, the pilot includes a broad-based systematic Copyright Awareness Program, which will be tailored to the needs of each participating university.

Chapter 8. The Nature of Copyright

1. The full title of the *Wheaton* case was *Wheaton and Donaldson v. Peters and Griggs*, Donaldson and Griggs being the booksellers. Wheaton sold the copyright only of volume 1 of his *Reports;* for later volumes he sold only a license to reprint. "Wheaton's publisher, lacking a copyright interest of his own in all but the first volume of *Reports*, demanded that Wheaton immediately engage counsel to protect their mutual interests" (Joyce, "The Rise of the Supreme Court Reporter" at 1367).
2. *Millar v. Taylor*, 4 Burr. at 2396; 98 Eng. Rep. at 251.
3. 2 Brown's Parl. Cases at 131 n. 1; 1 Eng. Rep. at 847.
4. On the scope of the common-law copyright, compare *Pushman v. New York Graphic Society, Inc.* (287 N.Y. 302, 39 N.E.2d 249 [1942]), which held that the sale of an unpublished painting included the copyright, with *Chamberlain v. Feldman* (300 N.Y. 135, 80 N.E.2d 863 [1949]), which held that the sale of an unpublished manuscript written by Mark Twain did not include the copyright.
5. See *Burrow-Giles Lithographic Co. v. Sarony*, 111 U.S. 53 (1884), which held that the Constitution is broad enough to cover an act authorizing copyright of photographs that are representatives of original intellectual conceptions of the author.
6. *Bleistein v. Donaldson Lithographing Co.*, 188 U.S. 239, 250 (1903).

Chapter 9. Copyright and Free-Speech Rights

1. The underexamined element here has been "the historical origins"; scholars have, of course, both recognized and analyzed the overall relationship of copyright and free-speech rights. See Paul Goldstein, "Copyright and the First Amendment," *Columbia Law Review* 70 (1970), 983. The late Melville Nimmer, long acknowledged as America's leading authority on copyright, also dealt with the issue. See *Nimmer on Copyright* (New York: Matthew Bender & Co., 1988) § 1.10; see also *Nimmer on Freedom of Speech* (New York: Matthew Bender & Co., 1984) § 2.05[C][2] "Copyright vs. Freedom of Speech."

2. See Patterson and Joyce, "Monopolizing the Law" at 719.

3. H.R. Rep. No. 2222, 60th Cong., 2d Sess. 7 (1909). See n. 16 for ch. 5, above.

Chapter 10. The Role of Fictions and Fallacies in Copyright Law

1. 1 Stat. 124; 1st Cong., 2d Sess., c. 15; 2 Stat. 171–72 (1845).

2. 4 Stat. 436–39 (1846).

3. 13 Stat. 540–41 (1865). The Supreme Court upheld the constitutionality of copyright for photographs in *Burrow-Giles Lithographic Co. v. Sarony,* 111 U.S. 53 (1884).

4. 37 Stat. 488–90 (1913).

5. H.R. Rep. No. 2222 at 15.

6. *Community for Creative Non-Violence v. Reid,* ___ U.S. ___, 109 S. Ct. 2166, 2174 (1989).

7. *Copyright Law Revision; Hearings on H.R. 2223 Before the Subcomm. on Courts, Civil Liberties, and the Administration of Justice of the House Judiciary Comm.,* 94th Cong., 1st Sess. 1853 (1975).

Chapter 11. The Scope of the Right to Copy

1. The 1976 Copyright Act makes use of the second distinction, that is, to copy by imitating an original, in defining the scope of copyright protection for sound recordings. Thus, section 114 provides that "[t]he exclusive rights of the owner of copyright in a sound recording . . . do not extend to the making or duplication of another sound recording that consists entirely of an independent fixation of other sounds, even though such sounds imitate or simulate those in the copyrighted sound recording."

2. 101 U.S. 99 (1880); 9 F. Cas. 342.

3. H.R. Rep. No. 1476, 94th Cong., 2d Sess. 61 (1976).

4. *Dowling v. United States,* 473 U.S. 207, 216–17 (1985).

Chapter 12. The Law of Authors' Rights: Moral Rights

1. William Strauss, "The Moral Right of the Author," Study No. 4, in *Copyright Law Revision, Studies Prepared for the Subcommittee on Patents, Trademarks, and Copyrights of the Committee on the Judiciary*, U.S. Sen., 86th Cong., 1st Sess., 109–42 (1960).
2. Strauss, p. 142.
3. Strauss, p. 142.
4. 17 U.S.C. § 203.
5. 811 F.2d 90 (2d Cir. 1987).
6. 811 F.2d at 99 (emphasis in original).

Chapter 13. The Law of Publisher's Rights: Monopoly Rights

1. 248 U.S. 215 (1918).
2. *Feist Publications, Inc. v. Rural Telephone Service Co., Inc.*, ___ U.S. ___ (1991) is discussed further in n. 9 for ch. 15, below.
3. *White-Smith Music Pub. Co. v. Apollo Co.*, 209 U.S. 1, 19 (1908) (Holmes, J., concurring).
4. The quote is taken from the PBS flyer advertising (and containing) the license for the off-air taping of the broadcasts.
5. Jessica D. Litman, "Copyright, Compromise, and Legislative History," *Cornell Law Review* 72 (1987), 857, 859–61.

Chapter 14. The Law of Users' Rights: Personal Use and Fair Use

1. Benjamin Kaplan, *An Unhurried View of Copyright* (New York: Columbia University Press, 1967), p. 57.
2. The industry perception is that in *Salinger v. Random House, Inc.*, 811 F.2d 90 (1987), and in *New Era Pub. Int. v. Henry Holt & Co., Inc.*, 873 F.2d 576 (1989), the Second Circuit has effectively eliminated fair use as a defense in an action for infringement of the copyright of unpublished material. In both cases, the court relied

on *Harper & Row Publishers, Inc. v. Nation Enterprises,* 471 U.S. 539 (1985), although arguably the reliance was unjustified in that the Second Circuit ignored the context of Justice O'Connor's comments. In *Harper & Row,* the Court's holding protected the right of first publication for a work that was in the process of being published, and which had been stolen and made available to the defendant. Justice O'Connor, in a carefully crafted opinion, limited her comments to avoid deciding issues not before the Court, and specifically recognized that fair use applies to all the rights protected by copyright, including the right of first publication.

3. As of this writing, legislation has been introduced in Congress to amend section 107 in order to make it clear that fair use is applicable to unpublished materials.

4. 464 U.S. 417, 432 n. 13 (1983).

Chapter 15. The Future of American Copyright

1. We cannot deal in depth here with all the implications for moral rights that the United States' adherence to the Berne Convention will entail. Authors and other creators clearly have much at stake, but the major media interests are strongly opposed to the whole concept of moral rights. Nevertheless, one important step has been taken toward more statutory recognition of these rights with the passage of the "Visual Artists Rights Act of 1990" (PL 101-650; HR 5316). Signed into law by President Bush on 1 December 1990, this act establishes the right of artists, photographers, sculptors, and printmakers to protect their work from unauthorized distortion, mutilation, or modification. The act currently excludes from its moral rights protection "any poster, map, globe, chart, technical drawing, diagram, model, applied art, motion picture or other audiovisual work, book, magazine, newspaper, periodical, data base, electronic information service, electronic publication, or similar publication."

2. 4 Burr. 2303; 98 Eng. Rep. 201.

3. 4 Burr. at 2398; 98 Eng. Rep. at 252.

4. Litman at 870.

5. Litman at 872.

6. *Copyright Law Revision: Hearings on S. 1006 Before the Subcomm. on Patents, Trademarks and Copyrights of the Senate Comm. on the Judiciary, 89th Cong., 1st Sess.* 66 (1965).

7. Thomas P. Olson, "The Iron Law of Consensus: Congressional Responses to Proposed Copyright Reforms Since the 1909 Act," *Journal of the Copyright Society of the U.S.A.* 36 (1989), 109–11.

8. Litman at 871 (citations omitted).

9. See *Feist Publications, Inc. v. Rural Telephone Service Co., Inc.,* ___ U.S. ___ (1991), a Supreme Court opinion (on a 9-0 vote) written by Justice O'Connor that supports our comments about both lower courts and the Supreme Court. In the *Feist* case—perhaps the Court's most important copyright decision since *Wheaton v. Peters* in 1834—the Court constitutionalized the basic requirement for copyright: a work of *original* authorship. The Court also said that the right of one to use much of the fruit of a compiler's labor without compensation is not "'some unforeseen byproduct of a statutory scheme.' It is, rather, 'the essence of copyright,' and *a constitutional requirement*" (citations omitted; emphasis added).

Justice O'Connor was specifically addressing the right to use uncopyrightable material in a copyrighted work. Her language, however, could be read to mean that there is a constitutional right to make a reasonable use of copyrighted material—a reading that would be consistent with the copyright clause, which empowers Congress to grant copyright only to promote learning. A reasonable use, that is, would be fair use.

10. Stanley M. Besen and Leon J. Raskind, "An Introduction to the Law and Economics of Intellectual Property," *Journal of Economic Perspectives* 5 (1991), 11.

11. For a discussion of both copyright estoppel and copyright misuses, see Paul Goldstein, *Copyright,* 3 vols. (Boston: Little, Brown, 1989), 2:sec. 9.5.2 and sec. 9.6. As Goldstein's discussion suggests, copyright estoppel may not be of much value in controlling the scope of the copyright monopoly until courts are willing to dispense with its technicalities, which are a manifestation of its underdevelopment. Copyright misuse may be a more viable doc-

trine for this purpose. For a recent case applying copyright misuse, see *Lasercomb America, Inc. v. Reynolds*, 911 F.2d 970 (4th Cir. 1990). Both doctrines have the same ultimate purpose: to prevent the copyright monopoly from overflowing its constitutional banks. Given the current state of the law, the flood plain for copyright is already very large, but (as the *Lasercomb* case suggests) the courts may be ready to reduce its expansion and rechannel the flow of knowledge.

12. See Jessica D. Litman, "Copyright Legislation and Technological Change," *Oregon Law Review* 68 (1989), 275, 346–54.

13. T. Solberg, ed., *Copyright in Congress 1789–1904*, Copyright Office Bulletin No. 8, 115–16 (1905), quoting from Journal of the Senate, 1st Cong., 2d Sess. (Washington, 1820), pp. 102, 103, 104; *State Papers and Public Documents of the United States*, 2d ed., vol. 1. (Boston, 1817), p. 15.

Index

ABA/BNA *Lawyer's Manual on
Professional Conduct*, 183–84
Abrams, Howard B., 250 (n.11)
Abridgment, 60, 67–68, 147
ADAPSO, 219, 220
American Society of
Composers, Authors, and
Publishers (ASCAP), 129, 191
*Apollo Co., White-Smith Music
Pub. Co. v.*, 75–76, 78, 255
(n.10)
Apsley, Lord Chancellor, 42, 43
Arber, Edward, 20
Art, 82–83
Ashurst, Justice, 39–40
Associated Press, 179–81
Aston, Justice, 34
Audiovisual material, 8, 9
Author, 78, 86; defined, 96–99
Authors' rights, 2, 3–4, 32–46,
62–64, 75, 77, 79–80, 115,
116–17, 163–76, 231;
constitutional law and, 5, 47,
48, 49–53; Copyright Act
(1790) and, 140; Copyright
Act (1909) and, 73, 74;
Copyright Act (1976) and,
120–22, 140, 164; copyright
ownership and, 77, 79, 87, 95,
96–99, 167, 188; duality of
copyright and, 111–22;
economic factors and, 64–66,
78–80, 186–89; monopoly
and, 62–64, 78–80; moral

rights and (*see* Moral rights);
and obligations under
copyright, 138–39, 216, 236;
public-interest principle and,
70–71, 72; as publishers'
rights, 33, 45–46, 77, 140–41,
144, 164, 171–72, 188;
purpose of, 2, 155, 186;
Statute of Anne and, 27–29,
32–33; of termination, 95,
121–22, 167, 169–70, 232;
unpublished material and,
214–18; work-for-hire
doctrine and, 86–88. *See also*
Copyright, common-law; Fair
use; Fictions, legal; Literary
property

Bagehot, Walter, 109
Baker v. Selden, 61, 69, 115, 147
Barzun, Jacques, 2–3
Beckett, Donaldson v. See
Donaldson v. Beckett
Berne Convention (1887),
166–67, 171, 261 (n.1)
Berne Convention
Implementation Act of 1988,
49, 167
Blagden, Cyprian, 25
*Bleistein v. Donaldson
Lithographing Co.*, 258 (n.6)
Booksellers, 33–44, 112–13
Boswell, James, 46
Brady, Matthew, 78